Caroline & Doug

W9-CLE-145

FAITHQUAKES

LEONARD SWEET

FAITHQUAKES

"For Christians
with the
shakes, who
know that the
church is the
last hope for
saving our
families, our
cities, our
businesses,
and the earth."

Abingdon Press
Nashville

FAITHQUAKES

Copyright © 1994 by Abingdon Press

All rights reserved.
No part of this work may be reproduced or transmitted in any form or by any means, electronic or
mechanical, including photocopying and recording, or by any information storage or retrieval system, except as may be expressly permitted by the 1976 Copyright Act or in writing from the publisher. Requests for permission should be addressed in writing to Abingdon Press, 201 Eighth
Avenue South, Nashville, TN 37203.

This book is printed on recycled, acid-free paper.

Library of Congress Cataloging-in-Publication Data

Sweet, Leonard I.
    FaithQuakes / Leonard I. Sweet.
        p.   cm.
    Includes bibliographical references.
    ISBN 0-687-12647-9 (alk. paper)
        1. Christianity—United States—21st century.   2. Twenty-first century— Forecasts.
    3. Church renewal.   I. Title   II. Title: Faith quakes.
    BR526.S94   1994
    277.3'0829—dc20   93-44455
                                                                                                CIP

Scripture quotations, unless otherwise noted, are from the New Revised Standard Version of the
Bible, copyright © 1989 by the Division of Christian Education of the National Council of the
Churches of Christ in the USA. Used by permission..

Scripture quotations marked RSV are from the Revised Standard Version of the Bible, copyright
© 1946, 1952, 1971 by the Division of Christian Education of the National Council of Churches
of Christ in the USA. Used by permission.

Scripture quotations marked REB are from The Revised English Bible. Copyright © Oxford University Press and Cambridge University Press. Reprinted by permission.

Scripture quotations marked JB are from THE JERUSALEM BIBLE, copyright © 1966 by Darton,
Longman & Todd, Ltd. and Doubleday, a division of Bantam Doubleday Dell Publishing Group,
Inc. Reprinted by permission.

Scripture quotations marked NIV are from the Holy Bible, New International Version. Copyright ©
1973, 1978, 1984 International Bible Society. Used by permission of Zondervan Publishing
House. All rights reseved.

Scripture quotations marked GNB are from the Good News Bible—Old Testament, copyright ©
American Bible Society 1976. Used by permission.

94 95 96 97 98 99 00 01 02 03 — 10 9 8 7 6 5 4 3 2 1

MANUFACTURED IN THE UNITED STATES OF AMERICA

CONTENTS

EarthQuakes

Tomorrow the Lord will do amazing things among you.   JOSHUA 3:5

This book is written for those who have "got the shakes."

That is not to say that this book won't give some people in the church "the shakes." Indeed, I "got the shakes" myself while writing this book.

I operate on the motto that "there is nothing so bad in life that a trip to Big Bear won't fix it." Behind in my schedule for writing this manuscript, I took off to Big Bear Lake, California, and the cottage of Anna Claire Mauerhan, a seminary trustee. A couple of catch-up, fix-it days would do wonders for soul and script.

The rocking back and forth of the bed awakened me during my first night there. I forgot where I was, and reached for my seat belt. A handful of covers led me to conclude I was dreaming about sleeping on board some boat. Then I realized the waves were not those of the ocean, but of the land—in this case the aftershocks of the strongest earthquake to hit California in forty years.

These shocks and tremors that I rode for a few days were no bigger than 5.6 on the Richter scale, but they were big enough to make Big Bear City a federal disaster area, to force many residents to sleep in their cars (and even some to leave Big Bear and California permanently), and to bring in the government psychiatrists and psychologists who work with children traumatized from disasters. These aftershocks were also warning signals of new faults in the making, a portent of "The Big One," the megaquake that is due eventually to strike the millions of people living on the San Andreas Fault. "The Big One" now seems to me all the more imminent.

Yet I was reminded by the waiter—who, serving us amid the quaking, finally burst out in tears, "I can't take it any more; my kids can't take it any more; we're moving back to Kansas"—that wherever one lives, one is susceptible to "the shakes." No place is "shake-free," even Kansas. For some "the shakes" come from tornadoes, for others from hurricanes and hail, for others from flood and fire, for others from ice storms, and for others from monsoons.

Shake-free living is inconceivable. The question is whether or not one prepares for the shakes that will come wherever and whenever one lives. It is a waste of life lamenting that we are caught between a wonderful past and a dreadful future, or hankering after some unobtainable "good ol' days." Will Rogers is reputed to have said "I get a little bored hearing about the good old days. They never were that good, you know. The good new days are today. And better days are coming tomorrow. Our best jokes are still untold; our loveliest songs, unsung."

A West Virginian was asked for directions to a certain place. After musing for a few moments, he replied: "If I was wanting to get there, I sure wouldn't have started from here." None of us, however, get to choose our starting place. Few of us can get to a better starting point from which to proceed. This book is less interested in railing against the vices of the age (there are plenty) or in cautionary tales for the new paradigm (that's another book) than in rolling up the sleeves to do something about them. We can argue about what has to happen before we can begin, or we can begin. We can beat our breasts about the evils of the day, or we can open up our hearts to the needs of the day and do our best to address them.

Those houses most vulnerable to the quakes at Big Bear were those poorly constructed, substandard structures that were built by owners defiant of earthquakes and foolish in whims. It is not as if these residents had no warning. No single shift or lone crack produces an earthquake. Seismic seizures come from the weakening of plates over time, sometimes over centuries. The pressure of the Earth builds up until one day, something has to give.

The good news? "The Big One" has already hit. The church is now living in the aftermath of one of the biggest social earthquakes in history—the postmodern reality rift, or the collapse of the Enlightenment project (the Modern Era) on a world-historical scale. Modern culture did not begin in USAmerica, but it reached its greatest fruition and found its global center here.

The bad news? "The Big One" has altered, and at places leveled, our landscape and lifescape. The world has come to an end—at least the world we knew. The lay of the land has fundamentally changed, never to return to its original form. This earthquake has made us strangers in our own land.

The church's Rip-Van-Winklery spirit—at once exuberant and escapist—still largely refuses to acknowledge the new world in which it finds itself. It keeps polishing and "perfecting" an ecclesiastical paradigm that resists transformation. The results have been tragic: The Church in Ruins (1991) is the title of one recent evangelical assessment of evangelicaldom.

The primary world in which I have lived most of my ministry—among the various theological species of the *genus academicus*—has been defiantly train-ing nuts-and-bolts leaders for a 1970s transistor world, a 1980s microchip world, and a 1990s designer genes world. I have a colleague-friend who dubs what I do as training "typewriter repairmen for a computer age."

This book is written to prove her wrong. At least this book is composed and edited if not read on computer (though I started to write "on paper"). I admit, as Mikhail Gorbachev observed after moving plates in the national conscious-ness had swept him from power, "History punishes those who come late." But it is still not too late for the church to be on time for the future, true to its time and place, aware of the directions the tectonic forces are moving. Indeed, it is about time the church began rejoicing in its God, a God who had the first word and who has the last word, the word whose ring (as Conrad reminds us) can shake both heaven and earth.

There are, no doubt, some who, after reading this book, will say that if this kind of future is gasping to be born, they vote for postponement. But it is not our future that is pulling us in. It is God's future. And in that future God will not be without a witness. God will be there.

Will we?

MindQuakes

> *We are witnessing a revolution of international relations toward increasingly open and mass-scale communication. And this greatly increases the role of creative and positive policies. But equally, it raises the price of mistakes—the price we must pay for outdated adherence to dogmas, routine and old thinking. . . . I'm convinced that we stand on the threshold.*
>
> MIKHAIL GORBACHEV, JUNE 1990
>
>
>
> *We are privileged to live at a moment of history like none most people have ever experienced or will ever experience again. We must seize the moment not just for ourselves but for others.*
>
> RICHARD NIXON, AUGUST 1991

Howard Weaver, editor-in-chief of the Anchorage *Daily News*, was asked recently by editor Deidre Sullivan what he is feeling about events that are going on in the world today and "What do we mean when we say God?" Here is what this thirty-nine-year-old influential Alaskan leader said:

A friend told me this story once. Imagine that there is a grasshopper sitting on a milkweed plant near the railroad tracks in Montana. And the Great Northern Railroad goes by, the Empire Builder, and it creates a huge ruckus and the milkweed starts to bounce and bob and weave and the grasshopper looks around. Does he know why it's happening? He doesn't. And that is sort of the way I feel about God. There is obviously something happening but it is beyond my understanding.[1]

Many people are calling what happened at the beginning of this century a cultural earthquake; we now live in the midst of the aftershocks. Renaissance scholar O. B. Hardison, Jr., for two decades head of Washington's Folger Shakespeare Library, argues that we are living in the aftermath of "the cultural equivalent of an earthquake"—an earthquake that occurred in Europe and America in the early part of the twentieth century, an earthquake that encompassed all areas of human endeavor. All the bedrock assurances in Western culture—humanity, nature, art, history, the self, language—are doing disappearing acts, or "disappearing through the skylight," as Hardison asserts in the title of his book.[2]

The years 324–325 A.D. were as decisive as any in human history. So are the years we are living. It would be an exaggeration to say that, like the early Christians of the fourth century who lived through another cultural earthquake (think of John Chrysostom and Augustine[3]), we live on the other side of a cultural divide where nothing in the new is like the old, hence there is "no way of communicating between the two worlds."

What would not be an overstatement is the assertion that the flux and fragmentation of end-of-the-millennium living is part of a "phase transition" or paradigm shift not unlike that from Roman paganism to Christianity in the fourth century. Think what it was like for those fourth-century

> *When the ground starts moving, all bets are off.*
> JOURNALIST/PLAYWRIGHT
> JOAN DIDION

Christians to negotiate a world where there were no Christian schools, no Christian weddings, no Christian calendar, little Christian art, and even less Christian poetry, into a world where Christianity became the established and majority religion of the West.

Today we are living when those processes and transformations are being reversed. We are witnessing the decline of a dominant culture—Western civilization. Indeed, "for the first time in intellectual history, we are more inclined to think that something is finished, than that something new has begun."[4] We are products of historical fracture, standing on the cusp of the modern and postmodern worlds. This explains why we find few terms in everyday language to convey what we are experiencing, making it almost impossible to express new experiences in old language.

Peter Drucker calls the speechless members of the clergy "the most frustrated profession" in the nation.[5] Many clergypersons identify intuitively with Picasso's harrowing *Guernica*, a masterpiece which cannot be explained without understanding the earthquake in Malaga that he and his family went through when he was only three. This conversation between my colleague Gordon Goodgame and his friend is taking place in many of our churches:

> An old friend dropped by my study one day. We entered seminary together, I just twenty-one and he in his forties responding to a call to ministry. . . . Twenty-two years later, we talked of his struggles in ministry, and he buried his head in his hands and cried. He said, "This is just not the world we were trained to serve in."[6]

What world have we been trained to serve in? A world that is no more—thanks to the earthquakes that have altered forever the landscape. There are only a handful of possible responses to an earthquake—and each of them has advocates in the church.

One response is *denial that there is an earthquake.* The Lilly Endowment recently convened a meeting of the former top executives from the oldline Protestant churches and asked them, among other things, "What have you learned?" Arie Brouwer, former General Secretary of the National Council of Churches (NCC), responded that he has learned that oldline churches "continue to act as if they are established institutions" in the social order when in reality they have largely been "sidelined" by the society in which they live.[7] Decades of denial have created in the church "major messes," in the words of William R. O'Brien, Director of The Global Center, as problems have been allowed to "metastasize," infecting the entire system.[8]

Another response is *preaching* to an earthquake, admonishing it to turn back and not bother you, or cursing it in the name of all that is old and established and familiar. One thinks of John Berryman's "I'm cross with God who has wrecked this generation." There are plenty of cross-with-God Christians in "the wrecked generation," who find the notion of preaching to a San Francisco earthquake inconceivable if not laughable, who simultaneously believe that the current cultural earthquake has met its match in their sermons. Jeannette Rankin once said "You can no more win a war than you can win an earthquake."[9]

Another possible response to an earthquake is the *hunker-in-the-bunker* sectarian withdrawal of "back to the catacombs." When the world quakes, the church trembles and hides—it finds safe shelter on some beachhead, saves itself as a "righteous remnant," or lives as if the continental drift of change had never happened. Far from changing the church's tack given the new windscape, the sectarian strategy nails the old colors and configurations ever more firmly to the mast, pulls down the shades to the stormy outside world, and insulates the church family against the popular or alien culture. Before long, these colony Christians develop chemical sensitivities, becoming allergic to twenty-first-century products and people, until they can only survive in a bubble.

Again, there are more and more Christians for whom *sect* is no longer a four-letter word. The problem with the church as a beachhead is that one can never venture above ground much less home again, the terrain is so altered.[10] This strategy is less an escape route than a death trap. It offers the false eternity of the mausoleum.

Another ill-fated strategy for surviving an earthquake is to *ride the falling rocks*. This condition of compulsively following whatever is trendy and fashionable is known as "faddiction," and the church has its share of faddicts who have never learned to "test the spirits" or to live out of a tradition. They can only climb aboard the popular and the new without biblical screening or historical scrutiny of the timeless over ephemeral values.

When the world quakes, the church need not tremble. Indeed, it is about time our faith itself, which two millennia ago started quaking the world when a stone was rolled away, gave the world "the shakes." For those deciding not to deny the earthquake's existence, not to preach away at an earthquake, not to whine away in a bomb shelter, or not to ride the falling rocks, there is another alternative. It is the Issachar alternative.

The Issachar Window is one of the most stunning of Marc Chagall's twelve Jerusalem Windows, and Issachar one of the most unusual of the twelve tribes of Israel. The tribe of Issachar was an agricultural tribe that worked hard and reaped an abundance from their labors with the soil. The Bible says Issachar's people loved their land so much that they would not leave it even to go to war (Gen. 49:14-15).

Tradition also has it that Zebulun and Issachar made a compact between them: Zebulun would enter the commercial arena to allow Issachar the time to spend in scholarship and study of the Torah. Hence the gift the Issachar tribe gave to David was this: we are the people who "had understanding of the times, to know what Israel ought to do" (1 Chron. 12:32). What if the church were to raise up some leaders who could be a people, like the sons and daughters of Issachar, who know the times and know what to do? It doesn't do any good to know what the signs of the times are unless you know what to do about them. Or in the words of Peter Drucker, "The best plan is *only* a plan . . . unless it degenerates *into work*."[11]

Herb Miller relates this about Thomas Carlyle:

[He] was dressed to go out for a Sunday speech before a large crowd. His mother was sitting beside the front door. As Carlyle passed her on his way out, she said to him, "And where might you be going, Thomas?"

13

"Mother," he replied, "I'm going to tell the people what is wrong with the world."

His mother responded with, "Aye, Thomas, but are you going to tell them what do about it?"[12]

> NOTHING IS INEVITABLE, IF WE ARE WILLING TO CONTEMPLATE WHAT IS HAPPENING.
>
> MARSHAL MCLUHAN

A historian once argued that history has its hinges or "plastic moments," those in-between periods of "overlap" (the Apostle Paul talked about his living in "the overlap of the ages") when the old has gone but the new has not yet arrived and when the course of history is more open to shaping and steering than at any other time. The postmodern era is such a period of plasticity. We are living in an era obsessed with origins and endings.[13]

But the future is not something that wins. The future is something that is created, something that awaits our shaping energies and actions. From a historian's standpoint, there are no sources weaker than those for the future. That is why this book is not about predicting. Is there any one among us who can tell what this very day may bring forth, not to speak of this year or this decade?

If this book is not about predicting, then what is it about? It is about semiotics, the science of signs.[14] It is about reading the signs of the times, and decoding the "semiosphere," the world of signs in which we live and move and have our being. It is about the semiotician's courage to be wrong, which counts for something in the cause of truth. It is also about "spiritual literacy"[15] and "deconstruction" that often precedes it. The semiotician in me is concerned with reading the text of what is already happening around us and what might happen to us if we opt for being victims in the world around us instead of authors. It is also about not insulting the future with our conservative projections and arrogant predictions.[16]

When Native Americans found their way through the wilderness, they engaged in what they called "reading sign." In this exploration of finding our way into the unknown terrain of tomorrow, an exercise I call "Faithquakes," it matters a great deal who we ask to be our guide. Because the church has invested very little in the futures market, we are forced to turn "outside," to those beyond the church, for help. Fortunately, there are many skilled guides out there to help us traverse the falling rocks. There is an influx of energy and direction coming from people like Tom Peters, Peter Drucker, John

> *Perhaps the time has come for all of us to rec-ognize that humankind's greatest goal, which outweighs lengthening life through medical advancements, is to evolve spiritually.*
>
> DR. DAVID O. WIEBERS,
>
> Chair of Scientific Advisory Council of
> The Humane Society of the United States

("Megatrends") Naisbitt, Joel Barker, Rosabeth Moss Kanter, Robert Theobald, and Faith Popcorn.

These economic and business futurists take care to monitor the weather patterns as precisely as possible. Each one takes pains to place his or her weathervane as high as possible. Weathervanes that are perched high on public buildings and church roofs shift with the true wind currents. They provide accurate registers of wind directions and velocities. Put a weathervane on the back porch, however, and it will shift with every slam of the door. To monitor the messages emanating from the twenty-first century, to discern the Spirit of God from the "with-it-ry" spirits of the age, we need to place our measuring instruments as high as we can get them.[17]

Too many of us have been taking cheap shots at the "spirit of the age." Changes in wind can be good—they stop the air from getting stale. The essence of enchantment is the break from the familiar, and changing winds enables everlasting enchantment. But, more than anything else, sophisticated weather stations track changes that have already occurred as well as alert us to what is coming. The "spirit of the age," like most spirits, has a hidden agenda, even gender. We must live alert to the spirits that every new cultural era brings. But then we must engage those spirits, challenge them, critique them, denounce them, and ride some of them.

Faith Popcorn gets her monitoring instruments higher than anyone else I know. Her *Popcorn Report: Faith Popcorn on the Future of Your Company, Your World, Your Life*[18] is a (not *the*) very present help in time of trouble. Popcorn herself (she was born Faith Plotkin) founded BrainReserve in 1974, a Manhattan-based research and marketing consulting firm with whom many of the Fortune 500 contract to help them develop new products and reposition old ones. American Express, Nissan, Eastman Kodak and IBM are among clients who pay up to $1 million for her consulting advice.

Fortune Magazine calls Popcorn the "Nostradamus of Marketing." Diviners of the future previously read tea leaves or entrails, frogspawn and rowan berries to decipher the signs of the times. Today's soothsayers read other things—like stock reports or soft drinks. Or, as my editor Paul Franklyn puts it, "At the end of the first millennium, diviners and fortune-tellers looked into crystal balls. At the end of the second millennium, they look into crystal computer screens." The *Wall Street Journal* keeps track of the orders for Coca-Cola at McDonald's as a highly sensitive economic indicator of a troubled economy and rising unemployment. Popcorn calls what she does "brailling the culture" or "reaching out to touch as many parts of it as possible."[19]

Popcorn is usually likeable, sometimes lightweight, but always lively and provocative. Nobody is going to be right about everything that's coming, and Popcorn makes no pretensions to infallibility. In fact, if Popcorn can be criticized for anything, it is putting too low a lid on the limits of future possibilities. *Newsweek* calls her predictions "blindingly obvious," and even her fans in *Futurist Magazine* admit that while her record is solid, "she is a bit short-term and says little that is radical or new." Much of what she says may sound radical and new to the church but that testifies loudly about our sealed-in spirituality.

Popcorn's genius is her eye and ear: an ear close to the streets, an eye that can see things in the world about her that the rest of us pass over without "seeing." She has an eye that catches the special, the vivid, above all the imperceptibly new commonplaces. One's breath is taken, and taken often, by the way Popcorn turns an everyday occurrence round and round like a conch shell until she sees or hears something in it that others had not noticed.

Even though Popcorn only "brailles" the culture of a socio-economic class with "their buns in the butter" it is this class that predominates the pews of USAmerica. The down-and-outs, or hard-living, trapped in prisons of poverty and degradation, are integrated into this book by an effort to be sensitive to class-specific issues. I have also tried to track multiple, interrelated changes by types of "church" and "person." Lumping all churches together is like analyzing "business" when the latter term includes everything from farms to antique shops to blue-chip corporations. Discussions about "the church" are "typed" when at all possible.

The generational divisions of USAmericans—into "boosters" (those 49 million born between 1927 and 1945), "boomers" (those 75 million born between one second after midnight 1 January 1946, the birthday of the original baby boomer, Kathleen Casey Wilkins, and 31 December 1960), and "busters" (those born between 1961 and 1981)—are also adopted by this book as well. Those born before 1927 are most frequently known as the "GI Generation." Some prefer the "Silent Generation" to "boosters," a leaderless group that may go down in history for being the first generation in American history never to generate a President. Since those born between 1961 and 1981—at 80 million strong, this group has numerically outgrown the "boomers"—are the thirteenth generation to live under the U.S. flag and the Constitution, some prefer to call them the "thirteeners" rather than "busters" or "generation X."[20] We still do not have a name for those after-busters born in the last twelve years, a generation that will reach from 1981 to somewhere just beyond the year 2000. Some are calling them "the millenniums," others the "Benetton" generation. Whatever name ultimately sticks, the now-in-place generation of the twenty-first century are already making their mark felt like no group of children in history before them.

The Popcorn Report is used as a foil for self-analysis that does more than map the bog the church presently inhabits. Self-analysis when done in tandem with trend-analysis is one of the most difficult of things to do—hence the need for turnaround specialists in business (Joel Barker) and in the church (Lyle Schaller), people who will ask the hard questions that examine if there is anything salvageable left to one's operation: Does the church bring people up short of the needs of our time, snugly preferring rote religion, or are we daring to enter those moments when the fires of change burn most searingly? Is our leadership willing to sacrifice and be reinvented, even to replace itself with more prepared, more skilled leadership if the church is to thrive, or are we clawing for our best interests over God's?

I know of no better study than *The Popcorn Report* on which to base such a self-analysis. It is time to match "market pull" with tradition push. Market pull is the church's response to members' wishes or perceived needs. Tradition push is the church's responsibility to explore and develop new areas of mission and ministry that are based on theological content, not consumer demand. Sustenance is to be drawn from the past, from tradition. But this does not mean that the way forward is through a cultural conservatism. New paradigm believers must not be locked into old paradigm responses.

Alfred North Whitehead described the danger he feared most—that events would outrun humanity and leave us panting and helpless, old-answer anachronisms. That nightmare seems to have come true. We are *leaping* into a new world philosophically, scientifically, technologically. We are *creeping* backward, crawling into the arms of an old, more comfortable time, there to set up residence. Of course, the church is no different from the world. Both are extraordinarily conservative, with powerful structures well positioned to do everything in their power to preserve the status quo and resist change.

The church is currently locked in a *kulturkampf* that is greater than the culture wars over social policy. It is a struggle over what symbols, metaphors, and ideas will organize and engage its communal life, which thus determine the limits to the wars over social policy. The establishment church is intellectually marginal, a theological shambles. It has lost the capability to address the intel-

17

lectual culture of the world of the "p" (postmodern) word. And what is most frightening of all options, it sees no need to.

Artemus Ward once said, "the trouble with so many people is that they know so many things that aren't so." There is massive confusion in the church today, primarily because a lot of things simply aren't working, and we know too many things that aren't so. The most dangerous condition one can be in is to function while holding blatantly dysfunctional and wrong-headed notions. Peter Drucker is fond of saying that "the most difficult thing to do is keep a dead horse from stinking." The church is frantically flailing horses that died in the 1960s. It is time for derelict churches to bury the carcasses and break-in new vehicles. "When the horse you are riding is dead, dismount."

The present time of believers is no longer determined by the past. It takes its definition from the future.

theologian JÜRGEN MOLTMANN

For the church to enter the postmodern world ("The Knowledge Age," "The Information Era"), it must rethink some oldthink notions about the decentralization of power, the place of and tolerance for unorthodox and innovative thinking, the employment of new skills (such as marketing research[21]) and new technologies, the use of information in the church (even the church as an informational community, an info-ecclesia), the environment and incentives for entrepreneurship in an enterprise culture, the role of risk-taking, community leadership and shared ideas and information—not to speak of an entire larger atlas of largely unknown and unexplored intellectual territory and theological terra incognita.

Faithquakes puts on a garage sale for old ideas—or at least builds a hospice where fatal assumptions and terminal customs can die gently and peacefully. Faithquakes also invites churches to visit those clearinghouses already there and cart away as many of the most creative living ideas and cutting-edge ministries of our time as we can take with us—always keeping in mind that imitation and impersonation are two entirely different things.

One of the first things to be gotten rid of is the political and theological thinking that divides the social landscape into old Left-Right maps. This dualistic schema is an irrelevance that is inapplicable to the most urgent issues facing our day. The question for USAmerica's 350,000 congregations is whether they will be found in the frontlines of mission and new paradigm ministries, or whether they hide out in the back as part of the rearguard, fighting the perils of the right or the pitfalls of the left.

Faith Popcorn's book is built around "Socioquakes" (each a consequence of what Robert Theobald earlier called "Mindquakes"). After eight of the ten[22] of these "cultural compulsives," as missiologists might call them, have been summarized and built upon, they will be followed by what I am calling "Faithquakes."[23] In each of these "Faithquakes" I have tried to break through the old ideological strictures of party politics and entrenched theological camps to present an AncientFuture faith—"the faith that was once for all delivered to the saints" (Jude 3).

An AncientFuture faith is as much remembered as imagined. If postmodern means anything, it means a new openness to the past and to the authority of tradition in the future. It was the Modern era that thought it was the only age to know anything. Memory provides identity. Loss of memory means loss of identity, perhaps the most serious outcome of the modernization of religion.

Hence AncientFuture. Time moves backward as well as forward—as we recognize the future in the past, and the pastness of the present. An AncientFuture faith yokes yesterday to today through a future filled with new-old thinking, living, and moving. You will find in these pages a lot of old saws. But the job of every new paradigm leader, and preacher, is to make old saws buzz again—to put a hum back in what has become humdrum. The AncientFuture mixture of oldfashionedness with newfangledness, the old and the yet to be born, is a surefire recipe for a faith that has fire power.

> *Whether these are the worst of times or the best of times, they are the only times we have.*
>
> humorist Art Buchwald

Whether all or none of these "socioquakes" is good or bad is outside the scope of this book. The church must enter the real world where people live and live out its life from there. Just as God loves me "just as I am," not as God wishes I might be, so God calls the church to love the world as it is, not as the church might wish the world to be. It is a waste of time accusing an earth-quake of untruthfulness. It is a waste to wish that people didn't think like they think or live where they live. Our job, as one of the founding fathers of the Society of the Holy Cross said to its first priests, is to "dig a pit for the cross, wherever we are."[24]

It is a poor memory indeed that only works backwards!

If each of us is a letter, as the Apostle Paul suggests, we get to decide the address where that letter will be sent. Will that letter be sent to our day, to our own time? Or will that letter be sent to some other time, some earlier day, ending up in the Dead Letter Office, like millions of Santa letters? Will the letters of our lives be little more than litter that future generations must find a way to dispose of responsibly?

HomeQuakes

SocioQuake 1: *Cocooning*

The first and fundamental right of a human being, many anthropologists insist, is the right to habitation. Faith Popcorn is the one who first observed and named one of the most significant changes in postmodern patterns of habitation—the now widely referred to cultural phenomenon of cocooning, the postmodern desire to circle the wagons and seek refuge in the inner circle of the home for relief from the harsh, nightmarish outside world.

> The last gasp of the eighties found Americans huddled in high-tech caves. Cocooning, the trend we first predicted in the late seventies, . . . was looking for a haven at home—drawing their shades, plumping their pillows, clutching their remotes. Hiding. It was a full-scale retreat into the last controllable (or sort of controllable) environment—your own digs. And everybody was digging in.[1]

Fear is a permanent feature of postmodern life. People are pulling in the reins, digging in their heels, battening down their hatches. Staying in has become as prized and valued as we once rejoiced in going out.

This form of psychological bulletproof living and spiritual snuggery is what Popcorn calls "reality retreat" or "hyper-nesting." I call it the cave syndrome. Popcorn reports that more than 70 million American households are now digging in the backyard, making gardening the most popular leisure activity in the U.S. She might also have mentioned that three of the biggest developments in the arenas of education, medicine, and religion during the 1980s were the mushrooming movements toward home schools, home births, and home churches.

Cocooning is another name for controlling our environment, for protecting ourselves. And Americans are into "protection" and into "protecting ourselves"—physically, psychologically, emotionally, every way—big time. We aren't going places unless our property is protected; we aren't going to do things unless we're protected. We send our children to private church schools, hoping that they will be protected. We seem to be needing protection like never before.

There is a good reason for all this cocooning. We increasingly do need protection. How many cities do you know where the night is safe? "For the first time ever in the history of mankind, the wilderness is safer than 'civilization,'" Popcorn writes. "There are no cracked vials in the wilderness, no subway murders, no asbestos, no Scuds."[2] Urban violence and wave after wave of urban terrorism are new ways of life. In fact, people of the twenty-first century will go "wildering" in nature (a phrase Popcorn has invented since her book), exploring and experiencing wilderness and natural wildlife as they previously explored and experienced cities and urban wildlife.

Some critics are arguing that we have moved beyond cocooning into "burrowing" and "hunkering." One will see this more frantic cocooning in the future as underground homes begin to grow in popularity due to people's desire to escape the surface pollution of air, noise, and infrared rays due to the loss of planet Earth's ozone shield. Even now one can purchase "P.O.P." protection—*campesino* hats fresh from Costa Rica marketed as "Personal Ozone Protection."

> Increasingly, we'll entrench ourselves in the privacy of the fortress—EveryHome in America. The purpose of the fortress? To make us feel safe. Sophisticated distribution systems will stock and supply the fortresses; the chore of shopping as we know it will be over—shopping has to become theater and diversion. The fortress will be the center of production (we'll work at home), the center of security (we'll make the fortresses intruder-proof), and the center of consumption. Penetrating the increasingly impenetrable fortress will be the primary challenge for marketers and manufacturers in this decade.[3]

The key understanding of socioquake 1 resides in this last insight from Popcorn about the cocooning phenomenon: "Leave our cocoons? Forget it. Instead, cocooning has moved into a newer, darker phase—breaking down into what we are identifying as three new Trend Evolutions: the Armored Cocoon, the Wandering Cocoon, and the Socialized Cocoon. Cocooning is no longer exclusively about a place, the home, but about a state of mind—self-preservation."[4]

What is the "armored cocoon"? Notice how we are armoring our homes. Security is big business, with increasing numbers of offices and homes even going so far as to install intercoms, infrared motion-detectors, and surveillance cameras. Fire departments around the country are raising $20,000 for a specially designed chain saw that can cut through steel. That old firefighters' tool the axe is no match for steel doors, steel bars, and other metal building materials used in fortress homes.

Ever notice how the higher the income, the higher the iron fence?[5] Ever notice how signs on the front lawns displaying owners' names have been replaced by signs on the front lawns displaying the names of security firms?[6] Every area in the country is seeing the growth of gated communities—planned developments that promise residents locked gates and twenty-four-hour security guards, some even with signs posted "Armed Response." Rural areas are not exempt from the increasing number of home invasions either. The FBI says that burglaries in rural counties are rising about 7 percent a year.[7]

There is even being marketed an "urban scarecrow" named Gregory that you can buy for $375 as the latest weapon in the war on crime. Gregory has a musclebound fiberglass body (and a thirty day guarantee) that you place next to you when you are driving alone or by a window in your home when you are out, and his physique and tough demeanor will scare away intruders.

The cocooning phenomenon Popcorn describes means that the mallification of America is over. The August 1992 opening of The Mall of America complex in Bloomington, Minnesota, a megamall of 360 retail stores replete with chaplains and services (built with the help of $100 million in state gas tax money to build access roads) and projected to draw more visitors than Mecca or the Vatican, is the last fire-breathing gasp of a dinosaur (USAmerica boasts more shopping centers than high schools, with 2000 added each year in the 1980s). Malls already have their future behind them.

The only way The Mall of America is making it is because it is not strictly a mall, but a mechanism for stimulating new desires, experiences, and distractions: it is part theme park, part child-care center, part sing-along bar, part rental services, part supermarket, part video arcade, and so on. Even those who do visit these town squares of late modern public life include almost as many "post-shoppers"—people who visit malls to consume images and brand-names rather than commodities—as chain-store "credit card junkies."

In one poll of mall shoppers, only 25 percent said they came to buy something in particular.[8] Three-quarters of them came to "gaze" and get their "eyeball kicks." Indeed, British sociologist John Urry elevates sight as itself a social activity for postmodern culture, what he calls the postmodern "gaze."[9]

Supermarket shopping is being radically "decentered" through food-purchasing clubs, interactive shopping channels, and personalized buying in the home through consultants.[10] In one of the more startling figures to emerge from Popcorn's book, she reveals that mail-order sales in 1980 were $2.2 billion. In 1990 mail-order sales stood at $200 billion. Shopping is now, and increasingly will be, an electronic adventure conducted from the safe confines of the home where the objects of gazing can be leisurely grazed. When people leave their homes to "shop," the "stores" they visit will be as much adventures in education, entertainment, and oblivion as they will be retail outlets (see e.g., "Nike Town" in Chicago or Atlanta, or Tandy's "Incredible Universe" megastores in Portland, Oregon, and Arlington, Texas[11]).

In the postmodern era, the migration of people to where the jobs are is ending. The jobs now can go to where the people are, giving new meaning to the word homework. The home office ("hoffice") now can be plugged into a planetary network of communications technology that can make one place every place and bring every place to one place. Indeed, if a person gets a computer, gets a fax, gets a partner with which to network, that person gets instantaneously a global corporation with anytime-anyplace-anyone linkages within the confines of his or her home. The "electronic cottages" Alvin Toffler predicted in *The Third Wave* (1980) are here faster than even he imagined.

What is the "wandering cocoon"? It is more than recreational vehicles, customized vans, or "motor homes." Sometime take a tally of what people in cars are doing as they drive the $100 billion Interstate Highway System, one of the largest public works projects in the history of humanity. Peter O'Rourke, director of the California Office of Traffic Safety, took just such a census. He found people doing the following things in their cars: changing clothes, shaving, reading magazines, brushing their teeth. At sixty miles per hour they're eating baked potatoes, canned food, and bowls of cereal. They're changing diapers and nursing babies, grooming their pets and playing the guitar, inserting eye drops and washing clothes. "One child was seen getting his hair cut while the parent was driving," says O'Rourke.[12]

Our 1.8 cars per household (worldwide, one person in fourteen owns a car) are becoming cozier, places that you might as well live in—car phones, car faxes, voice pagers, voice activated minicassette recorders, laptop computers (for traffic jams), cassette and CD players, portable refrigerators, portable ovens, everything you need for work or play for drive-time cocooning.

Kurt Vonnegut, in his *Fates Worse Than Death*, offers this description of his son: "He is now a pediatrician in Boston, with a wife and two fine sons, and two fine automobiles."[13] To a culture that is in love with "car talk," that is awash in vanity plates, and that gives pet names to its cars, the car as just another member of the family cannot seem all that strange. Even though I drive a glorified Ford Escort, my pheromones do handstands at the sight of a Lexus. The Lexus has the option of a steering-wheel car phone that automatically turns down the radio volume whenever you get or make a call. Future models will be introducing a microwave in the glove compartment. Mercury's Villager minivan boasts separate entertainment system controls and headphone sets for each passenger, along with two-zoned climate systems and temperature controls for each seating position. I've already picked out the name I'd give my dream car, which now migrates from a daydream into my nocturnal dream life.

> *The interplay between humankind and the Earth has often generated ecosystems that . . . are more interesting and more creative than those occurring in the state of wilderness.*
>
> RENÉ DUBOS

What is the "socialized cocoon"? According to Popcorn it comes in two parts. The first part she calls "Huddling and Cuddling": "inviting a few close pals . . . in for a cozy evening in the cocoon. Probably not your clients or your boss or your suppliers. Nobody you don't like."[14] Eating out will be increasingly defined as a small indulgence (see socioquake 3) rather than as standard fare (as hundred-dollar dinners-for-two were in the extravagant 1980s). Dining at home will be developed into an art form, and table culture may become as important to postmoderns as it was to premoderns.

"Hearthing" is a postmodern phenomenon that returns the family's gathering spot to the kitchen. Kitchens in many ways have become the new family rooms, and *Metropolitan Home* magazine celebrated the arrival of *The Big Chill* kitchen by dubbing it "The Living Room Kitchen."[15]

This does not mean boomers and busters will finally learn to cook in their elaborate kitchens. Sixty percent of "Frugal Gourmet" viewers do not cook anything from the show. The cookbooks that boomers buy in best-selling quantities will be consulted more for the kind of stemware required by a Mexican-theme table than for the kind of sauce that goes with Beef Wellington. Cookbooks are prominently displayed more for ambience than for recipes, their insides consulted more for secrets of how to concoct a creative menu than for how to prepare a *crème brûlée*. Now that the accent is on "fresh," "healthy," and "light," and patisseries everywhere, an elegant meal can be put together without a lot of preparation. All one needs to make a premade meal special is one homemade dish (raspberry sauce) or some fresh berries soaked in brandy.

"Huddling and Cuddling" has even infiltrated kid culture in a significant way. A favorite new group game is called "nesting"—getting six or seven kids in front of the TV, playing Nintendo all at once. Or try out on busters the old games of Monopoly or RummyTile without them getting hooked. A new "Trivial Pursuit" is just around the corner.

The second part of the socialized cocoon she calls "Saloning and Salooning": the salon movement or what some call the "salon craze" is one of the most neglected social movements in our day and one of the best indicators that participatory democracy is still alive and well. Part discussion, part debate, part old-fashioned jam session, people are gathering together in homes and cafes, churches and libraries on a regular basis for learning, listening, and laughing about the hottest topics facing our world today. With so much time spent alone receiving an electronic flood of information and ideas, Neighborhood Salon Associations (NSAs) are popping up all over USAmerica to help community-starved people achieve intellectual, if not relational, intimacy with others. Some names of salons include the ARF (Addicted Readers' Forum, Schaumburg, Illinois), The Cincinnati Rads (Reading and Discussion Society, Cincinnati), and Untethered Talk, WNQR-FM (We're Not Quite Ready For MENSA). A global network of Internet mailing lists has been formed to create Electronic-mail Salons, offering the unique feature of truly transcultural perspectives on the issues of the day.

"Salooning" is "close-knit packs" going out for an evening to restaurants or bars.[16] No one "dates" or "has dates" any more. People "get together," "go out with a gang of friends," "meet at a party," everything but "go out on a date." Despite a brief comeback of the date in 1986, emphasis among teens today is casual "group dating" (the language as well as the intensity of "double dating" is outmoded). Dating en masse is now more popular than serious couple courtship. Dating is increasingly a shared group experience that emphasizes social, recreational, and friendship components (video parties, skating parties, house parties, bowling parties, etc.).

Time magazine's look into the century ahead, the theme issue called "Beyond the Year 2000," even predicted somewhat humorously that by the year 2020, "casual dating" will be a popular arena sport. "People too terrified to pursue something so hazardous themselves will witness actual live human beings who, for big money stakes, will eat dinner with and then perhaps (if dinner goes well) become intimate with people they are attracted to but basically know nothing about."[17] Sound like any shows already watched on television?

FaithQuake 1: *HomeQuakes*

1. GOOD-BYE FROG EVANGELISM: *Hello Lizard Discipleship*

Don't expect people to "come to" church anymore. You've got to "go to" them and reach them in their cocoons.

FROG / LIZARD EVANGELISM

Ignostic

Frogs sit and wait until their food walks, flies, or swims past. Then they pounce. Lizards go out in search of food. In the frog world everything comes to those who wait. In the lizard world everyone would die if they sat and waited. The postmodern climate is not conducive to frog ministries. "Come-to" strategies no longer work. It's a "go-to" world.

Twin forces have caused this: cocooning and the deregulation of the religious marketplace. Enough has been said about the former, except perhaps to remind us of Woodie Allen's definition of what it means to be middle class: to be middle class, he says, is to take life very seriously—to take with equal seriousness God and Carpet.

The second shaper of this "go-to" world is the cultural disestablishment of the Christian religion. No longer does culturati favoritism go to Christianity. Religion in America does not mean any more simply the Christian religion. Indeed, religion in America increasingly means "other than" the Christian religion. Or in the language of the sociologists and their ubiquitous questionnaires, the "nones" or "none of the aboves" (Protestant, Catholic, Jew) constitute the fastest growing segment of American religious life.

Pastors and church boards used to be able to count on as regular churchgoers and supporters those who sincerely consider themselves Christian but for whom establishment religion was only a marginal part of their lives. No more. How many people actually read the religion ads of newspapers, much less respond to them? We have come a long way from the world novelist Eudora Welty remembers in her growing up: "we grew up in a religious-minded society. Even in high school, pupils were used to answering the history teacher's roll call with a perfectly recited verse from the Bible. (No fair 'Jesus wept.')"[18]

George Hunter talks of people today as being "ignostic"—they simply don't know what the church is talking about with its insider language and intramural debates.[19] The dilemma of the church today is that those who know its words think they know what *sin* and *salvation* mean, and they are not interested. Those who don't know the words are not interested in something they don't understand.

Postmoderns find it no longer culturally advantageous to conform to Christianity's rituals and rhythms. It would be a mistake to look on these people as being less committed (though the pathological individualism of the 1980s was almost obsessive about refusing to commit). Postmoderns can be just as committed, but in different directions. The "boomers" are already being known as "America's most God-absorbed living generation."[20] For those who will become committed Christians, their commitment will be more to Jesus and less to church.

No longer can we expect people to fit into the church's rhythms, rhythms that reflect a lost paradise of rurality and the agriculturally based economy of

27

stop offering people an institution.

early twentieth-century village life. The rhythms of people's lives today don't match the "rurbanity" rhythm of the church's life. What could happen if the church responded to socioquake 1 with the same imagination and integrity as the forty-two-year-old interfaith advertising council Religion in American Life, which has transformed its media campaigns from trying to get people to go to church to urging people to invite friends to go with them to church? Garrison Keillor's life is a good example. Keillor was brought up in a fringe group of Plymouth Brethren Church. You have probably heard him tell how fire and brimstone evangelists left him hoping that Jesus would not return until he had gotten married and had sex, at least once.

Finding the church's heavy legalisms and dullness offputting, Keillor stopped going to church. From then on people would ask him, "Do you go to church?" And he would say, "No." Then they would say, "Why don't you go to church?" And he would tell them.

That ritual exchange served him well for many years until, not too long ago, someone (a Lutheran no less) engaged him in the two stock questions, "Do you go to church?" "Why don't you go to church?" But then this person surprised him with a third question: "Why don't you come with us?" Never having been asked that before, Keillor didn't have a stock answer. And before he knew it, he found himself saying yes. A centerpiece of his week, along with his family and job, is now a new-found family of faith.

In short, give up church evangelism. Going to church is less and less the defining experience of religion. The time for getting people to come to church is over. It is time now to get people to come to Christ. The church must give up its "organized religion" and stop offering people an "institution." The church must take up its "Way, Truth, and Life" and start offering people a life-way, a lifetruth, and a life.

Replace centripetal evangelism that tries to draw outsiders in with centrifugal evangelism that drives insiders out. The new-paradigm church will give up church evangelism or membership evangelism. It will take up "missiopreneurial"[21] evangelization: it will be a sending church rather than a gathering church. In other words, as discipleship professor David Lowes Watson insists, we must "decouple" the identification of evangelism, which is focused on God, with church membership, which is focused on institutional concerns. The church has too long operated as if they were one and the same.

A centrifugal evangelism offers a designer discipleship into the body of Christ through life-style evangelism that is consistent with McLuhan's acknowledgment that the medium is the message. The church might also consider developing a type of in-formational evangelization in which the communicator lives in conscious formation and congruence with the Divine Information (Christ) being communicated to and through a variety of communication receptors.

A truly postmodern form of centrifugal evangelism is "re-membering" evangelization. The phrase is that of poet and novelist Meridel Le Sueur, today aged ninety-two and still writing. In her 20s when she crafted the phrase, she was part of a community of prairie populists known as the "Wobblies," the Industrial Workers of the World, whose heart was with those society had cut off and cut away—the exploited immigrants, non-whites, and migrant workers.[22]

Re-membering evangelization is based on obedience, a word that comes from the Latin *obaudire*, which comes from the root *audiere*, which means "to listen." To obey means to listen, to pay attention, to love. Re-membering evangelization involves listening with God to hear what God—who has the greatest authority—hears: the poor, the outcast, the marginalized, the dismembered. Listening to the cry of the poor and dismembered leads the hearers to remember their own unfulfilled dreams, unexpressed memories and lost members. By re-membering the future believers are empowered to re-member the dismembered, and by so doing build up and integrate the body of Christ into a whole, healthy force for God in the world. The future is the memory of the past.

In terms of centripetal evangelism, people will choose churches on the basis of recommendations of neighbors and friends. Relational evangelism's one-on-one conversation, whether by kinship netweaves or friendship netweaves, is more important now than ever before. Such "conversation" is more hearing and presence than speaking and witnessing. The same goes for "response" evangelism or "event" evangelism—both of which are based on respecting and responding to the felt needs of people.

In fact, postmoderns will do well to rethink if not give up *evangelism* altogether (hence the preferred term *evangelization*). Lesslie Newbigin, missionary to South India for almost a lifetime, makes this case better than anyone I know:

> It is, is it not, a striking fact that in all his letters to the churches Paul never urges on them the duty of evangelism. He can rebuke, remind, exhort his readers about faithfulness to Christ in many matters. But he is never found exhorting them to be active in evangelism. For himself he knows that he cannot keep silent about the gospel. "Woe is me if I do not preach," he says. There is an inner constraint; the love of Christ constrains him. But he does not lay this constraint upon the consciences of his readers. Mission, in other words, is gospel and not law; it is the overflow of a great gift, not the carrying of a great burden. It is the fulfillment of a promise: "You shall be my witness, when the Holy Spirit comes upon you."[23]

2. Focus on Real Families

The best way into the postmodern home is through the family. Take it from Steven Spielberg, who commandeered J. M. Barrie's story about Peter Pan and transformed it into a mounted platform—the movie *Hook*—to preach the gospel of parents spending "quality time" with their children.

The family is *not* in decline. The family is reshaping itself in new and old and unexpected forms. Unfortunately, the family is making less of a comeback in the church than in the culture. Religious leaders must help parishioners ritualize their family lives, set aside more time for family commitments, and find ways to celebrate families (not just nuclear family patterns, but binuclear, extended, cooperative, etc.). The church has for too long been an assortment of individuals rather than a collage of families.

This is not a bathing in Norman Rockwell nostalgia for the "nuclear" family. As one study puts it, "The American nuclear family, as an institution, is beginning to resemble a nuclear catastrophe."[24] Of the wide variety of familial relationships, the nuclear model is one of the most troubled. Indeed, we need to give up the notion entirely of "the family."

There is no such thing as "the family," only "families." Families have demassified along with everything else—single-parent families (single motherhood, single fatherhood), "sandwich" families (middle-aged couples responsible for both children and parents), stepfamilies, live-together families, extended families, intentional families, gay families, and so on. Wherever one comes down on the "homosexual issue," gays and lesbians are not a threat to the family.

Different varieties of family can offer their members a tradition-rich family life. John Wesley, recalling the words of Jesus (Matt. 12:46-50) in context of a visit to the home of Mary Bosanquet, a rich, young, unmarried woman who turned her home into a residence for the homeless of Laytonstone, said that this was "the only perfect specimen of a Christian family" he ever witnessed.

Families come in all shapes and sizes like people do.

ACTRESS/PRODUCER CYBILL SHEPHERD

The church's only consolation is that it is almost as "out of it" as the United States Census Bureau, which defines a family not as "a group of people who love and care for each other," as one would think and hope it would, but as "two or more persons related by birth, marriage, or adoption who reside in the same household."[25] Fewer than 27 percent of the USAmerica's 91 million households in 1988 fit the traditional model of family.

The "average" American? A thirty-two-year-old single woman. Almost three out of ten homes are single-parent families. Sixty-six percent of African American children are being born to single women, according to the latest figures.[26] The population of singles in USAmerica is skyrocketing—in 1970 the percentage of US population age 18 and older that were single was 32 percent women, 22 percent men; in 1990 it had climbed to 40 percent women, 36 percent men. From 1960–1990, the proportion of adults living alone tripled, from 4 to 12 percent of the population. The most recent census counts 22 million people living alone, over 1 in 4 households.

> June! I'm home.
> WARD CLEAVER,
> "LEAVE IT TO BEAVER"

Is the church caring for their well-being and celebrating and helping these families? Are there "Divorce Recovery" or "Re-builders" programs? How many churches have classes for children of divorce where kids whose parents are divorced or are in the process of divorcing can come and have their questions answered, their identities strengthened? Since the divorce rate will continue to go down as couples struggle to "live together" and "stay together" (fear of AIDS, financial pressures, the failure of disposable relationships are all driving the divorce rate down), are there "Marriage Recovery" groups that can help marrieds fall in love with one another again?

What if the church were to provide people the kind of intimacy that family offers—place where people laugh and cry together, look out for one another, take care of their weakest members? What if the church took seriously Jesus' mandate to care for the marginalized, the disenfranchised? What if the church took seriously the needs of "non-marital children" (how demeaning that old phrase "illegitimate")? What if the church began providing families without fathers the father-figures they need, especially since the more sociologists learn about children growing up in homes without fathers, the worse the picture gets—and not simply for reasons having to do with income. What if the church helped prevent families themselves from cocooning by getting families outside themselves: have multiple generations from a family visit a nursing home on a regular basis, as a family unit volunteer for the local Red Cross, and so on.

New forms of human community and "being" community are already coming out of communications technology. If the church does not reflexively condemn these new forms of family life, the church can help shape them morally and ensure that families will be rich and authentic and uplifting of the human spirit.

31

3. Make House Calls Without Entering the House

The church must be careful how it treats people's cocoons. Pastoral "calling" will always be needed. But the types and variety of calls must change dramatically.

I was startled into this perspective by the spouse of a trustee, who one summer day in the midst of a meal at their Pennsylvania farm pleaded with me as president of a seminary to do something about old-style pastoral "cold-call," "drop-in" home visitation with a new generation of leaders.

I asked what she could possibly mean. My mountain culture background celebrated the "poppers in." Didn't people like being visited anymore? "Like being visited," she exclaimed. "Are you kidding? These 'drop-by' visitations require 'drop-everything' responses from the visited. Do pastors today really think we live in a world where there are people doing nothing but waiting for them to drop by?" she demanded. "Don't they know that time at home is precious, that it is carefully planned, that a 'drop-by,' three-hour visit can wreak havoc in a home schedule?" I suddenly realized that the amount of psychic effort and physical energy that goes into "hosting" someone in one's home is only dimly appreciated by clergy.

If one's home is one's castle, and the sizes and styles of people's armored cocoons increasingly suggest they are, then it is very different from the castles or "great houses" of the medieval period, which provided havens of hospitality and openness to strangers, travelers, peasants, relatives, refugees, and so on. Whereas in castles safety was in numbers, today safety is in seclusion.

Home is now a hiding place, not a gathering place. Doorbell rings bring anxiety, not anticipation. We run from, not to, knocks at the door. People do not welcome unsolicited or uncontrolled intrusions into their postmodern castles, which are havens from, not hospices for, the needs of the world. It is for this reason the lid is fast closing on telemarketing for new church development. Increasingly people are showing themselves resentfully resistant to anything that impinges on their safe, well-regulated enclaves.

A better place for the church to show up is in people's work worlds, anyway. Call at the office. The old paradigm church hasn't been interested in people's workaday worlds. It has too often conveyed the opposite message to "take your job and love it"—and we'll help you do it. The best way to reach people in their cocoons and bring them out of them is to show that you care about their work. This is where people spend their lives. Since this is where people make their "living," this ought to be where the church shows people how to truly live. The gospel changes bad habits of living and bad habits of thinking into successful patterns of whole-life living and thinking. It transposes one's work into a divine key.

For men (i.e., male-order living), who have gone from bar crawls in college to boardroom brawls in business, this often means helping them see how some lost meanings of macho-ness and success are well lost. For women, who have to run faster than men just to keep in place, this often means showing them how to shuffle unmanageable demands and convergences, and distribute responsibility for the 51,000 major meals they have traditionally attended to during one lifetime. For both, this means positioning people to turn weekly setbacks and daily sunsets into something like new dawns.

The church should be the one place that shows people practically how to live a life at home and at work that can be something both more and less than ODTAA—"one damn thing after another." Life at work and at home can be truly ODTAA—one dawn thing after another. When the church is seen as the place that helps people look for the "new thing" (as Isaiah 43 puts it) that God is wanting to do in them and through them at work, at home, and everywhere, people will come crashing out of their cocoon.

"House calls" can be made without ever entering the home—through phone counseling and phone prayers, handwritten notes, faxes, walking the town's streets or "hanging out" where the community hangs out, and a host of other "pastoral visits."

4. Every-member Ministry

Every-member ministry is the larger point here anyway. Visitation is something that should be done by the people. The church is most dynamic and growing where it is a lay movement. Ministry is not the clergy's job. Ministry is the people's joy. The job of the clergy is to see that ministry gets done, and that the people doing it are properly prepared and educated.

Volunteers willing to visit homebound folks while delivering sermon tapes and Sunday bulletins are a given at new-paradigm churches. Volunteer healing teams of laity should be visiting the sick and infirm, praying with the diseased and depressed, and anointing the sick with oil blessed by the elders. The whole people of Christ must be employed in the preaching/teaching/healing ministry of the church.

Or as Rick Warren, pastor of Saddleback Valley Community Church in California puts it, "The church is measured, not by its seating capacity but by its sending capacity." Indeed, at Saddleback it is the people who are the ministers and the pastors the "ad-ministers." In direct opposition to the prevailing custom of most churches, the Saddleback pastoral team does the maintenance work of the church while the people do the ministry. There are over 100 lay pastors at Saddleback visiting the sick, the shut-in, and the new residents of the community. The business clergy are in, as Warren puts it, the business of "giving ministry away."

The postmodern era will witness the deprofessionalization of psychological and spiritual care. Care has been for too long something that "caring professionals" specialize in rather than caregiving as something that belongs to us all. The pastor is not paid to show people the church cares. The pastor's job is not to care for people. The pastor is paid to train the church to care and to make sure the members are caring for people. It is the members of the church who care for people and show the world how much the church cares. The pastor trains and educates the church in how to care. Ministry is not about we pastors doing it. Ministry is about we pastors helping others do it. Empowerment is the name of ministry.

It is the function of the clergy to call and commission people to high commitment and to high levels of ministry. Sometimes clergy will accompany lay healing teams and bring the sacrament. But it is not the function of the clergy to be parish "visitors." This does not mean that home visits will never be done. But when they are, these home visits should be significant ritual experiences, with home prayers always, home blessings sometimes ("house blessing" rituals will increase in importance), and home teaching often.

5. New Architectural Feel

One of the biggest obstacles to aliveness in the postmodern church is the architecture it must work with and around. High-ceiling gothic architecture no longer feels "homey," for example, as more and more people are returning to the original architectural feel of the early Christian "house churches" of the first century, before they became the special church buildings of the second century (see the Christian church in Dura-Europos) or the great basilicas of the Age of Constantine, and before the clerical retreat from the nave back to the chancel behind a rood screen of high liturgy and holy language where access is reserved for the *cognoscenti*.

Smart churches—like smart cards, smart cars, smart houses, smart highways, smart everything in the future—find ways to make the church feel more like home. One church in Tucson, Arizona, built an educational wing that included space for the "boomers"—a carpeted room (both floors and walls) with no furniture, only stacks and piles of different sized pillows. Members of the "Boomer Class" come into the room, select their pillows, plop down on the floor, get out their Bibles, and start saloning.

Another church holds a "Teddy Bear Sunday" each year when everybody, adults and children alike, bring their teddy bears to church (whatever size). They find there is no better mass ice-breaker and body-builder than this one. (The first year the church treasurer showed up with his four-foot teddy bear.)

6. Connect, Don't Cocoon

Instead of reaching people in their cocoons, the church itself is cocooning. Instead of making the church as comfortable as the home, the church is itself

tele-hermits

constructing fragile fortresses. When the church goes into a cocoon, there is no telling what sort of creatures will emerge from it.

The future of the oldline churches is endangered, not because they are not religious enough, but because they are too religious—obsessed by therapies, filled with superstition, afraid of being public much less "going" public. The REM song "Losing My Religion" might be a good theme song to move the program-based church into a more people-based design. It states "Oh no, I've said too much. I haven't said enough," which captures nicely the way the church is saying more than it should say about some things and at the same time not saying enough to help about the things that really matter.

The indoors-insider-ingrown spirituality of the church must be broken. We must push the church out-of-doors. It's time the church lost some of its religion to gain its life. The biblical story of the disciples ripping apart the roof to get to Jesus someone who needed healing is best told from the perspective of the man who owned the roof. The disciples probably did not destroy this roof without first talking to the owner of the home about the situation. Here obviously was a man who cared more about human need than about his house. Make that owner a patron saint.

Feasting on the bounty of the earth is not our sin. . . . The pitfall comes as we eat in isolation from the needs of the poor.

KEN SEHESTED

7. Give a Hand-Up

A cocooning First-World church has offered the Two-Thirds World its "handouts" rather than justice. But as Dom Helder Camara reminds us, "handouts" are not just food and clothing (too many of these "hand-outs" are "hand-me-downs") and charity. Handouts can also be resolutions and policy statements.[27] The modern church's "social concern" (how patronizing a phrase!) has generated far too many hand-out resolutions and far too few hand-up resolves.

Marshall McLuhan's romantic vision of the global village created by electronic communication most resembles the "fake togetherness of a honeycomb of hermits' cells in a cave wall" in Colin Morris's unforgettable words.[28] Christian "tele-hermits" must come forth from their caves and stretch out their hands in the service of justice and beauty and truth.

8. Keep Your Distance

In the Third Millennium P.C. ("politically correct"), anti-Christian sentiment will continue to rise. Far from the Christian church as a majority force in culture, in postmodern culture the Christian faith is a minority movement, its influences being expunged from the larger culture. This is the basic reason for mainline Protestant membership loss, according to sociologists Johnson, Hoge, and Luidens: "declining commitment to the church and to Christian faith and witness."[29]

The new Knopf picturebook of Hans Christian Andersen's classic story *The Wild Swans* (1992) excises all Christian symbolism and referents from the tale. Elisa never "prays" to God or reflects on God's "goodness." There is no "crown" of nettles. "Church bells" become merely "bells." In fact, the spectacle of people running off to court to get every trace of Christianity extinguished from public life, as the "crèche" scenes of Santa and Mrs. Claus and Frosty and Rudolph testify, seems almost normal.

Already P.C. sentiment has almost come to the point where the only jokes deemed nondiscriminatory to the disability du jour are Christian-bashing jokes. In the Alice Thomas Ellis's new novel *Pillars of Gold* (1992), the most loathsome epithet in teenager Camille's vocabulary is "Christian." Comic novelist Michael Carson has made a good living poking fun at the astringencies and absurdities of establishment religion. The magalogue with the provoking name *Real Goods News* can hawk its energy wares by announcing that "There is a significantly better chance of saving the planet through solar energy than through Christianity" and get hardly a twitter of protest.[30] Martina Navratilova penned a fund-raising letter for the National Gay and Lesbian Task Force demanding that the gates be splintered, and power be stripped, from "straight, white, Christian men."[31]

In the first century the Christians were accused of "atheism" because they refused to worship more than one God. The church should prepare itself for similar statements and treatments in the future. Novelist and pagan revivalist Gore Vidal has already begun the crusade with *Live from Golgotha* (1992), a celebration of the postmodern revival of paganism and an indictment of the great unmentionable evil—monotheism and its three barbaric and antihuman "skygod religions," Judaism, Christianity, and Islam. Arthur Lubow writes: "Vidal is a devout pagan. 'The greatest disaster ever to befall the West was Christianity,' [Vidal] says. He has equal contempt for the other two monotheistic religions, Judaism and Islam."[32]

Another pagan revivalist, celebrity historian Camille Paglia, while supporting the right of the church to set moral tones for society and draw ethical boundary lines, mocks the Presbyterian Church's report on sexuality and its recommendation to learn from marginalized groups: "We can move tender, _intimatedistance_

safe, clean, hand-holding gays and lesbians to the center—but not, of course, pederasts, prostitutes, strippers, pornographers, or sadomasochists. . . . I wrote in the margin, 'No lobbyists, I guess!' "[33] But expect celebrations of paganism and polytheism to be heard within the family as well as without: "The most rewarding quality of polytheism is the intimacy it can make possible with one's own heart. . . . An attitude of polytheism permits a degree of acceptance of human nature that is otherwise blocked by single-mindedness."[34]

The postmodern era will find its own creative ways of throwing Christians to the lions. Political philosopher Christopher Hitchens calls Mother Teresa a "leathery old saint" and a "prostitute" to neo-colonialism and capitalism."[35] (She apparently can't win.) In fact, the number of postmodern "marketplace martyrs" and "living witnesses" may necessitate reconsideration of Menno Simons's ranking of persecution as one of the six marks of the true church. On rare occasions the scorned may become the exalted, and the postmodern coliseum come alive with cheers and applause for the Christians. But these chants are not to be trusted, and certainly not to be dignified by a Sally Field response, who upon receiving her Oscar from the Motion Picture Academy shrieked "You like me! You really, really like me!"

> _TAKE HEED THAT YOU DO NOT OFFER YOUR BURNT OFFERINGS IN ANY PLACE THAT YOU HAPPEN TO SEE._
> DEUTERONOMY 12:13 (RSV)

The church must remember in its relationship to postmodern culture that while it must never lose the common touch, it is not "one of them." It must never "go native." Its relationship to the culture is one of what J. G. Melquior calls in another context "official marginality" or what I call intimatedistance. In its relations with the world, the church will be often misunderstood and maligned. It must also stop expecting its values and opinions to be those of the majority. Too much coziness between the church and the culture will jeopardize the church's mission and devalue its ministry.

All effective leadership requires the art of intimatedistance—the establishment of sufficient intimacy for trust while at the same time enough social and psychological distance for drama to be created. The church must be intimate enough for the culture to be able to access it and identify with it (hence this book). But without the quality of "distance," one is too close for respect (is there one among us who got the parents we think we deserve?). Without the reserve of "distance," familiarity breeds parity which breeds confusion, uncertainty, and misunderstanding. Without "distance," mystique dies.

37

9. Encourage Observer-Participants

It is the observer-participant mode of tension that best transforms anonymity into intimacy in the postmodern era.

Instead of descending on newcomers at church with all sorts of "friendly" gestures (one of the unfriendliest of which is asking them to stand and be gawked at—uh, I mean "greeted"), give new faces and new families plenty of space and plenty of freedom to be an observer-participant—to feel at home and to find their identity without the immediate pressure of "Can I sign you up for the womens' club?"

10. Deconstruct and Deconvert

Postmodern society is in the puzzling throes of transition from a rational, scientific, bureaucratic "modernity." The Western Enlightenment model of reality, founded on the principles of materialism and anthropocentrism, no longer "work" operationally in the world in which we live and move and have our being.[36] Hence people are being forced, one way or another, to deconstruct the old order and to "deconvert" from a safe, establishment mode of being in the world to another more risky way of living.

The spiral of transformation involves going back before going on or beyond. One form of deconstruction is defamiliarization, a conscious, chosen path of regression to one's origins. "Deprogramming" from old beliefs means making habitual assumptions and commitments seem strange.[37] Overheard on a New York subway was this exchange: "Be reasonable, Phyllis. I made this date with Rita months before we were married!" After giving one's life to Christ, there are some prior commitments one simply cannot keep.

Defamiliarization is a concept that entered postmodern thought from Russian formalism, especially the work of Victor Shklovsky who proposed defamiliarization as the aim of all literature.[38] Polish psychiatrist Kazimierz Dabrowski calls this "positive disintegration," a healthy and positive period of disorientation and despair that leads to "higher psychic structures and awareness." To hear things afresh, to see things anew, there needs to be a break with the expected, a pivotal estrangement or defamiliarization of the material so that one can experience it on ever deeper levels. Hence the disorienting, destabilizing function of art.

Part of deconversion is weaning people away from bad concepts of Jesus, or wooing people away from religious abuse.[39] Visit any Sunday the fast-growing St. Francis of the Foothills in Tucson, Arizona or Glide Memorial Church in San Francisco. Both these churches have as their primary ministries deconversion, taking the fallout from fundamentalism or weaning wary seekers away from bad concepts of Jesus. The words of a T-shirt worn to Glide Church one Sunday morning states this process most graphically: "Jesus, Save Me From

Deconversion

Some of Your Followers." I am a Christian today because the most powerful religious experience of my adolescence was a deconversion from Christianity.

Paul Ricoeur has offered a helpful dialectics of deconversion which he calls a "hermeneutics of suspicion" and "hermeneutics of retrieval." A hermeneutics of suspicion uncovers the underlying distortions and latent illusions that are warp and woof of any given interpretation of the world. A hermeneutics of retrieval or restoration reaches back into the past to recover and recreate the bedrock traditions lying dormant but upon which the best of our interpretation of the world is based and out of which new meanings and imaginative formulations will emerge.[40]

Deconversion is more important now than ever before for another reason. It used to be that the values of the culture were Christian, but not any longer. This is not a Christian culture, and if deconversion doesn't take place when people become Christian, their Christianity gets piled up on previous beliefs, and faith becomes more an exercise of adhesion than conversion. Christian spirituality has heretofore involved both *conversio* and *aversio*—a choice *for* was also a choice *against*. Choices of conversion/aversion are no longer popular, as people have difficulty deciding firmly to live in one way and not another and prefer to stockpile spiritualities on top of one another. Many postmoderns find it in no way conflicting to serve multiple gods.

To relive is not to relieve. Sometimes one has to unlive and throw off one's past before the abuses and burdens of that past can be integrated into new and whole life. In the postmodern era, deconversion will often precede true conversion. The church must learn to do the "hermeneutical retrieval." Exhume the dead myths of the past and bring them back to life as myths and "mythemes" that can be ours today.[41]

Experience-Quakes

SocioQuake 2:
Fantasy Adventure

Get me Out of Here!" is the fantasy-adventure cry of overmediated, overmedicated, oversourced, overconsuming, two-income cocooners. In their off-screen life, postmoderns exhibit what I like to call the Yearning-for-Yonder syndrome that summons us, in Popcorn's words, to "escape physically into our cocoons looking for comfort and security, escape emotionally into our fantasies looking for release."[1]

These latter days of the twentieth century find us absorbed with travel and "soft" or pseudo-adventures (e.g., doing things that look more dangerous than they are like sea kayaking off Orcas Island or bungee-jumping off the Brooklyn Bridge). In their cocoons, where postmoderns are constantly "plugged-in" to screens, their experiences are derivative and secondary, the events around them defined electronically. When postmoderns leave their cocoons, they become positively ravenous for primary experience. The ageless USAmerican quest for a good high has perhaps never been higher.

Postmodern culture looks forward and backward at the same time. The irresistible combination of the familiar and the exotic is part of the AncientFuture phenomenon in which one seeks to both change the world and conserve the past. The nostalgic tug of the past is especially strong among postmoderns rushing pell-mell into the unknown. When the past's contradictory virtues of the accessible and the exotic are joined to the future, as in Chrysler's AncientFuture contribution known as the Viper, the appeal becomes virtually a spiritual experience. The curvaceous styling of this car is a throwback to the 1950s, while at the same time having a futuristic look.

The only thing more predictable than our fixation on the lives of the rich and famous (*People* magazine, *Vanity Fair*, *Town and Country*, *Architectural Digest*) is our fascination with the world of the bizarre and unusual (*Nose Mag-*

azine, The Realist). Hence our tabloid culture's insatiable appetites for trivia, junk food, and scandal ("Marilyn Monroe Really a Russian Spy"). Hence today's desire for fantasy environments in shopping malls. Postmoderns are not about to waste their funs, or funds, on the commonsensical. Whimsical is the name of the game.

So too is nostalgia in and of itself. Contrary to Francis Fukuyama's "End of History" thesis, postmoderns find themselves not at the book of Revelation but at the book of Genesis, facing a new world "without form and void."[2] It can be frightening. Joyce Carol Oates once noted that nostalgia was the vice of a people fascinated with the past because they are afraid of the future. If you want easy growth in the twenty-first century, be a hypertraditional church with all the "smells and bells." Old hat is the new wear. But more than that, the cult of "newness," or what Harold Rosenberg calls "the tradition of the new," belonged to the old project called "modernity."

Retromania rules in the "heritage" marketing of antiques, museums, and historical villages (Old Sturbridge, Williamsburg, Deerfield, Genesee Country, etc.). There is nothing intrinsically wrong with a high nostalgia quotient, or "looking forward to going back," or "saving yesterday for today." The postmodern pace of change is so fast that affection for old buildings, slow-motion experiences, ancient objects, and hyperreal historical re-creations can be a healthy way of maintaining contact with the past and coping with stress.

For example, the summer resort Chautauqua Institution, "the most American place in America," has capitalized on the nostalgic possibilities of architecture, music, literature, and religion in creative and even salvific ways. At its best Chautauqua represents a nostaliga, not for the past itself, but for those traditions and values which our ancestors have created and preserved but which we have frittered away or carelessly flouted. Nostalgia gets obsessive, however, when a heritage culture gets chosen over one's living culture. Nostalgia gets compulsive, furthermore, when what is recent must be magically transformed through the alchemy of nostalgia into the ancient through a process scholars are calling "the invention of tradition." A morbid and moribund ancestor worship can be the result of one; an escapist romp in unrealities the result of the other.

Socioquake 2 explains the boom in tourism, "ecotourism" (which conservationists define as travel that promotes conservation of natural resources) and "cultural tourism." The astonishing recent boom in travel writing is fueled by these "fantasy adventure" forces. In one generation, travel has gone from being a privilege to being an "unalienable right" (e.g., Duane Hanson's "Tourists II" sculpture). About 10 percent of the USAmerican population leaves its boundaries in any year. Forty percent of free time is spent in travel of one sort or another, necessitating a burgeoning new major in undergraduate education known as "Tourism and Travel"; agents are licensed after two years of study and five years of experience.

The economic significance of tourism is reflected in the fact that even the most conservative estimates project world tourism to be the largest source of employment by the year 2000.[3] The United Nations estimates that by the year 2000, the world's most important economic activity, the world's richest industry, will be tourism. According to the *Travel Industry World Yearbook*, worldwide travel expenditures top $2.5 trillion annually, about 12 percent of the gross international product. As it is 1 in 15 jobs worldwide is travel-related.[4] This already would make travel and tourism-related services the largest and fastest growing industry in the world, and one of the most powerful social and economic forces at work in the world today.

The freedom of the "away," the power of the "other" are postmodern rites of passage from the profane to the sacred. The bicycle and the kayak, sampaning and spelunking, are the monk's cells and the eremite's grottoes of the postmodern era. Anthropologists have only begun to study "tourism" as something more than a safety-valve and escape capsule for twentieth-century living. But some exciting work is being done on "tourism" as group pilgrimages with religious significance.

Pilgrimage is still one of our primary reasons for travel, and it is on these pilgrimages that most of us come the closest to mystical experiences. Visits to "sacred" sites yield spiritual renewal. The reason for the pilgrimage? Benefits conferred by the undertaking include better understanding of the scriptures, even the cultivation of eternal youth, as well as allowing oneself to be taken up with moods, gestures, visions, and epiphanies that transcend one's normal plane of existence.

British Catholic novelist and literary theorist David Lodge's *Paradise News*, for example, is a wonderful allegory of tourist rituals and practices as sacred pilgrimage. If this is so, then the church must be sensitive to how "tourism" can be as spiritually-motivated as leisure-directed. Perhaps a key mission of the postmodern church is to turn "tourists" into "travelers," to transform journeys from consumption rituals into identity rituals, even with the pastor as spiritual "travel agent" (as the laicized priest Bernard puts it in Lodge's novel) and the church as travel agency.[5]

There are two top tourist attractions in USAmerica. Or put more precisely in anthropological terms, there are two meccas for postmodern USAmerican pilgrims. Every parent feels both physical and emotional tugs to take the kids on two group pilgrimages, and will travel long distances, spend way too much money, and endure steamy heat and long lines to enter these sacred spaces: Washington D.C. and Disneyland/World. The 1989–1990 season was the first time that Disney attracted more visitors than the nation's capital.

43

"Nowhere" is a postmodern issue, since things look more and more alike and the real is disappearing (or has disappeared, argues Jean Baudrillard[6]), replaced by the simulacrum. DisneyWorld is the archetype similacrum. Mickey Mouse (who would have been named "Mortimer" had it not been for the strenuous objection of Walt Disney's wife Lilly, who insisted on the name "Mickey") ranks as an icon up there with Marilyn Monroe and Elvis Presley. Some critics have dubbed the $4 billion Euro-Disney a "cultural Chernobyl." But most everyone is a failed cynic when it comes to the Mickey and Minnie cites, creations, and characters. Everyone comments on how "amazingly happy everyone appears" at Disney: "I have never seen such collective, uncomplicated, lump-in-the-throat happiness, and no matter where it comes from, no matter what abuses and horrors it might be concealing, it's really rather a moving spectacle about which I find I cannot be cynical."[7]

Faithquakes 2 seeks to learn some things from Disney in helping the church to become a vital presence on Main Street in USAmerica. At the same time we learn from Disney, we must not become like Disney. There are those who say that if you learn from Disney, you become like Disney. And it is a danger. The Disney methods for attracting members can also be methods for corrupting the Christian faith if the church succumbs to pandering or palavering to Madison Avenue. The spirit of Christ is very different from the materialistic, consumerized spirit of Disney. We are all, willy-nilly, marketeers of visions and values. We do not have to turn into Mouseketeers, however.

We must also critique the Disney-style adventure in which pleasure is thoroughly white, totally suburban, totally controlled, totally commercial. Christians can consume brand new experiences like brand new sneakers, creating a consumer religion that collects new experiences like some people collect old furniture. Sociologist Christian Smith, critiquing the way the Christian faith becomes just another in a long line of products offering health and beauty, warns that "imitating the problem" doesn't "solve the problem."

> Can "ClergyCard" take on MasterCard and win? Can Heritage USA take on Disney World and win? Through our direct-mail evangelism we jump into a sea of direct mail trash, where we are drowned by Publisher's Clearinghouse and the rest. Our methods match the world's in worldliness and banality—and we wonder why the power of the gospel gets lost.[8]

Disney's Main Street, U.S.A. "exudes prosperity, shuns pluralism, and is a haven for white America," especially the white America of Disneyland's opening in 1955, writes cultural historian Judith Adams. "It is popular culture sanitized of its most creative and energetic elements, static in time, and reserved for the financially comfortable."[9] Disney's lifegiving amusements can be deathmaking for non-Western cultures and traditions. "Whose world order are you talking about" is the response from the Southern hemisphere to discussions about an emerging postmodern "New World Order." It is a question that haunts every faithquake.

FaithQuake 2: ExperienceQuakes

1. "Living" Worship

To say that the church's worship has become as dull and lifeless as a museum would be an insult to museums—which express postmodern culture architecturally in ways the cathedral and skyscraper expressed medieval and modern cultures respectively.

> Big wind, lotta dust, no rain.
> American Indian chief
> after attending church

Today's museums are reaching out to the MTV generation and coming to life as "living museums." Thomas Hoving, whose efforts to "make the mummies dance" at New York's Metropolitan Museum of Art transformed the museum world, envisioned museums as institutions that were obliged to serve the community and reach all classes of people where they were. Long-gone glass cases have been replaced by hyper-media technology and interactive, hands-on exhibits for museums like the Academic Italiana—where touch-sensitive screens in the "Rediscovering Pompeii" exhibit let you take "your own journey into Pompeii;" or the Sainsbury Wing of the National Gallery; or the Museum of Discovery and Science at Fort Lauderdale, Florida, where you can maneuver a satellite on a simulator; or the Oregon Museum of Science and Industry in Portland, where visitors build and launch boats in water tanks; or the Fernbank Museum of Natural History in Atlanta, where scientists in five labs help you examine your own cells, or use a laser.[10] Museums now feature electronic learning and "edutainment." They are reaching out to less highbrow cultures like working class constituencies.

In short, the church wouldn't even make a good museum any more. Museums are more fun.

Edmund Wilson spoke of the novelist's "unpardonable sin"—to write something that "fails to live." The preacher's "unpardonable sin" is to preach a gospel that "fails to live." Most divinity students have at least one professor who makes it an original statement that the preacher's only unpardonable sin is to be boring: "Do anything in that pulpit, but don't make the gospel boring.

It is the only unpardonable sin." Mary Midgley explains concisely why the church must become less grindingly dull: "Dullness is the enemy, not of frivolity—it is easy to be both dull and frivolous—but of wisdom."[11]

2. Worship "in Spirit and in Truth"

Worship has become a dry and disembodied business, scarcely calibrated to make most hearts skip a beat "at the sound of his name." Worship has almost become a slow-motion, avoidance experience that protects us from having a life-changing experience of God. Liturgy is not a lecture; it is a celebration. Postmoderns are hungry for more interactive, participatory, aroused, tactile worship.

Theologian Robert Hotchkins of the University of Chicago writes, "Christians ought to be celebrating constantly. We ought to be preoccupied with parties, banquets, feasts, and merriment. We ought to give ourselves over to parties of joy because we have been liberated from the fear of life and the fear of death. We ought to attract people to the church quite literally by the sheer pleasure there is in being a Christian."[12] Worship should be an explosion of joy.

> ## PREACHING IS NOT TO INFORM BUT TO TRANS-FORM.
> ### DR. SUNDO KIM

A veritable revolution in worship is coming, and in some cases is already here. In the postmodern era two styles of worship "celebrations" promise to induce transcendent states of consciousness: the realist mode (more ritual and prescribed liturgies) and the abstract mode (more spontaneity and free-form liturgies). The abstract mode is sometimes triumphantly referred to as "contemporary Christian worship." It may be helpful to enumerate the realist and abstract worship styles by referring to the two styles and strategies that have proved successful in bringing some life back to cities.

The first is the hyperreal historical re-creations like one finds in Lowell, Massachusetts. Umberto Eco calls them "travels in hyper-reality"[13]—"living museums" of themed historical eras in which replicas make antiquity feel new and clean. Ur-Christian worship that does high liturgy exceptionally well, that re-creates the past better than the past did it, page by slowly turning page, will have much appeal for many postmoderns. The primitive, old and familiar, however, must be comfortably reupholstered in romantic and relevant material for postmoderns to sit down and make a home there (hence the fake Chief Seattle speech[14] that has almost reached liturgical standing in some alternative worship experiences).

The nostalgic marketing of ancestral voices through live relics attracts a homesick culture as it struggles with its sense of loss, searching for a lost home, or, as the singer Madonna captures so powerfully in a recent song title, a search for a safer and saner place to live, "This Used to Be My Playground." Anything that takes on the patina of the ancient or old-fashioned will be greeted with distanced affection by hoping-it-might-be-so postmoderns, as the world of baseball is proving in its glut of "Old Timers Games" and its nostalgia movies (*Eight Men Out, Field of Dreams, The Babe, A League of Their Own*) or as the world of publication is proving in its highly successful genre of reminisce magazines.[15] Riding the nostalgia wave is the revival of "Big Band" music, ubiquitous Elvis events, TV westerns, and The Nostalgia Television cable network, which in seven years since its founding (1985) has fourteen million viewers. Spiritual neuralgia seeks the comfort of historical nostalgia.

There is another group of postmoderns, however, for whom high liturgy is high lethargy. These are the people who enjoy and are energized by the celebrative "festival marketplaces" for which James Rouse is justly famous (Fanueil Hall in Boston, Harborplace in Baltimore, etc.). This abstract mode of worship experience might be called ludic liturgy—liturgy that is playful and participatory, worship that is experiential, existential, experimental.

Glide Memorial Church is a more extreme example of this type of worship experience. "This is Glide. You have to fight to get a seat here," sighs its pastor Cecil Williams (as he tries to find space for a beyond-standing-room-only crowd). "We're not into religion here, we're into spirituality," announces Williams.[16] Glide is one of the fastest growing United Methodist churches in America, and one of the most comprehensive nonprofit providers of human services in San Francisco. Glide's only visible symbol in front of the sanctuary is not a cross, not an altar, not a baptismal font, but a fire extinguisher. That one fire extinguisher on the wall speaks loudly each week about the ashes-worries, not dust-worries, this worship-style brings.[17]

The abstract mode of worship will find ways to minimize or get rid of pews and pulpits (see-through lucite lecterns at best) and bulletins. For the bulk of church history there were no pulpits, only ambos, and these were for the reading of the lections. Pulpits didn't make their way into parish churches in England until the twelfth and thirteenth centuries. In much of American history sermons were delivered from what were called "reading desks." How many reading desks have you seen lately? That's about how many pulpits you may see a hundred years from now. Sackcloth and ashes were important features of the reverent and true worship of God in Jesus' day. How many sackcloths and ashes do you see today?

Postmoderns are distressed by authorities who hide their knees. The Oprahfication of preaching (Oprah Winfrey, the talk show hostess, in case you listen only to national public radio) could make interactive, in-context, exposed-knees exchanges a key form of proclamation in the future. I have worshiped with congregations where, even if they had bolted down pews, they were an irrelevance as people walked on them, over them, and sat everywhere, including the floor and window-seats. Abstract worship's high energy, tight timing, deep flow, and crescendoing spirit make the event of worship a real "do," with red-rubbed eyes, running noses, and clapped-chapped hands a badge of having been where something "happened."

The greatest challenge as well as the greatest returns will come to those churches that manage to bring both tendencies together in creative ways, that incarnate an AncientFuture faith. This does not mean glorifying everything ancient, or everything future. Ancient Christianity saw bathing as decadent and voluptuous. Future Christianity will be far too casual about theological matters. What an AncientFuture faith puts together is an awareness of the past and an attunement to the future. We have been this way before, but it was different.

What is the same for both realists and abstracts, however, is the quest for "living out God" or theopraxis, as theologian Andrew Sung Park defines the term.[18] What drives both groups to worship is the passion for lived experience or "consciousness," as philosopher Daniel Dennett defines it.[19] The modern era gave out graduate degrees in doubt. The function of worship thus became giving Enlightenment doubters "something to believe in." Worship pointed toward life's meaning and purpose amidst a prevailing skepticism that pared down faith to a defensible kernel. Worship left modern Christians with patches and snatches of prose without the poetry of religion.

In the postmodern era worship celebrates being alive to life, offering people an experience of being alive in Christ. Postmoderns are not going to invest their one and only life in dullness and doubt. If the haunt of our common nature in the modern period was doubt, the postmodern haunt is belief. Whereas good preaching in the modern era struck thoughts and struck attitudes, good preaching in the postmodern era strikes chords and invites poetry.

Postmodern worship doesn't help people doubt it, but helps them shout it.[20] Worship generates song and poetry. Worship must set vibrating in the soul the full chord of God's awareness.

Both realists and abstracts expect worship to help them "experience" life, to unclench spiritually, so as to better hear the wind and see the fire. Worship that is not fresh, preaching that is preplanned will increasingly have the same reception as clothes that are "prefitted" and products that are "prefabricated." Postmoderns can stand hot air—but only in fresh air.

Worship is not something postmoderns want to "attend"; worship is something postmoderns want to enact. It is not too far wrong to say "When a past-[forty] adult misses church he will ask, 'What did he say?'—meaning 'What was the sermon about?' The under-forty adult is more likely to ask, 'What happened?' "[21] Both groups judge worship primarily on the basis of whether or not they were caught up in something , and most of all, whether joy is felt!

Both the abstracts and the realists emphasize enacted worship—"hands on," bodywork worship that uses physical actions and gestures as well as words. Both abstracts and realists are what the church used to call "knee crawlers." Praying is done with the hands and knees as well as lips; singing is done with the hands and even hips as well as vocal chords. In both abstract and realist bodywork worship, there is the full use of the senses through the ritual movement of the liturgy.

Homiletics specialists are inclined to recommend shorter and shorter sermons to accommodate postmoderns' shorter and shorter attention spans. Charles L. Rice, whose text on preaching wants us to "make less" of preaching so that the world can "make more" of it, argues that since the longest television viewers go without a commercial break is fourteen minutes, sermons should stay within the fifteen-minute range.[22]

But the question is not so much how long the sermon goes as how goes the sermon. People who sit down to hear a sermon do so with different expectations than when they sit down to watch a soap opera. In African American traditions of preaching, which are highly interactive, participatory, metaphorical, and performative, sermons can go on for hours without diminishment of attention because something is "happening." Fifteen-minute sermons that are linear, point-making, position-taking and intellectualist are fourteen minutes too long.

It will not be easy for religious leaders to make this transition to less linear styles of worship where participation replaces representation as the culmination of liturgy. I shall never forget my attempt at leading a field communion chapel service at United Theological Seminary. I preached on "The Square and the Circle," a sermon that explored the difference between "getting things right" and "seeing things straight." Sometimes "right" is "circuitous," not "straight."[23] There occurs a metaphysical convergence of these basic geometric shapes in the worship moment just before one opens one's hands to receive the elements from the priest (a half-circle) just after one has made the sign of the cross (a horizontal and vertical line) while kneeling at the altar.

After the sermon I then invited the community to come to the communion table, which had been brought down to the nave. I asked them to come not "like mourners approaching a funeral bier," or to return not "looking as though they have viewed the body," but to come as "an Easter celebration of thanksgiving, not a Good Friday observance of despair."[24] Piled on top of the table were fourteen massive loaves of bread, representing the continents of the world (Norwegian flat bread, African round bread, French long bread, Arab pita bread, Jewish challah, Swedish limpa, English muffins, Spanish tortillas,

49

Communion

German pumpernickel bread, Russian rye bread, Southern cornbread, San Francisco sourdough bread, Australian outback bread, Italian garlic bread), a mound of assorted colors and shapes at which the congregation had been staring throughout the service.

Every one of us boasts an ethnic pedigree from a continent where these breads are baked. Every student in worship that morning was also going to or had already visited one of these continents as part of a graduation requirement of a transcultural study experience somewhere in the world where the church is in ministry. In light of this, I asked the members of the community to come forward when moved by the Spirit during the singing of praise songs led by a synthesist, and to gather around the table in family-style fashion and take some chunks of bread from those places around the world that were of personal or familial significance. Four stations were positioned around the sanctuary, signifying the gospel's girdling of the globe, and people were invited to stop at multiple points of the compass to intinct their bread.

Even after all this prep work, I watched in amazement how the Spirit supposedly "moved" this congregation—once again in supermarket-style, grocery-store check-out, row-by-row (starting with the front) fashion. Even my own community couldn't break away from the standing-in-line mode of taking communion to gather around the table as a global family responding to the Spirit's call.

If you do not raise your eyes, you will think that you are the highest point.
Argentine writer ANTONIO PORCHIA

3. Lighten Up, Loosen Up

Why doesn't the body of Christ have a funny bone, for so many people? An old English saying has it that a surgical operation is needed to get a joke into the head of a Scotsman. Why do we try to make the disciples look like one of El Greco's sunken-eyed, skeletal ascetics? Why are Christians so hung-up?

Why is the God-look strait-laced and sober-faced? Why do we find it more congenial to see Jesus as a man of sorrows, acquainted with grief than a man of joy, acquainted with celebration and jubilation? Is it really holier to be nonsexual than sexual? Is Christianity rightly portrayed in cultural studies as a body-denying, sex-hating religion? Why do we celebrate those who pass up paradise rather than those who know how to enjoy the garden of earthly delights? Why is it more saintly to begin the day with saying, "Get thee behind me!" to yourself than to say, "Here I am Lord," to God?

> *We are all born sexual creatures, thank God, but it is a pity so many people despise and crush this natural gift.*
>
> MARILYN MONROE

If people are open to out-of-the-ordinary experiences, is there anything more out-of-the-ordinary than a gospel that turns the world upside down? That finds self by losing self? Is there any more radical idea than that? Georges Bernanos said that the only true adventure in life is the adventure of sanctity or holiness. The life of faith is not a set of problems and difficulties to be solved, as the modern era saw it; the life of faith is a destiny to be accepted, a journey to be explored and enjoyed.

4. No "Adult" (Adults-Only) Communities

Throughout history, God has spoken to us through a dazzling multitude of media—burning bushes, talking donkeys, raining frogs, invisible-inked walls, fiery chariots, dancing bones, naked prophets, harpist psalmists, and the most radically creative of all, God-made-flesh. Unfortunately, God's church is not nearly so open to the unexpected.

Establishment religion has, and one can say this without hesitation, done diddly to make electronic communication a form of communion. Indeed, establishment churches have virtually sainted electronic virgins, demonizing those who have made peace with "the Devil's blinking box" (i.e., television).

This shows unconscionable contempt for the spiritual well-being of a book-flipping, channel-switching generation with acute visual sensitivity. The church is not yet tele-literate when its own children are already "aliterate" (with a preference for electronic, polycentric modes of communication over print sources). Boosters' constant condemnations of the television as "the boob tube," "chewing gum of the eyes," a "cultural barbiturate," a "vast wasteland," a "golden goose that lays scrambled eggs," and so on is an insult to three generations now that have fallen in love with television the same way boosters themselves fell in love

> BEFORE LONG, AMERICANS WILL THINK OF THE TIME WHEN PEOPLE SAT AT HOME AND READ BOOKS FOR THEIR OWN SAKE, DISCURSIVELY AND SOMETIMES EVEN ALOUD TO ONE ANOTHER, AS A LOST ERA— THE WAY WE NOW SEE RURAL QUILTING BEES IN THE 1870s.
>
> ROBERT HUGHES

with books. New paradigm communities of faith need to stop warding off the "Evil Eye" of television.

In one sense, however, it is already too late. For the era of broadcast television is almost over. The era of tele-computer has just begun. The "broadcast" medium of TV is now obsolete; its plumping for "general" audiences has been trumped by the "niching" of cable and "narrowcasting" and the interactive technologies of the "teleputer," soon to be available on fibre optic phone lines. But the larger issue is the church's response to electronic media.

"And that's the way it is," Walter Cronkite's signature sign-off, stands also as a signature of an electronic culture, where the way-it-is is given to us by the media. Who has real power in any cultural system? Whoever defines our world. Whoever tells us "how it is." It is the information media that defines our world and is in charge. To claim an electronic culture for Christ necessitates the claiming of an electronic media for Christ.

To offer but a couple of examples out of hundreds that might be marshaled, the use of automated phone calling software to call parishioners on Saturday, giving them a personal message about worship in the morning, asking them if they have any prayer requests, and ending with a special prayer or Scripture verse that prepares them for the morrow. Pastors who have tried this are amazed at how members experience this as a caring call. Similarly, if "denominations" are to have a useful future, they must begin to use the new technology to create a lay-driven, desk-top, user-friendly, 800-number structure of accountability to the church at large. What next? Church Online.

The ability of the church to be user-friendly with an electronic culture is absolutely critical if the church is to try reach its own kids. Unfortunately, by and large the church's goal has not been, in the words of Elie Wiesel, "to prevent future generations from inheriting our past as their future." Youth work too often is seen as hack work. It is not.

Nor is children's work. Indeed, few ministries are more important to boomers and busters than "children's ministries." Here is where boomers expect the quality to be highest, the creativity most obvious: from teachers wearing costumes of biblical characters, to pace-setting quality children's newsletters, like the one a pastor's spouse in Milford Mill, Maryland, produces with some volunteers, which is sent weekly to each child in the church with a personal note attached.

5. Automagic Living

The relationship between mind and body is one of the central themes in biblical faith, but it is also one of the least acknowledged aspects of contemporary theology. Indeed, most of modern theology developed with little or no reference to the human body, as if the body weren't even there.[25] New paradigm churches will find ways to acknowledge both the pneumatic and somatic features of the Body of Christ.

Maurice Sendak, author and illustrator of 100 books, tells of receiving a touching fan letter from a little boy who wanted Sendak to know how much *In the Night Kitchen* had meant to him.

In reply, Sendak sent him a postcard decorated with the boy's name and a scribbled drawing. Sendak thought no more of it, until a few months later he received another letter from the boy's mother. So pleased was her son to receive Sendak's postcard, she reported, that he promptly ate it.

"'What greater pleasure?'" asks Sendak. "'With children, it's always a body pleasure.'"[26]

The gospel is always a body pleasure. It makes the body whole again: it brings together not just mind and spirit but also matter. Thanks in part to the women's spirituality movement, the body is no longer seen through the lens of shame but through the eyes of faith and wonder.[27] The church must help bring postmoderns back to their bodies. It is time to come home to the body; for the church to help people listen to their bodies and trust their body's wisdom.

Suffice it to say here in experiencequakes that there is now even the possibility of body pleasure in learning. The future of technology will be far afield from the passive audience of the medium of television. Just as art is moving from passive to active; so too is computer technology moving from interaction to participation, providing people the sense of having had life experiences that enliven and enrich our everyday, non-virtual reality.

Here is a Taoist legend adapted for virtual reality by Michael Heim:

The commission money was good and the artist arrived on time. One of the executives from corporate design was there to meet her at the door. After touring the facilities, the artist was left alone to begin painting. Each day the mural materialized a bit more, section by section, spreading a ribbon of color across the large gray wall at the end of the lobby. First a green patch of forest glade appeared, two blossoming plum trees, three sky-blue vistas, and a Cheshire cat

53

on a branch. Finally the day came when the tarp would fall. Employees gathered around plastic cups and croissants. When the speeches were over, the room grew hushed for the unveiling. The crowd gasped. The wall came alive with paradise, an intricate world of multicolored shapes. Several employees lingered to chat with the artist. Once the congratulations died down, the artist strolled to the center of the mural, stopping where the garden path leads into the forest, and, with face to the crowd, she smiled, bowed, and turned her back. Walking into the green leaves, she was never seen again.[28]

Homo Electronicus (a phrase coined by Joseph Pelton, telecommunications director at the University of Colorado) constitutes a new species of human for whom success and access is measured in neurons and nanoseconds rather than bullion and ballistics. It is possible now to give humans an endless number of mindbending experiences by hooking up our five senses to computers and interactive media. It is also called virtual reality.

Much of the promise of virtual reality is yet unrealized and unfulfilled. But the role of technology is redefining the relationships between humans and computers, even to the point of creating a new way of being Christian, much as print created new ways of being a Christian. The conceptual software and hardware of media technology is mind-boggling—interactive multimedia, virtual realities, cyberspace, authoring environments, DVI, CDI, HMDs, Data-Gloves, and much, much more pops up all the time. As computers get smaller and more mobile, and as people get more freed from the keyboard (voice recognition holds the greatest promise), the day of transparency between humans and computers is not far off. Some experts are already talking about cellular telephones implanted in individuals' heads.

Virtual reality technology, which made its public debut in the Gulf War, stands to be more than just a new interactive technology. It promises new dimensions of human experience and expression, some say the "Ultimate Experience." The potential for abuse is great. Talk show host Dennis Miller predicts that virtual reality will become an electronic drug that will "make crack cocaine look like Sanka."

Virtuality (as the deluxe video arcade game is called) involves "first-person" or "direct experience" sensory immersion inside an image or three dimensional interface that exists only inside a computer, but which appears as much like "the real thing" as the real thing.[29] A trip to Futuroscope outside Poitiers in France, "The European Park of the Image," gives an image of our "virtual" future.

Information-rich multimedia databases yoked to media technology now is making possible life lived "Automagically" (Brenda Laurel's phrase). Through the use of computer goggles, helmets, data gloves with built-in movement sensors and pressure sensors, and other devices to project our bodily motions and facilitate physical interactions, virtual reality offers even at its current state of development an "empty space" in which participants can exercise some of the highest forms of self-expression, self-discovery, and self-disclosure.

Once any "world model" or environment has been digitized, one can choose the space one wishes to live in for a while. Then enter a "total experience chamber"—the world of virtual reality—and you can fly _____, explore _____, dive _____, visit _____, race _____, join the "action" at _____, just fill in the blanks. As Meredith Bricken puts it, in virtual reality one can be "captain of his or her own ship in an ocean of one's own making."[30]

First applied with aircraft simulators and Omnimax projection systems (where the audience is submerged in engulfing images under a huge hemispherical dome), virtual reality is best defined as "multi-sensory media environments in which the viewer can interact with the information presented as they would in encountering the original scene." The viewers are "free to choose their own path through available information rather than remain restricted to passively watching a 'guided tour.' "[31] Its promise is that of a multiple, "viable, 3-dimensional, alternative realities providing the maximum number of individuals with the means of communication, creativity, productivity, mobility, and control over the shapes of their lives within the new information and media environment."[32]

"Cyberspace" even gives people virtual bodies in virtual realities. Randal Walser, manager of the Autodesk Cyberspace Project, envisions cyberspace as a form of theater, and calls it "a cyberspace playhouse for sports and fitness, a new kind of social gathering place where people go to participate in three-dimensional simulations."[33]

Instead of giving "edutainment" technology to Hollywood, or Wall Street, or the Pentagon, or Penthouse ("cybersex" or "dildonics" is already being proposed as the ultimate answer to "safe sex"),[34] why not get these new technologies into the hands of educators, both in the fields of general education and religious education. We are at the first time in history when we can help others to see and hear the story of Jesus in three dimensions. We are also at the first time in history when technology—orthotics, robotics, virtual reality, and so on—promises to close the gap between the outside world and those with devastating impairments.

No longer is it a matter of whether interactive two-way television (ITV), or extended classrooms, is going to become a major force in education. Dramatic changes in telecommunications industries through a variety of transmission technologies—microwave, cellular radio, fiber optic cable, satellite transmission—has already made ITV the medium of the future. It is only a matter of whether the church and its intellectual centers will capitalize on this medium and appropriate an omni-media curriculum of education that has print, audio, video, and computer components.

Postmodern culture is not either-or, but both-and. When a media revolution occurs, one doesn't lose a media form. One gains others. The written word succeeded but did not replace song, dance, and gesture.

It is like the addition of low or no-calorie sweeteners to the table. They have not cut back U.S. sugar consumption. In 1978, Americans consumed 13 pounds of sugar substitutes per person; by 1988, they averaged 20 pounds. During that time, sugar and other caloric sweetener consumption increased by 7 pounds a person.

My seminary has gone through four distinct phases in its use of computers. First came the large central mainframe. Next came the personal computer. Next arrived on the scene the "networking" of microcomputers. Now we are working on the netweaving of "networks." What is so significant, however, is that the seminary still uses a mainframe for student registrations and financial accountings. The mainframe was not superseded by distributed data processing, which in turn was not replaced by pc networks. Each new phase supplemented but did not supersede the previous phase.[35]

Similarly, the book is prospering as never before. Desk-top publishing has not threatened publishing companies, nor has home video made Hollywood tremble. It is not so much that the culture no longer has any "men of letters" (look at Garry Wills). But it now has "women of cds" and "men of electronics" as well.

There are many unresolved moral and philosophical issues relating to virtual reality.[36] If virtual reality is the ultimate learning experience, the potential is immense for helping the Bible to come alive in new and fresh ways for postmoderns. Proposals I have heard talked about include "Doorways to the Bible"; "Doorways to Missions"; "Bible Explorations" through "personalized television safaris" in which one could actually go down the streets of Jerusalem and decide what streets one wanted to go down. Or in a course on history or theology, using a "glove gesture" the student could interact with the crowd on Palm Sunday, or personally travel with Martin Luther or John Wesley, or interview Jürgen Moltmann.

Until we arrive at our virtual reality future, there are steps we can take to get people prepared. The American Bible Society has already issued an electronic translation of the story of the Gerasene demoniac that can be purchased for use in Bible study classes and youth groups. It comes in the form of an interactive, multimedia hypertext that is as state-of-the-art as anything one finds in business or education.[37] Or one can use computers in worship instead of a bulletin and worshipbook, as one pastor from Newburgh, Indiana, is doing. The computer operator pulls up messages, prayer requests, hymns, and so on on a screen in front of the congregation throughout the service.

The monograph has stood for centuries as the Enlightenment model of truth. The world of theological education must move from academic monographs in a print media to academic multigraphs in hypermedia (print, visual, audio, electronic). The church must find ways to synthesize literary functioning into an electronic context.

6. Body Freedom and Soul Food

Erotic life in our day is far from easy, which makes bringing together *logos* and *eros*, soul and sensuality, extremely risky. This is partly because postmodern culture is both a highly sexualized culture and at the same time one of the most "disembodied" and "anti-sensual" of all time.[38]

The late French philosopher Michel Foucault argued in his study of the history of sexuality that it is precisely centuries of repression by church and state that has brought us to this unerotic but "sexualized" state of affairs. A prevailing "angelism" strips the flesh from the soul, which explains the ubiquity of pornography as we reach for the lost bodies that are no longer a part of us.

The church is acutely sensitive to anything sensual or sexually arousing. But the church, founded by the "God made flesh," betrays its founder, the "God deep in the flesh," if it does not take this risk and exercise leadership in erotic relationships and erotic affirmations. As Martin Luther stated at the Marburg Colloquy (1529), "the only God I know is the God made flesh." New paradigm spiritualities are sensuous spiritualities. We must treat the eros of body pleasures in a new God-centered, not sex-centered way: as a gift from God, and as food for the soul.

First, there are erotic relationships with one's self. It is time the church gave up its angelistic notions of releasing the "good" soul from the "bad" body. It was axiomatic in the modern era that the gospel has everything to do with the spirit, something to do with the mind, and very little to do with the body.

Nothing could be farther from the truth. It behooves the church to put back together what the modern era cast asunder—mindbodyspirit, or bodysoul. But before we can experience body pleasures, however, the soul must be more in harmony with the body. As important as it is for some Christians to "get soul," that important is it for postmodern Christians to "get body."

The earlier saints of the church have not been nearly as inhibited about this as we are. They talked about living so as to touch Christ's "garment," to taste his "body," to hear his "voice," to see his "face," to smell his "presence." They believed the divine could be smelled, tasted, touched, heard, and seen. They enjoyed sufficient body freedom to engage in bodyworship.

"Don't just sit there. Do something!" Bodyworship is worship that doesn't just sit there, but does something: it sings, chants, shouts, hugs, cries, claps, kneels, runs, jumps, dances, laughs, dreams. "Do something" worship may even get people on the floor (kneeling in prayer) and in the aisles (clapping and clasping in praise) again like some of our "shouting" ancestors.

It's time the church came to its senses. It need not fear sensual delights. In

57

contrast to American literature, which from Hawthorne to Updike has specialized in the interconnections between religious and sexual experience, American ecclesiology has run the other way.[39] It is time to enter anew the realm of the senses through renewed appreciation of body praying, body signs (the sign of the cross), iconography (even rosaries), movement prayers where there is physical conversation between humans and God (also known as liturgical dance), drama, breathwork, mind-training disciplines, and practices of contemplation and meditation.

For example, bodyworship helps bring back the thunder. I grew up in the holiness tradition where when one prayed one "heard the thunder." Our bodies moved when we prayed because we almost always prayed on our knees. But the thunder started to roll as soon as the person leading in prayer said "O God, ..." Those were almost the last words anyone heard from the prayer leader until "in Jesus' name we pray, Amen." For everyone in worship prayed together—out loud.

James Lofton, one of the pastors at Christ Church, Memphis, has found a way to hermeneutically retrieve the thunder—except he begins with a thunderhush. During what is customarily called "the pastoral prayer," he asks the worshipers to stand, turn around, find someone's hand, and form concentric small circles throughout the sanctuary. He then invites everyone to spend time in silent prayer. This stage of prayer time is followed by people within the circles praying out loud if moved by the spirit. After this season of thunderous communal praying the pastor concludes with a brief prayer. All that is missing in Lofton's hermeneutical retrieval of the "thunder" is the thunderclap, which occurs when every willing worshiper prays simultaneously.

Second, there are the erotic relationships with others. In particular, the church can help lead in the developing of healthy perspectives on sex, which John Updike in *Rabbit at Rest* calls "soul food." A good place to begin might be the celebration of the fact that the Vatican has the world's largest collection of erotica (the British Museum comes in second). A good place to begin might also be the recognition that some biologists and taxonomists are arguing that humans should be reclassified as a third chimpanzee, alongside the common and pygmy chimps, *Pan troglodytes* and *Pan paniskos*. *Pan sapiens* would be an acknowledgment that humans share sexual life with the wider order of creation.

The church has already lost out in terms of who is shaping people's perspectives on sex: "Madonna has done more to affect the way young people think about sexuality than all the academic gender theorists put together."[40] Or what pastors attempted to pile upon them for that matter. The girl Fuchsia in *Gormenghast* gave the world the first use of *make love* for *have sex* [41]—a change in meaning that symbolizes a great deal of social change. We have given up

God's free gift of sex in favor of the learned techniques and earned knowledge of a modern Western invention called "sexuality." No wonder humorist James Thurber's quip that Americans are so confused "they can't tell love from sex, lust, Snow White or Ever After." If America has this trouble, how much more do Christians?

People are desperate for leadership that will guide their erotic relationships with others in moral directions other than what is legal and illegal, what is "safe" and "unsafe." Many of the expressions of what are defined as "sexual love" (pornography, pimping, advertising, etc.) are nothing more than violent fantasies and a sign of faith-life gone awry. Jesus taught that the sins of the soul are more grievous, partly because they give rise to the sins of the flesh. The church must not be bashful about proclaiming that what may be a riot for a time, may bring ruin forever if the gift of sex is misused. No can be the most life-affirming word in language. But at the same time the church must help people "say no" in ways that say yes to a sensuous spirituality.[42]

Unfortunately, the church is as fixated on sexuality as the rest of the culture. The only difference is that its fixation manifests itself as an obsession with sexual or pelvic sins. *Esquire* obsessions create *Esquire* scenarios, which helps explain the church's messy sexual state. As any executive session of any denomination's annual meeting painfully reveals, it is not just politicians that are afflicted with what William Safire has called the "bimbonic plague." Regardless what one thinks about homosexuality, it is not "the mother of all issues" as one pastor tried to tell me it was—although some gays and lesbians do not make it easy on Christians to be Christian when some artists seem to make a defense of offense or when certain novelists make Jesus Christ into a lover of boys.[43]

Third, there are erotic relationships with the world. Who we are as sexual beings has less to do with one aspect of life than with the whole of living and moving and being in the world. Ironically, the ascetic Shakers understood these sexual components of everyday living better than most in American religious history. Shakers deemed fresh baked bread so sensuous that they outlawed it.

Joanna Macy has argued that the world needs to be seen, not as some moral or psychic battleground or as a prison that entraps us and from which we must escape, but as a "lover," an intimate partner with whom we fall in love in all its splendor and spend our life getting to know. Macy tells the story of a poet friend who suffered a nervous breakdown, moved to New York City to live by herself, and walked the streets for months until she found healing and wholeness. "A phrase of her echoes in my mind: 'I learned to move in the world as if it were my lover.' "[44]

7. Get a [Fantasy] Life

If life is what Clement of Alexandria said it was—"a divine children's game"—it is time for the church to come to terms with unused play and unlived fantasy. Since the church has not been willing to resource the role of play and fantasy and imagination in life, Disney takes it over. Indications that the church is beginning to house fantasy and play are evident in Jerome W. Berryman's proposal of a learning methodology for religious education he calls "Godly play." As much a style of living as a method of learning, Berryman describes the life of faith as "playing with God," whereby "the player, other players, and God's earth can all join in the game."[45]

Jesuit Indian psychologist Anthony de Mello is one of the few to have acknowledged the "unsuspected and untapped source of power and life in our fantasy." In fact, withdrawal into a fantasy world is at almost the opposite pole from escape from reality. Indeed, true fantasy helps us "plunge more deeply into present reality—to perceive it better and to come to grips with it with renewed vigor." In de Mello's words, the difference between fantasy and memory is that "in fantasy I actually re-live the event I remember."[46]

To be in an absolutely fantastic universe with at best atrophied powers of fantasy and ossified imaginations is an abomination unto the Lord. It has also been one of the besetting sins of modern culture. Those beloved fairy tales that moderns read to their children did as much to discourage playfulness, squash curiosity, and stifle the imagination as postmodern culture's so-called "boob tube."[47] The church must help people develop the power to fantasize—to relate to God with imagination, to pray with imagination, and to become a play community.

> *Religion is lost with the repression of the high hope of adventure.*
>
> ALFRED NORTH WHITEHEAD

Some good examples of the church responding creatively and faithfully to the need for adventure ministries include "biblical hermeneutical field trips," the well-known Vacation Bible School "Jerusalem Marketplace," and the new "Journey to Bethlehem." African American biblical scholar Cain Hope Felder initiated the "biblical hermeneutical field trips" at Howard University School of Theology, where he required his students to take biblical texts to the streets and see how the Bible reads differently after visiting places "other" than one's familiar habitats. It is a model of biblical study worthy of wide adaptation.

"Journey to Bethlehem" was the North Riverdale Lutheran Church's Christmas gift to the Dayton community. "Journey to Bethlehem" is a form of living theater that takes one on a twenty to thirty minute journey back two thousand years into the marketplace, inn, and stable. Live animals, costumed townspeople tending their shops, roaming Roman soldiers bring alive the sights, aromas, and sounds of Bethlehem. You can stop and chat with the artisans, musicians, and merchants and learn about their lives and hear their version of the nativity. At the end of the tour a reception and free refreshments await the traveler, with members of the church present to answer any questions.

8. Wing It

Learn to ride those spiritual air currents that lift life above the ground and help one soar through each day "on a wing and a prayer."

Postmoderns are eager to break the molds of spiritual mediocrity through an active devotional life, ritual exercises, spiritual travel adventures, and so on. Madonna evidences the universal nature of this postmodern need to spiritually "wing it"—pray and read scriptures like people take an aspirin, "on a wing and a prayer"—by her practice before every concert (see Truth or Dare[48]) of gathering together her performers for a circle prayer.

There will be increasing importance attached to the devotional practices of prayer, fasting, and meditation, which in their essence combine the oxymoronic forces so beloved by postmoderns. For example, in meditation one is "at one and the same time both unusually relaxed and unusually aware."[49] Meditation is at once escape and engagement; a simultaneous centering and decentering. "Meditation is often proposed as a way of handling stress, but it is also a way of unlearning the addiction to entertainment and its accompanying vulnerability to boredom."[50]

In the deterministic world of modern science, prayer didn't make sense. The postmodern world where ultimate reality is spirit has virtually returned us to a more biblical outlook on the world. In the words of Nancey Murphy, "changes in philosophical approaches in understanding causation, and changes in science itself, have in effect removed the major obstacles to belief in God's continuing action in the world."[51] Little wonder Ken Briggs writes in the New York Times Magazine, "A prayer revival is the most powerful, least documented development within modern American religion today."[52]

It will be important for postmodern Christians to revitalize ancient and contemporary prayer forms that provide the church with a solid prayer base, as well as develop new forms of family devotions, daily offices, Christian mantras, and so on. One way might be to substitute old "family bedtime devotions" with nightly storytelling sessions.

My image of postmodern praying is having a tuning fork in one hand and a pitchfork in the other. The pitchfork image is obvious; a true prayer is not something one does with one's lips but what one does with one's life. Each of us is called to become in as literal a sense as we can understand it the Lord's Prayer. But the mission of pitchforking the eternal into the temporal can begin only when we have put that tuning fork to use.

Prayer is attunement. Our body is an instrument, tuned for the right pitch, which is God's pitch. But we all get out of tune very easily. We become out of tune with God. Part of prayer is lifting life toward God. Prayer is getting in tune with the eternal. Jesus is our tuning fork for the eternal. Jesus is God's Perfect Pitch.

We live in a universe that resembles one immense, interconnected information system in which a thought or a task undertaken in one corner has unpredictable effects on other corners of the system. Prayer is turning down the volume controls to the outside world, tuning out diversionary frequencies and, through ritual and fasting, turning on the divine frequencies and tuning in to God. Whereas, in traditional Christian thought, fasting was supposed to be an act of self-abnegation and sacrifice, in postmodern terms fasting is conceived of as an exercise of self-fulfillment and service. By fasting one not only loses weight, but purges the body of years of accumulated toxins, identifies with the marginal, relieves tension, sharpens the mind, and tunes the being.[53]

Soldiers throughout history, when they come to a bridge, break step. They have learned from experience that their marching cadence gives off a frequency that, in rare instances, matches the frequency of the bridge. When frequencies match, there is achieved technically a state of "resonance" or sympathetic vibration that can literally collapse the bridge and everything on it. Remember the Ella Fitzgerald memorex commercial? When singers modulate their voices upward until their frequency matches the frequency of something else in the room, whether a drinking glass or a pane of glass, there is achieved a state of "resonance," a sympathetic explosion of energies, a vibrating, pulsating exchange of energies until something has to give or rattle.

This is precisely what happens in prayer. Prayer is attuning our beings to the frequencies of the Spirit until "resonance" with the divine is reached. When we reach those rich, full registers where mysterious things happen, then something has to give, and our lives are transformed, transfigured, if you will, into the divine image. Our minds and bodies then vibrate until it's as if they have wings. When people not just individuals combine their thoughts and tune themselves together to the divine, then act in harmony on the basis of those vibrations and pulsations, there is a rhythmic entrainment of group conscious-ness[54] until the church becomes literally what the Bible says it should be: the Body of Christ on planet Earth.

Jesus' resurrection released a power in the universe—a power that can raise life to a higher power. That is what resurrection does: raises up. One day our raised bodies will be raised in power and raised in glory. But the resurrection powers that have been released and unleashed in the universe can raise our life to a higher power right now. We can begin eternal life now.

But this can be done only through attunement. New paradigm churches will help postmoderns develop a rich personal and communal "prayer life" through natural ways of praying, not prayers bogged down with a slag-heap of spirit-breaking, mind-numbing jargon. It is time for some hermeneutical retrievals of the old-fashioned "prayer meeting," the "concerts of prayer," and "prayer breakfasts." It is also important to celebrate "answered prayers" publicly, some-thing already being called by some as "thank you notes to God."

The postmodern hunger for prayer rites and styles that can "raise them up" is manifest in the success of the "Prayer for Peace." Introduced ten years ago with the blessing of Mother Teresa and now translated into forty languages, this prayer makes explicit the connection between peace within ourselves and peace in the world. It has now become a favorite way for many postmodern families to say grace before a family meal.[55]

9. No Euphorics Without Euphonics

Music is the means to God for much of postmodern culture. There can be little enchantment without a chant. The re-enchantment of the church as well as the re-enchantment of the world hinges on whether the soul can find its voice again.

As Prince and Madonna evidence with every world tour, music is in itself a spiritual experience, with or without the church. In one of the most suggestive passages of Gerard Manley Hopkins' spiritual writings, he speculates that the origin of evil began when the angel Lucifer became so enraptured with the beauty of his own music-making that it captured him within it. In contrast with Christ, who led the angelic choir in singing harmonious notes of "Venite Adoremus" to God, Lucifer sounded "his own trumpet" and hymned "his own praise" until "it became an incantation: others were drawn in; it became a concert of voices, a concerting of selfpraise, an enchantment, a magic, by which they were dizzied, dazzled and bewitched."[56]

New musical forms will be required if churches desire vibrant ministries, espe-cially to boomers, busters, and after-busters. If the postmodern world is not to be "dizzied, dazzled and bewitched" by the power of countermusic (MTV has been called the first postmodern television network), new paradigm churches must create for their members a rich and varied musical life, both at home and in community. Whether through writing new lyrics to fit contemporary rock or country and western tunes, as Doug Murren recommends in "Roll Over, Chuck Wesley!";[57] whether through attaching favorite hymn lyrics (e.g., "What a Friend We Have in Jesus") to familiar pop tunes (e.g., "Scarlet Ribbons"); whether through a variety of worship teams that teach new music; one of the most effective forms of postmodern communication and evangelization is through the ministry of music.

Music-making that has spiritual integrity intones the music of the spheres, not of the self. In 1938 Ludwig Wittgenstein visited St. Patrick's Hospital in Dublin, and was especially drawn to one mentally-ill music-lover. "This man is much more intelligent than his doctors," Wittgenstein is reported to have claimed. "I asked him what was his favorite instrument in the orchestra, and he replied, 'the big drum.'" Every one of us knows the Luciferic attraction of beating on that big drum of the self. But "the big drum" is not the path to mental wholeness or spiritual salvation.

> *There let the pealing Organ blow,*
> *To the full voic'd Quire below,*
> *In Service high, and Anthems clear,*
> *As may with sweetness, through mine ear*
> *Dissolve me into extasies,*
> *And bring all Heav'n before mine eyes.*
> JOHN MILTON, *Il Penseroso*

Music is an absolute imperative if postmoderns are to move outside of themselves, connect with others, and build community. One can motivate and move individuals to an experience of God without music—perhaps. But to have a community experience of God's presence, to bring a community of faith to a "catalytic moment" (as African American preacher DeForest Soaries would put it), music is a must.

Indeed, group singing and interactive musical experiences are the chief communifying forces of the postmodern era. No one is arguing this more forcefully than Jill Purce, author of *The Mystic Spiral* (1974) and advocate of perceiving the body as a "vibratory system" with multiple resonances. In the past, church was a "tuning" place where people could sing, chant, and intone together, thereby tuning their mindbodyspirits to their families (in this way the family could be "in tune with itself"), their village community, and their geographical place and time in history.

The importance of the church's liturgical calendar was that it enabled communities of faith, no matter how remote, to tune together with the whole of Christendom by enacting the same rituals in similar ways and similar times. "Through sonorous means every thing or being was resonantly embedded in a greater meaning."[58] Or to express this more theologically, as Dietrich Bonhoeffer does, "It is the voice of the Church that is heard in singing together. It is not you that sings, it is the Church that is singing, and you, as a member of the Church, may share in its song."[59]

Purce shows how in the modern era society and souls went silent. The mechanized world of the industrial era became the chief music-maker, as "we shifted the whole emphasis from a natural world full of natural sounds—birds, the wind in the trees, and within it, ourselves singing and chanting as we praised the Divine—to a noisy world within which we ourselves are silent." Of course, we paid and paid well some "professionals" to make the sounds for us, as we sat back and listened. Then "we put the sounds of these professionals inside a machine," and excluding all other natural and human sounds, "put the machine over our ears, as close to our brain as possible. Then, unfortunately, since headphones impair our hearing, we end up silent and deaf in a noisy world!"[60]

A life silent of "joyful noises unto the Lord," or a worship life where others (whether choirs or soloists) make those noises for you, is a life lived out of tune; we become out of tune physically, mentally, morally, spiritually, and socially. Through the resonant fields created by liturgy, the whole person comes together and becomes alive through music, and from the heat of that aliveness individuals weld together to form a community. Singing in worship is indispensable, because it is by singing that we tune ourselves to each other, and tuned together we then turn to God and tune ourselves to the music that is God. It is by singing that we become a vibrating community, resonating with the divine music of the spheres.

If there is "a part of the soul all made of tunes," as composer Charles Ives insisted, the postmodern soul is filled with praise tunes. How sad, to take but one example of our noiselessness, that in the midst of a worldwide musical "praise" revolution, establishment churches have so far insisted on largely sitting the "hosannas" out, content to mock from the sidelines these "schlocky little Jesus songs."[61]

But as biblical scholar John Koenig argues, praise and thanksgiving are one of the threads that stitch the Scriptures together. Indeed, he has found more than two hundred occasions in the New Testament alone to give God thanks and praise, regardless of whether there appear reasons for being glad and grateful.[62]

65

Augustine defined a hymn as "the sung praise of God." The prayer Jesus gave his disciples to pray begins and ends in praise. One of the first examples of hymn-singing in corporate Christian worship is a simple praise song: "O magnify the Lord!" (Ps. 34:3; see also Rev. 4:8: "Holy, holy, holy, the Lord God the Almighty, who was and is and is to come"; Rev. 4:11: "You are worthy, our Lord and God to receive glory and honor and power.") In singing praises, we join our songs to those of the heavenly choruses already magnifying God with their voices. Praise choruses are to music what chocolate is to food. Worshipers come today with rather a sweet tooth, which requires some careful rationing of how much is served. But only a severe spirit refuses guests the sweets of faith.

One person bragged to me that the church he attended enjoyed music every Sunday "just this far from the Met." Unfortunately, as the almost three-digit cost of opera tickets might suggest, opera is not the primary way God is speaking musically to postmodern culture. But neither is "Kum Ba Yah" campfire music. Perhaps now that its composer is dead, the church will declare a moratorium on "Kum Ba Yah" for a few years. It may have been the kind of music kids were singing at summer camp in 1935, when seventeen-year-old Marvin V. Frey wrote it while attending a Christian Crusade camp. But "Kum Ba Yah" is not the normative sound for summer camps of the twenty-first century.

Even music critic Virgil Thomson understands this more profoundly than do most "tall-steeple" pastors. While music critic for the *New York Herald-Tribune*, Thomson was criticized for the inadequate coverage of church music in his column. His response is a classic:

> Church music . . . is not presented to the public at all, at least in principle, but to God. And God does not necessarily judge acts of worship by professional standards, since sincerity in His eyes may well make up for technical inefficiencies.[63]

The heart of worship is *eucharistia*, the offering of praise and thanksgiving for what God has done in Jesus Christ. It is hard for moderns—educated critically to say No—to sing songs (like praise hymns) that only say Yes. Biblical scholar Leander Keck, who at the same time bemoans the way in which much contemporary worship has reversed the opening lines of the Westminster Confession, "for now the chief end of God is to glorify us and to be useful to us indefinitely," argues that unless "purposeless praise of God is restored to its central place in worship, mainline Protestantism will not be renewed." "Purposeless praise" is praise to God for who God is, "not for what our fulsome talk will get [God] to do for us. Indeed, if the gospel is reliable, God is to be praised because of what has already been done for us, and will be done for us, that we cannot do for ourselves, because that is the kind of Reality God is."[64] And song is the best way to praise the grace and goodness of God. "Your statutes have become my songs," intoned the psalmist (119:54).

In fact, it was not simply the Methodist movement that was "born in song," thanks to "Chuck" Wesley and his 6000 hymns. Most of the powerful spiritual awakenings in history have been sung before being lived out with intensity and integrity. This is why Jewish theologian Abraham Heschel insists that "Praise precedes faith. First we sing, then we believe. The fundamental issue is not faith but sensitivity and praise, being ready for faith."[65]

To be sure, communities must join intercessions for the world to these praise songs—the other part of *eucharistia* that the church must contribute to this growing "praise revolution" around the world. After all, it was the prophet Amos who interrupted a worship service at ancient Bethel because of its lack of "concerns and announcements" about the world. Thomas W. Mann suggests that Amos' "praise hymn," with which he interrupted their worship, might have gone something like this (set to the liturgical tune of Old Hundredth):

> *What the word makes clear, music makes alive.*
>
> FRIEDRICH SCHLEIERMACHER

> May God curse you, you hypocrites;
> You'll soon end up in the obits;
> If you don't change your unjust ways,
> You soon will see your final days.[66]

There is also the need for postmodern Christians to be bimusical—to be able to express one's beliefs in more than one musical tradition, and to know a second musical language and tradition almost as well as one's own.[67]

But the challenge of making these two corrections to the "praise revolution" should not slow the church from adopting the musical forms in which God is speaking to the culture in which we live. Postmodern communities of faith need pianos (and pianists), organs (and organists), and synthesizers (and synthesists, experts in electroacoustic music). Postmodern celebrations also need worship spaces where there is great sound, and where song leaders can open up and reach the whole person to receive the gospel in song and sermon.

Song leaders should be brought back to worship and valued for their key role in building community. These song leaders are not just metronomes with a human face standing in front of towering million-dollar pipe organs. Song leaders in new paradigm faith communities see their role in celebration as body builders—breaking down barriers between people, and building bridges among the diversity of people present so that there can be two-way traffic between heaven and earth. Combining ministers of music and fine arts would also highlight the importance of aesthetics in the life of faith.

A cricket in Asia is known to become so enraptured by its song that it consumes its own legs. Postmoderns are human crickets who are eating out their hearts for a song—and a resonant spirituality. It is time the church played the kind of music that would rescue crickets from having to cannibalize themselves.

MicroQuakes

SocioQuake 3:
Small Indulgences

Popcorn's socioquake of "Small Indulgences" is based on the "I-Deserve-Its" (IDI) Syndrome. Manifested most openly in the busters' "twentysomething" generation, the "IDI" worldview or "IDI-ology"[1] places a premium on the needs of the self at the same time it espouses a belief that "You get what you deserve"; "There's no free lunch"; "You deserve it"; "You deserve a break today"; "Go ahead. You earned it." According to the IDI syndrome, having a "meaningful relationship" meant someone was "meeting my needs."

The proprietor of a West Virginia country store adamantly refused to purchase for his shelves something the salesperson was touting as the "latest," "best-selling" fad. "You must remember," the storekeeper said, "that in this part of the country every want ain't a need." Consumer culture has come to regard luxuries as necessities, virtually abandoning the concept of "needs" or a "needs"-based social order. When "needs" no longer were needed or wanted, we got the 1980s, when consumers went from "need" to "want" to "deserve." Or as a 1970s graduate student replied to my incredulity at her working herculean hours to purchase a blatant luxury, "I want it, Professor Sweet, therefore I need it." The 1980s added "I want it, therefore I need it, therefore I deserve it." That is also, some have added, why I'll kill you for your sneakers.

The "Small Indulgences" socioquake of the 1990s gives way to all sorts of cultural bingeing: overdosing on data, overdosing on food, overdosing on relationships. There is but temporary exhilaration in bingeing. When life returns to normal, and addictions are conquered, postmoderns quickly get interested in much smaller, and more modest, scales of living. Postmodern consumers are "downshifting" in their buying, shopping for the best and bargain prices on everything, trying out low-end goods, setting limits on spending, and abandoning long-standing loyalties to brand-names.

For example, the buster and after-buster generations are not as money-obsessed as either the boosters or the boomers. Admittedly, the evidence here is contradictory. At the heights of the 1960s (1967), when asked by the Higher Education Research Institute (UCLA) whether they were going to college to develop a "meaningful philosophy of life," 92.9 percent of college students said yes. In 1987, that figure had dropped to 39.4 percent. What about going to college to become "well off financially"? In 1970, 39.1 percent said that was their main reason. By 1987, the figure had soared to 75.6 percent.[2] But the late 1980s and early 1990s have registered a dramatic reversal of engines. Indeed, busters seem to be leading the way in living less hedonic states of existence, in simpler, less acquisitive life-styles. They are picking wilderness camping over Winnebago campers.

"MOBYs" (Mommy Older, Baby Younger) and "DOBYs" (Daddy Older, Baby Younger) and WOOFs (Well Off Older Folks) and PUPPIES (Poor Urban Professionals) and SKIPPs (School Kids with Income and Purchasing Power) and NILOKs (no income, lots of kids) and SINKs (single income no kids) and DINKs (dual income no kids) and DINS (dual income no sex) and SINS (single income no sex) have begun practicing little economies. But these noble little economies enable the MOBYs, the DOBYs, the PUPPIES, the WOOFs, the SKIPPs, the DINKs, and the SINS to be naughty every now and then. Busters scrimp and save—"nouveau cheap" *The New York Times* dubs this phenomenon—so that they can splurge in one area.

Busters are much more pessimistic than their pragmatic forebears, an attitude that glistens through the prism of food. There is a growing preference for sourish or sweetsour taste stimulants over pure "sweets"—hence the rise of kiwi fruit, grapefruit/cranberry juice (great mixed), and carambolas. Postmoderns will likely be tempted by the quirky and sourish flavors of rhubarb, quince, persimmon, gooseberries, and so on.

Hence the "small indulgences" socioquake: "choosing one small category in your life and buying the best you can buy in that arena."[3] After reading about this in Popcorn's book, I walked off the plane into a Texas terminal, there to be greeted by a newly opened store named "Small Indulgences." Their wares? Expensive chocolates. How else does one explain the Starbucks coffee craze of the Pacific Northwest, or the super-premium Ben & Jerry's ice cream frenzy of North America: even if I can't afford the Ralph Lauren shirt or the Lexus car, I can buy the best frothed latte or the best double-dutch chocolate made on this planet.

As Popcorn puts it, people today want "Some small material 'reward'—some little lift of luxe—. . . and damned if we don't deserve them." Consumers are willing to pay more for premium brands, buy more exotic products, and choose products that express a personal sense of style while sacrificing in other areas of life. Postmoderns need to feel periodically pampered, even at times naughty. If they've dieted all week, they deserve one binge on the weekend. In the Lake Michigan resort community of Petoskey, Michigan, a TCBY (The Country's Best Yogurt) went belly-up. Why? A newly opened homemade ice cream parlor featuring such memorable mouth-watering flavors as Swiss Chocolate Almond did them in. People dieting all year on non-fat, sugar-free yogurt feel deserving of some real ice cream on vacation.

FaithQuake 3:
MicroQuakes

1. *Grace Upon Grace*

The challenge for the postmodern church is this: How do you preach grace to a society that is under the illusion that they deserve everything they can get and have gotten?

At Christmas and Easter many communities across the U.S. have begun community sing-ins where amateur singers can gather in an auditorium to join together in singing *The Messiah*. They call these gatherings "Do-It-Yourself-Messiah." That is precisely what God has become: a do-it-yourself-deity. A do-it-yourself spirituality of sweat and self-denial fashions a salvation through works rather than grace. A thirty-four-year-old widow, Marjory Kempe, in Lynn, Massachusetts, in 1667 received this word from the Lord: "More pleasing to me than all your prayers, works, and penances is that you would believe I love you."[4]

Postmoderns need fresh understandings of grace. One of the most amazing phrases in all of the Scriptures is found in John 1:14, 16, where it says of our Lord that he was "full of grace" and "From his fullness have we all received, grace upon grace." Grace upon grace: this is stockpiling, accumulating, unlimited grace; one grace following another grace; grace that is greater than we can ever ask or think or even need. This is the grace God makes available to each of us on a daily, as-needed basis.

The problem is that postmoderns think they have done it themselves. Historian Nathan O. Hatch, in his recent "The Perils of Being a Professional," lists as the third great peril, indeed the mother of all perils, the belief by boomer professionals that "they deserve" the career and financial success "they have achieved."

> Yet a Christian has to check the impulse that says, "I deserve it." How does this square with other biblical truths—that our standing before God is not as accomplished experts, but as miserable offenders desperately in need of grace? Furthermore, all of our gifts, our creativity and good health, our time and energy, are themselves God's good gifts. Their end must not be self-exaltation, living the good life, but the service of Christ and his kingdom.[5]

> ## LESS IS MORE.
> ### GERMAN PROVERB

For Christians the whole point of entering the professions is not success or the good life or career—rather it is "to serve rather than to be served."

2. The Celling Out of the Church

Give up congregational (or "single cell") thinking, which is basically "mass" thinking in ecclesiastical garb. Think "micro" to get "macro." Jesus said that until we have become "faithful over a little," we will not be given the large. Honor your gifts, especially the smallest ones: Become "small-minded" if you want to get "big-hearted." The Law of the Microcosm (as well as the Spirit of Christ) exalts the smallest components, the smallest systems, the small things of life. Those communities of faith who will do best in the future will score the highest in attention to detail. Coca-Cola has built a worldwide empire on close attention to tenths of a percentage point. Coke is 99.8 percent water and sugar.

Postmodern culture makes an axiom of "one can always do more if one will do less." It thinks "nano," "micro," "meta," "mini," and so on. There is a new appreciation of "small-mindedness" that is evident everywhere, including surprising places—from the way we domesticate the rich and famous by devouring the small print of their lives to the scaled-down feel of toys (especially adult electronic toys).

In the divine calculus taught by Jesus, the loss of one threatens the survival of all. The one lost sheep is worth as much as the ninety-nine sheep that were never lost—that is, one person saved is worth the inconvenience and risk of everyone else—because the fate of the ninety-nine hinges on what happens to the one. What happens to the whole depends on how the smallest parts are treated.

When the former Secretary of the Interior (Manuel Lujan) asks in exasperation, "Do we have to save them all?" there can only be one answer: "Yes." No species is an island, separate unto itself. All species are related. In a postmodern world of Medicare and Medicaid, the disease of any one of us is a day of reckoning for the rest of us. Your decision not to take care of yourself (e.g., smoking) doesn't just increase your chance of dying from lung cancer 11 fold, or double your chances of dying from heart disease; it also imposes a cost of 34 percent greater risk of lung cancer among your loved ones, not to mention greater health care costs for every taxpayer in the country.[6] Rather than the response to the downtrodden of "There but for the grace of God go I," the authentic response is "That's me!," or more biblically yet: "There by the grace of God go I." If we fail to see ourselves in others, we fail to see the God of us all.

This mathematics gave birth to Jesus' very simple ecclesiology: where two or three are gathered in his name. Or as someone has summarized it, "If two's company for Jesus, three's a church."

The ecclesiology of the early church was almost as simple: a small group of no more than fifteen to thirty members gathered together in members' homes forming a "pneumatic democracy" known as "house churches."

The church has wandered too far from its ecclesiological roots. Church programming expert Loren Mead, former head of The Alban Institute, makes the correct diagnosis—"the congregation is at a critical point of change"—but then seeks to "save" the congregation by "reinventing" it.[7] Perhaps it is time to give up "congregational" thinking and program-based community life entirely. This story explains why.

"This retreat is the last chance nine of us couples are giving this church." With these words I began a weekend retreat for a small-town church outside of Indianapolis. The town was experiencing an influx of young couples, but the church could neither attract nor keep many of them. What was wrong? Congregational thinking.

I asked a vibrant professional woman to give me an example of her problem with the church. She told the story of how nine new couples to the church, all with kids under two years of age, stumbled into each other one Sunday morning over coffee in the Fellowship Hall. The conversation turned to issues of Christian parenting. Someone suggested they get together for a while to work on how better to raise kids in a Christian climate and to build a Christian home. Everyone thought it was a great idea. They even came up with a name for themselves: COPS (Couples of Preschoolers).

"That's a great idea," I enthused. "What did you do next?"

"We took it to the pastor," she replied.

"Another right idea. What did he say?"

"Well, he said we'd have to take it to the Administrative Council to get permission."

I didn't say anything for a moment, and then ventured: "Were you asking for any money?"

73

She shook her head. "No, we just wanted to do it in the name of the church, and hoped for some help in resourcing."

"What happened next?" I nervously inquired.

"I drafted a proposal for COPS, and waited for the next monthly meeting of the Ad. Council. They put me on at the end of the agenda, and I sat there during the meeting waiting to make my proposal. When it came time for miscellaneous business, the Chair turned to me and asked to distribute drafts of our COPS proposal. I made the appeal for the formation of this group, and that's when the proverbial you-know-what hit the fan."

"What do you mean?"

"Well, the first person to respond to the proposal was a single mother who asked if she too could join our group."

"What did you say?" I prompted.

"I said, 'Well, I guess so. No, well, I guess I'll have to ask the group. There's already eighteen of us, which is a large group to begin with, and all of us are couples. I'd have to ask them.'"

"Then what happened?"

"Then a grandmother who said she had primary care for a two-year-old wanted to know if she and her husband could join our group. They were a couple, she said."

"What did you say?" I asked.

"Well, I guess I said the same thing: I'd have to ask the group. All of us were under thirty, and we conceived COPS as something for young couples."

"How did it all end?"

"Dr. Sweet, it ended when they took a vote, and tabled the proposal until I could submit to the Board a more 'inclusive' plan that would encompass the entire congregation in it's design."

I shook my head. The Spirit of God was moving in that church that evening, even in spite of all the bureaucratic hoops and hoopla that this creative layperson was put through. How many small groups or cells were wanting to be born that evening? At least four (one for couples with kids under two, one for singles with kids under two, one for grandparents with kids under two, and one for a hodge-podge with kids under two). But because this church could not relinquish its congregational thinking, instead of four new groups it had none. It also lost eighteen new members.

I repeat: Give up "congregational" thinking altogether. This means giving up being a program-designed church and becoming a people-designed church. This means taking up niching and people-based ministries. A tent-making preacher-friend, a shepherd from Indiana named Darrell Borders, faced the challenge of how to get the men in his rural community to take church seriously. So he first took one of their cultures, the outdoor-male culture, seriously. What he came up with has astounded everyone in its success: occasional Saturday evening fellowships that conclude a day spent hunting in the woods—a Squirrel Fry, a Rabbit Fry, and who knows what else he'll fry next.

Think small. Get small. The key number of the meta-church is ten, although even smaller numbers like four (Holy Club) and five (Haystack Prayer Meeting) have had great effect. Keep cells small—there is power and strength in small-scale. As Peter Drucker says, "You can't motivate the masses"; or in its converse form, "The smaller the group, the greater the motivation."[8]

Actually, the "group" may even be made up of one. This is what is being called a "new paradigm politics"—a one-person, one-project, one-issue politics that uses SWAT-team strategies. This is being pioneered in the enviromental arena, where Renée Askins, founder of the Wolf Fund, is a model. Her single, monomaniacal vision is the reintroduction of the wolf to Yellowstone National Park, a goal which began to gel when she wrote a paper for a college theology course on the role of the wolf in religion. When that goal is accomplished, Askins will get on with her life, and the Wolf Fund's sunset clause will go into effect, and the fund will no longer exist.[9]

> The love of country is a spendid thing, but why should love stop at the border?
>
> PABLO CASALS

Big numbers in and of themselves mean nothing. Argentinean pastor Juan Carlos Ortiz writes "God began speaking to me about the condition of the church. He said that we were not growing. My reply to that was, 'Lord, we are growing. We have gone from 200 to 600 in two years.' And God said, 'You are not growing'; you are just getting fat!' "[10] Or in the words of Baptist evangelist Vance Havner, commenting on the impact of evangelicals on USAmerican culture, "We may be many, but we ain't much."[11]

The cutting edge of missionary churches is double-edged: more megachurch and more micro/alternative church. Both will grow in the future, as will decentralized traditional churches. In megacongregations there is an immense use of resources—land, money, materials, and so on. In fact, the rule of thumb for suburban growth is one hundred to one: worship attendance cannot grow greater than one hundred times an acre of land. That means an attendance of one thousand requires one hundred acres. By contrast, the micro or alternative church are light on the land, use very few natural resources, and are reluctant to invest capital in buildings and their upkeep.

75

New nontraditional models of "being church" in ministry to the world include the microchurch (house churches, base communities, covenant groups, intentional communities, twelve-step groups, etc.), perimeter-satellite, "hub-and-spoke" churches; metachurches; nonchurches; co-churches (named after the "co-housing" movement; in this version multiple churches share the same facilities); transchurches (multistaff, multilocations, multi-ministries, yet with a single identity, a single mission, and a single force of leadership and governed by the entire members from all the parts); and megachurches, the emergence of which Peter Drucker calls one of the most significant social changes in late twentieth-century America. One-half of the people who attended church last week attended one-seventh of the churches.[12] These new models of the missionary church are associated with particular communities like the Church of the Saviour in Washington, D.C.; The Circle Church in Chicago; New Hope Community Church in Portland, Oregon; Saddleback Valley Community Church in Mission Viejo, California; Bear Valley Baptist Church in Denver, Colorado; the house churches in China; the base communities in Latin America; and the Yoido Full-Gospel Church in Seoul, Korea.

Of all these new models, the metachurch is by far the most significant. The metachurch model revolves around two events: small groups or cells (also known as "affinity groups," study groups, TLC, or CTTC groups [Cut Through The Crap groups]); and large corporate worship/celebrations. The closest thing to a sure-fire formula, a one-size-fits-all model for any church is one that the metachurch understands best:

He who would do good to another must do it in Minute Particulars. General Good is the plea of the scoundrel hypocrite and flatterer, for Art and Science cannot exist but in minutely organized Particulars.

WILLIAM BLAKE

cells + celebration = body-life church

Indeed, the metachurch graphically illustrates the postmodern ability to do oppositions that are not contradictions: the dual tendency to get more micro (specifically niched small groups) and macro (inclusive, large communities) at the same time. In the metachurch the primary care givers are not the "clergy" but laity and decentralized home discipleship centers. Unfortunately, a missing part of many metachurch formulas is the reason for the church's being in the first place: the mission of God in the world.

3. Less Is More, Little Is Much If God Is in It

A new austerity has gripped the postmodern world; it is bad taste in the 1990s to flaunt possessions. Ostentation is out. There is emerging a Reign of Quality over Reign of Quantity. People are getting tired with a life of getting as much money as possible in as short a time as possible with as much show as possible. They are learning to do more with less.

> MY DEAR WATSON, IT HAS BEEN AN AXIOM OF MINE THAT LITTLE THINGS ARE INFINITELY THE MOST IMPORTANT.
>
> SHERLOCK HOLMES

The meaning in life is in the small numbers, not in the big numbers. The same week Wilt Chamberlain makes his pathetic boast about having sex with 20,000 women, Magic Johnson makes his announcement about being HIV-positive, caused also by casual encounters ("A matter of numbers," he said). In the words of historian John G. Stackhouse, Jr., we have been taught to "like things big. Big events. Big projects. Big institutions. Big budgets. Big personalities."[13] We are searching for the "big time," and not finding it in bigness. Growthism is unfulfilling. We must get over our disease of gigantic achievement and give up our get-big-or-get-out mentality.

> The longer the title,
> the less important the job.
>
> GEORGE MCGOVERN

Wisdom moves toward less, not more; the small, not big. Paradoxically, the megametaphor for a devolutionary world is "micro." The big time is small town. Why can't the church lead the devolution revolution? It can if it thinks small is beautiful, gets small and launches small-scale projects in alternative living.

The metachurch reflects niche-or-be-niched principle of small-town thinking at work. A metachurch is not so much one church as a network of small churches. Ironically, megacongregations are better miniaturists than small membership churches. It is those churches balking at balkanization who are the most quarrelsome and opposed to higher levels of integration and cooperation.

The think-small "principle applies everywhere. In the Negev Desert, the Israelis are perfecting traditional "water harvesting" techniques. Instead of gathering rainwater into large centralized reservoirs, they are carefully channeling every precious drop of precipitation into hundreds of local cisterns, with minimum loss of precipitation through evaporation and a remarkable 95 percent water efficiency. The most generative scientific minds alive today are not part of the big science establishment, but are working at small outposts in Santa Cruz (Ralph Abraham), Devon, Canada (James Lovelock), the University of Massachusetts (Lynn Margulis), and Paris (Francisco Varela).

A symbol of importance is not how many keys you have on your chain, but how few. The point is to progressively get rid of keys, not gain more of them. The point is not to build up assets in some bank account, but to respond to Christ's call to give away every good gift we have received. The point of life is not that "the one who dies with the most toys wins." The point of life is, as media mogul Bob Buford (founder of Leadership Network) puts it, "The one who bounces his last check wins."[14] To say that one "died penniless" is the point, not the problem. Jesus' words to the rich young ruler apply universally: We have no choice but to give it all away. The question becomes, To whom shall we give it?

How much is enough? A massive social movement underway says it is time to moderate our desires, moderate our "mod cons" (modern conveniences), and moderate our claims on what life owes us, declare an end to the "ACID" rat race (ACID is eco-philosopher Sigmund Kvaløy phrase for "Advanced Competitive Industrial Dominion") and Jonesism (as in keeping up with, that is). If the world's population is broken down into three classes, as Alan Durning has done—the poor, the middle income, and the consumers—almost all North American Christians are in the consumer class, the 1.1 billion people who earn more than $7,500 per family member.[15] The church must help postmoderns restore faith in simple pleasures, simple relationships, simple loyalties—or what the Stanford Research Institute calls "living in a way that is outwardly simple and inwardly rich."[16]

> I'd like to live life like a poor man with lots of money.
>
> PABLO PICASSO

Christmas makes a great time to begin this life of "enoughness." Some parents are already adopting the policy of allowing their children to play with all their toys until January 1, at which time they get to pick the three toys they will keep. The other toys they must give away personally to a homeless shelter, or a family in the community with kids who could use them. The Troy Annual Conference, one of the smallest of the 73 annual conferences of the United Methodist Church, is leading the way in helping Christians dream of a green Christmas. Led by author and environmentalist Bill McKibben, the conference passed a "Hundred Dollar Holiday" resolution encouraging all church families to covenant with their church to start a new Christmas tradition by limiting spending to no more than $100 in gifts. USAmericans spend $37 billion in Christmas presents annually, a figure which is higher than their total annual donations to charity. In the words of one of McKibben's short speeches, "Christmas spending contributes environmentally damaging luxury consumption, sends many families deep into debt, diverts funds that could be better spent on pressing human needs, and makes the church look hypocritical to many outsiders."[17]

But resolutions are one thing; resolve is another. To build this resolution into a movement the conference hosted a series of mini-celebrations in every district—folk singers, gospel choirs, and Christian rock groups teamed up with McKibben to provide a festive evening of music and fun while the "Christmas Project" was explained and encouraged. A poster of a Christmas tree decked out with alternative, noncommercial ideas for commemorating Christmas was passed out at these events. The biggest bonanza of this attempt at a "Simply Christmas" celebration was the raging debates that went on in the local news media. One man wrote a column wondering "why churches don't stick to religion and leave Christmas alone."[18]

Ernest McClain, professor of music at Brooklyn College and an expert in musical harmonies and number symbolism, expresses microquake 3 in the language he knows best:

> It's certainly true that we live in a culture with an enormous respect for accumulations of wealth, accumulations of power. Certainly we've been reminded by modern philosophers that public values seem to be going downhill in the sense of some kind of reign of quantity, some dynamism run amuck—it's never possible to have enough nuclear weapons, or enough billions in the bank. In ancient

times, the smallest numbers are the most prestigious ones. The most important number to the ancients is one, unity. Any unity is a point of reference. The other numbers, two, three, four, can be thought of as simply replications of unity. Two is a collection of units, three is a collection of units; all the numbers are generated from one in a sense. . . . in the ancient Neo-Pythagorean Neo-Platonic values systems, virtue and value are seen most clearly in the ratios of small numbers, not in the relations between very large numbers. . . . So, if you want to look for God, if you want to look for absolute truth or for meaning, you look at the smallest numbers.[19]

God incarnated divinity into the world in a microscopic cell. The infinite was entrusted to the finite, the largest to the smallest. The greatest things in life are miracles of smallness—the miracle of birth, one cell from mother, one cell from father, coming together to form the complex, many-celled creative beings that you and I are.

Throughout history, the Spirit has been at work most often in single cells, in smaller communities that served as nerve cells for the regeneration of society and the church. The story of these *ecclesiola in ecclesia* Howard Snyder traces expertly in *Signs of the Spirit* (1991). Ironically, the genius behind this "critical mass" or "nerve cell" kind of thinking was John Wesley. Russell E. Richey has a marvelous book, *Early American Methodism* (1990). He demonstrates that earliest Methodism in America stressed close-knit, intimate community through small groups and spiritual structures, but was overlaid in 1784 by a non-fraternal episcopal system. He shows how quarterly meetings and annual conferences were in the beginning big celebrations or "camp-meetings," as we came to call them, but as Methodism grew in size and scope, camp-meetings were separated off and sidelined while the "big event" developed into mere business meetings.

4. Model Down

Shamgar had an ox goad, David had a sling,
Dorcas had a needle, Rahab had a string.
Sampson had a jawbone, Aaron had a rod;
Mary had some ointment, but they all were used for God.

So goes the old Sunday school ditty, illustrating the way God lets the truth hang by a thread, committing the future of God's purposes to insignificant things and unnamed, unknown people. There are no little things. There can be no cup of water without thousands of small drops. There can be no hour of caring without thousands of small seconds.

> **MORE WILL MEAN WORSE.**
>
> BRITISH AUTHOR
> KINGSLEY AMIS

Celebrate the ministry of small things. Small acts of faithfulness are often great acts of courage. The most difficult step in a "mustard-seed faith" is mustering the courage to begin an authentic, faithful relationship with God, and believing that God's spirit will never abandon you in your journey.

> *I am done with great things and big things, with great institutions and big successes, and I am for those tiny, invisible, molecular forces that work from individual to individual, creeping through the crannies of the world like so many soft rootlets, or like the capillary oozing of water, but which, given time, will rend the hardest monuments of human pride.*
>
> WILLIAM JAMES

Perhaps one of the smallest of "small things" that can be used by God to evoke faithfulness in this postmodern era is the microchip. Computers have changed the way we work, the way we play, have increased our expectations, and have shortened our attention spans. By 1982, there were more computers (from microprocessors to mainframes) on this planet than people. The church must accept the challenge of learning how best to communicate the gospel in nanoseconds. "Imagine two computers conversing with each other over a period," Geoff Simons asks in *Silicon Shock*. "They are then asked by a human being what they are talking about, and in the time he takes to pose the question, the two computers have exchanged more words than the sum total of all the words exchanged by human beings since *Homo sapiens* first appeared on earth two or three million years ago."[20]

However timid about technology we may be, God has always called people of faith to "serve the *present* age, our calling to fulfill." By exploiting to the fullest the invention of moveable type, the Protestant reformers were able to put the word of God into every person's hand. What will twenty-first century Christians be able to accomplish for God with silicon chips or gallium arsenide?

This is not to romanticize the "small," however. God knows no big or small churches, no megachurch or microcommunities of faith. Only the Body of Christ, of which we are all part. If we stop seeing churches as "big" or "little," we will perceive that each community of faith has a special calling of God for ministry and mission in their unique context.

In Ralph Waldo Emerson's "Fable," a mountain and a squirrel are having a squabble. The quarrel ends with the squirrel saying:

> If I'm not so large as you
> You are not so small as I;
> And not half so spry,
> I'll not deny you make
> A very pretty squirrel track.
> Talents differ.
> All is well and wisely put:
> If I cannot carry forests on my back,
> Neither can you crack a nut.

5. The Power of One

The connectedness of the cosmos helps us to give up our feelings of powerlessness to bring change and to see that one small change can make all the difference between life and death. Individual complicity in public good and public evil is enormous. The fact that I am human implicates me in the promises and perils of planet Earth: in the famine in Somalia, in the carnage between the Croats and Serbs and Muslims, in every drug transaction, in every tree that is chopped down in the rain forests, and so on.

Nikki R. Keddie, editor of the new journal *Contention: Debates in Society, Culture, and Science*, discusses the predictability of revolutions by attacking the widespread fallacy that "big results . . . must have discoverably big causes." The truth is that small, minute, even chaotic shifts can trigger changes that will take the course of history in very different directions.

Chaos theory has taught us that small shifts of orientation, slight differences of initial conditions, often produce massive changes and wide variations. Belgian physicist David Ruelle, one of the founders of chaos theory, defines *chaos* as another word for "sensitive dependence on initial conditions." How sensitive? Ruelle answers this question by using some mathematical theories and calculations developed by British physicist Michael Berry, French mathematician Emile Borel, and Russian probability theorist Andrei Kolmogorov. He tells it in the form of a story about a "little devil" who wishes to change the course of your life.

All that "little devil" needs do is start with an infinitesimal deflection of a single electron somewhere at the edge of the known universe. In a tiny fraction of a second a new set of consequences are set in motion from this altered air molecule that radically reshapes the reality of the entire universe. Of course, if you're the one being tormented by the "little devil," you don't notice anything yet. After about a minute, however, the changes are so significant that they begin producing macroscopic effects, although still without visible notice. But after a few hours, or a day, things are quite different. The whole climate around you has changed. You start to notice that things are different. The blue sky is now turning gray. The clouds are changing from cirrus to cumulonimbus. After a couple of weeks, the changes are global.[21]

> Suppose then that you have arranged a weekend picnic with your sweetheart (or your boss, I don't care). Just as you have spread your tablecloth on the grass, a really vicious hailstorm begins, arranged by the little devil through careful manipulation of initial conditions (yes, this little devil is a jilted lover). Are you satisfied now that the carefully planned course of your life may be altered? Actually, the little devil wanted to crash a plane in which you would be flying, but I talked it out of that, out of consideration for your fellow passengers.[22]

Ridiculously small changes can lead to radical transformations in very short periods of time. Even Harvard sociobiologist Edward O. Wilson has taken to appropriating the ancient metaphor of the web to illuminate the highly interdependent system we call life. One motion anywhere in the web jiggles the whole.[23] Or as theoretical physicist Richard Feynman jotted down on the last page of his address book, which was found after he died:

> Principles
> You can't say A is made of B
> or vice versa.
> All mass is interaction.[24]

The popularity of the Wolf Petersen movie *The Never Ending Story* was precisely from this awareness that the individual can make a difference, even to

Large streams from little fountains flow
Tall oaks from little acorns grow.

DAVID EVERETT

the point of saving a universe (*Fantasia*). Jack McDevitt, associate director of the Center for Applied Social Research (Boston) and a specialist in hate crimes, is convinced that if there had been simply "one more officer" in the Los Angeles Police Department who would have dared to speak out "about the use of language that went on over public communication channels, Rodney King would have been saved."[25]

It is this new sense of the power of one, the awareness that "I can make a difference," that one's faith and actions reverberate throughout the universe, that is giving rise to such aberrations as the "I AM" Movement, or as it is better known, the Individual Activism Movement. People are very wary of bureaucratic grids or highly structured movements. They are also, unfortunately, suspicious of one another. In the words of George Kovanis from the *Detroit Free Press*:

> As Individual Activists, we don't rally in front of Tom Monaghan's house to protest his conservative politics when we can conserve our valuable time by simply refusing to buy his Domino's pizza. We don't collect petition signatures because we know they will just be forwarded to a corrupt, male-dominated government. We don't send money to charitable organizations that use donations to pay for rent and office staff when we can simply hand over $50 or a couple bags of groceries to someone who is needy. We look around and ask ourselves, "Who's the one person I can count on to do the right thing?" I AM.[26]

A key postmodern paradox is this: the more we know, the more vast the universe appears, and the more insignificant we seem in it. Yet the more we probe the mysteries of the universe, and the more we understand what is going on, the more we appreciate how great an impact seemingly insignificant things can have on the whole.

Part of the mission of the church is conveying this knowledge that what each person does will make a difference. For each of us has been gifted by God with three world-making, world-shaking, world-saving powers: the power of spirit, the power of mind, the power of body. In the same way Jesus mysteriously multiplied small loaves and fishes, so God multiplies our one-moment-at-a-time, one-step-at-a-time endeavors to change the course of history.

At the same time, the Power-of-One leads to thoughts of what might be rather than what is. Postmodern anxiety and caution is advised before any might-be thoughts are given either horns or hoods. For example, if our wanton acts of kindness and our random simple acts of alternative living at Christmas were to succeed, and after ten or twenty years North America had cut annual Christmas consumption in half (though the goal of $100 maximum per family, we really aspire to a cut of 80 percent), we would have more than ten million people out of work in this country (not to mention Japan). A reduction of Christmas consumption to this level would more than double the unemployment rate for those who produce and distribute the goods that are consumed. One's successful random righteous act against the consumer culture is linked to another worker's nightmare of hunger and despair. Am I prepared to spend the money saved by cutting my consumption to feed and clothe the displaced workers who are cursed by my righteous acts, especially since the rest of society is not likely to be so generous?

6. Be a "Seven-Day-A-Week Church"

Not a Sunday-only church. Also known as the people church, the full-service church" or the seeker-friendly or user-friendly church (George Barna), this seven-day-a-week church" successor to the big Sunday morning church of the 1950s is, in Lyle Schaller's words, "one of the most significant developments of this century."[27]

Schaller has found that the vast majority of new members born before 1930 when asked, "When did you first set foot on this property?" respond, "Sunday morning worship." When this same question is asked of those born after 1950, the waning power of Sunday morning as an evangelistic hinge event manifests itself, as the vast majority of boomers and busters point to a weekday or weeknight event as their initial entry point into the church.[28] In the words of one of the nation's most creative seven-day-a-week pastors, Minneapolis' Leith Anderson: "The primary entry into church is not one big Sunday morning door, but a plethora of little doors that open seven days a week. Churches must be less and less of a Sunday morning phenomenon, and more of a seven mornings, seven afternoons, and seven evenings every week phenomenon."[29] Each regional church should think of itself as a mini-denomination.

Choice no longer is a choice for postmodern culture. Choice is now a value and virtue in and of itself. It is hard to give people enough choices, although there can come a time of "option paralysis" when too many choices leads to no choice at all.

> A typical supermarket in 1976 had 9,000 products; today it has more than 30,000. The average produce section in 1975 carried sixty-five items; this summer it carried 285. (Kiwi has hit the top 20 list.) A Cosmetic Center outside Washington carries about 1,500 types and sizes of hair care products. The median household got six TV stations in 1975. . . . That family now has more than thirty channels. The number of FM radio stations has doubled since 1970. A new religious denomination forms every week. . . . In 1955 only 4 percent of the adult population had left the faith of their childhood. By 1985 one-third had. In 1980, 564 mutual funds existed. This year there are 3,347.[30]

A good example of providing people with "choices" is the proliferation of Saturday Night Alive/NightLife/Night Light Services. Already between 3,000 to 4,000 churches have begun offering alternative-day worship experiences for their people, especially young families, singles, and others who work on Sundays.[31] This not only "offloads" Sunday morning, but offers an opportunity for providing people with more contemporary styles of worship including synthesizer, band, drama, testimonies, informal dress, and more interactive and participative modes of preaching.

At the same time the church maximizes people's choices, consumer-sensitive must not become consumer-driven. USAmerica's national economy has become two-thirds consumer spending: in other words, our economic health is driven by our number one economic disease: consumption. "Compulsive shopping syndrome" can apply to the church as well as the mall. We can consume excitement and collect experiences just as we can consume ice cream and collect shoes. The church with the gospel of Christ is poised to challenge a culture that spends more time shopping than anything else other than work or sleep. We can replace the ersatz joy of consuming with the ecstatic joy of Christ.

7. A.Y.O.R. (At Your Own Risk)

Truth or Consequences. Rational Choice theory says we express our values in our choices—case by case, situation by situation, plan by plan. These choices over a long span of time show remarkable regularity. The choices we make on a regular basis have major consequences for our lives as well as others' lives. As our choices have increased, so have our responsibilities.

Hence A.Y.O.R. We are free to choose. We are not free to choose the consequences. Consequences come with choices. As *Newsweek* Washington correspondent Steven Waldman notes, "the more choices there are, the more wrong choices there are—and the higher the odds I'll make a mistake."[32] We are free to make our own choices, but not free to choose our own consequences. Certain choices come with specific consequences attached.[33]

Faith is more than a matter of personal choice. John 15:17: "You did not choose me. I chose you." It is not so much that we are a "chosen people" as that we are a "choosing people" created in the image of a "choosing God." It is one function of the church to make sure that the world doesn't get exclusive rights to define the choices that are available to people.

That's the catch of a choice culture—we are all expected to choose. Not to choose is not to be, and we need to choose one of the options that are given us. Amidst the many choices offered us, it may be that there are no good options offered. Then the church's responsibility is to respond to the choices offered to us with, "None of the above." It is up to us to provide the world with another option, the Jesus option.[34] One of the gifts that Christ's presence in our lives offers is not freedom of choice but freedom from choice under certain circumstances. When choices do not engender beauty, truth, and goodness as their "consequences," it is time to declare freedom from choice.

An AncientFuture church keeps before a choosy culture the ethic of duty and moral obligation. How ironic that Andrew Morton's book *Diana: Her True Story* (1992) vilifies Prince Charles for putting his public duty above his personal happiness and his wife's wishes.

8. Dis-Gracing the Creator

Far from blocking "sin" like their modernist forebears (e.g., Karl Menninger's *Whatever Became of Sin?*), postmoderns are not greatly concerned about personal wrongdoing, and can actually celebrate it. Theologian Mary Daly's motto is "Elemental being is sinning: it requires the courage to sin." Or as one scholar made the "Great Commandment" of the postmodern dispensation: "Go, and sin some more!"[35] "Practice what you preach" is being eclipsed by a defiant moral approbation of preaching what one practices.

This is a culture that wants words of grace without words of judgment. It is a culture that lacks all menace from its deity, that wants a God "who demands of us no more than our politics require," as historian Eugene Genovese puts it. This kind of God "warms every atheist's heart."

> Besides, if God is finite, progressive, and Pure Love, we may as well skip church next Sunday and go to the movies. For if we have nothing to fear from this all-loving, all-forbearing, all-forgiving God, how would our worship of him constitute more than self-congratulation for our own moral standards? As an atheist, I like this God. It is good to see him every morning while I am shaving.[36]

In every era of the church godly men and women have been able to say both "I love myself " and "I abhor myself." It is the puffed-with-pride, red-with-shame language of Job, of Isaiah, of David, of Ruth, of Daniel, of Mary, of Paul. It is the honest language of truth. In 1929 C. S. Lewis found his atheism in jeopardy when he looked inside himself and beheld "a zoo of lusts, a bedlam of ambitions, a nursery of fears, a harem of fondled hatreds." Every one of us is a sorcerer's apprentice, stirring up elemental forces for good and ill beyond our control.

Episcopal lay priest Garrett Keizer relates one of his favorite anecdotes about the man known as Curé d' Ars, eventually St. John Vianney. "At one point in the career of this uneducated and irritatingly zealous rural priest, a number of his flock circulated a petition declaring him 'unfit' to hold his post. When at last the Curé was able to get his hands on the petition, he signed it."[37] Christians throughout history have known exactly how he felt.

All who come to God do so with mixed motives. The underside of the human heart—its byways and bypasses—is both a pretty and ugly place. A postmodern sense of "living in sin" will remind Christians of the heights to which God is calling us and at the same time the horrors we inflict on one another. The terrifying truth unveiled in the modern era was that it is ordinary people, not monsters or the mad, who do horrifying things to innocent people.

The poor are not created by God's nature or by Mother Nature. They are created by human nature. They are the by-products of an "ego" that is good and decent and hardworking and honest—these are all defining characteristics of Lucifer—but an "ego" that is an acronym for envying God's omnipotence and "edging God out."[38] Evil is not the result of souls being sold to Satan. As Colin Morris put it long ago in some of the most insightful words ever written on "sin," our problem is not that we worship the devil, but that the devil worships us. "He does not set himself up against God as a candidate for your allegiance. He encourages you to set yourself up against God. He confirms you in your pride. He is your greatest fan. He coddles you in well-being and reflects for your satisfaction your highest estimates of yourself."[39] It is these egoistic tendencies to which none of us are strangers that stand us in such need of prayer.

> *HE SHOWS HIMSELF WORTHY, IN THAT HE CONFESSES HIMSELF UNWORTHY.*
>
> St. Augustine

"Confessions" in the new paradigm church will be much more collegial and creational than in modernist paradigm churches. "Bear one another's burdens" (Gal. 6:2) has been taken literally at certain times in Christian history, with families actually joining forces and sharing penances with the penitent to reduce the burden and the time required. "We're-all-in-this-together" rituals strike resonant chords with postmoderns.

Since we "sin" not just against one another but against the cosmos as well, church goers appreciate public expressions of contrition for our degradations of planet Earth. Such was the case in the Russian church, where the common people during the Middle Ages introduced liturgical acts of reconciliation with the earth—bowing to the earth, kissing it, wetting it with their tears, cleansing their hands with it. The Novgorodian Strigol'niki of the fourteenth century even confessed to the Earth, refusing confession to the church because of a deep mistrust of the hierarchy.[40]

9. Need Not to Need by Needing

Postmodern culture is a culture of needs. This need *du jour* phenomenon is especially prevalent in the church, where people need to need the ones who need them. No one has pointed this out better than John Guare, Broadway's current favorite writer, whose play *Six Degrees of Separation* (1990) shows how someone's dependency can make others feel and come alive.

In a culture of "cupboard love," where people come to one another for what one can get from the other, the temptation is for God to become for people simply a Jehovah-jireh God—a provider of needs. Or as a popular Southern gospel song entitled "Bankrupt Heaven" puts it, "God would bankrupt heaven to meet my needs." The insatiability and instability of personal needs is matched only by the inability of a "needs" culture to see the neediness of others in that culture. Maturity is the deabsolutizing of one's own demands, emotions, and sensitivities. In Wendy Kaminer's *I'm Dysfunctional, You're Dysfunctional* (1992), she laments the absence of anyone in any recovery program she has ever studied saying, " 'Some people suffer more than I.' For all the talk about sharing and caring, in recovery there's more evidence of self-pity than compassion."[41]

Don't become a Christian because God meets your needs. Become a Christian because the gospel is true, and Jesus is the way, the truth, and the life. Don't become part of an organismic body of Christ for psychological support and intimacy. Become a flesh-and-blood member of community because that is how God can be glorified in your life and belong in your midst.

Sociologist Robert Wuthnow worries about a culture that does good in order to feel good. Can you imagine Jesus ever saying to his disciples, Wuthnow asks, "Take up your cross and follow me—it'll make you feel good."[42] Some needs don't need to be filled, but emptied. Indeed, God is not going to meet all of our neediness. Some people are worse off with Christ than without him. Even if Christ did meet all of our needs, we'd find some more needs because human neediness is such a bottomless pit.

Admittedly, the gospel "meets" our deepest need to live the truth and to give birth to the truth within us. The gospel definitely and defiantly does not meet our surface needs, which are as changing and clinging as sheep. In the words of narrator Cain in the Howard Jacobson novel about the prototypical family, "The Lord was our shepherd. We did not want. He fed us in green and fat pastures. . . . Excellent, excellent, had we been sheep."[43]

We want God to "meet our needs" by which we mean to remove our needs so that we will need God no more, so that we will need one another no more. Why are we such good givers and such poor receivers? Why do we have this compulsion to fix whatever is broken?

God does not remove all our neediness because neediness is inherent in our creatureliness (see 1 Cor. 12:14-17). We will always, everywhere, "need" one another. Jesus does not lead us to a condition of independence from God but to a state of absolute dependence on God and a state of relative dependence on one another. We read from Paul in 2 Corinthians 11:29—"Who is weak and I am not weak? Who is made to fall, and I am not indignant." (RSV). We read in Hebrews to "Remember those who are in prison, as though you were in prison with them; those who are being tortured, as though you yourselves were being tortured" (Heb. 13:3). Jesus came for the sick. The well have no need of a physician (Matt. 9:12, paraphrase).

The cross is not Jesus being lost in the love of God. The cross is not Jesus offering himself to God by giving himself up to God. Jesus offers himself up, yes; Jesus gives himself away, yes. But not to God. Jesus gives himself away to us—to you and to me. That is the scandal of the cross. Love is self-expenditure for the sake of others. Love is John 15:13 "No one has greater love than this, to lay down one's life for one's friends." Love is communion—bodies broken; blood poured out.

10. Target Your Community

Targeting is a laundered word (at least for Christians) for what George Barna calls the "M-word"—"marketing" or a "receiver" orientation.[44] Stop trying to be everything to everybody, and carve a niche for your church from your surroundings. Target the audience God is calling you to serve, contextualize your ministries and functions to this audience, and be faithful to this mission. No church, no community can meet all the needs of any community. No church, no community can write a formulaic "how-to" program that will work across the board. Every target audience must write its own formulas.

Thriving Christians become sensitive to the needs of the culture that gives them shelter and the needs of individuals both within and without shelter. After all, the only alternative to a needed ministry—a ministry to the needs people have in their lives—is an unneeded ministry. These words of Adam Clayton Powell, Sr., demonstrate the fact that market-driven and tradition-driven exist not in antagonism but in creative tension: "When a neighborhood church begins to define its ministry by its members and not its neighbors, then the church has lost its ministry."[45]

It is dangerous to raise a pulse without first taking it. It is a healing step for the church to discover what members need and want but aren't getting. The church must meet people where they are, not where we wish they might be. The church must listen to its members more, not less. Indeed, "ask them," seems to be the hardest thing for the church to do. To those who express disinterest or distrust of marketing, I reply: "You mean you *don't* want to get closer to your people? You *don't* want to know who they are, what they value, and how their dreams and expectations may be changing?" Ordained ministers can revitalize their work as they become close to the concerns of those whom they seek to lead in ministry. This can happen through surveys, focus groups, by asking questions, and by finding out a person's opinions. And in this process of canvassing we learn not to rely on memory—the average person forgets 75 percent of what is heard in twenty-four hours.

The church's investment in "getting real" with its own people promises one of its biggest returns. Don't write off members that you think you've lost. Try to woo them back by addressing what chased them away. It is no less evangelistic, and often easier, to bring back the bored, lapsed, and marginal (we used to say "backslidden") than bringing in the new and untutored.

Churches that are in touch but not in tune with their times work at critiquing everything they do. They show no fear of feedback, and demonstrate a no-holds-barred orientation toward criticism. They order their lives around those ministries that are reaching people where they hurt the most. For example, Salem First Church of the Nazarene in Salem, Oregon, decided that its mission would be singles and divorced persons. In 1988–1989 the church added nearly 1,000 persons to its membership.

George Barna has discovered about successful churches, in one of his most revealing findings, that "programs were developed around a ministry that already existed. *It was rare in growing churches for programs to precede existing forms of outreach.*"[46] But there is no simple and direct line between what people most want and what the gospel offers. In theological terms *want* does not equal *need*, does not equal *deserve*. The gospel challenges our needs as well as fills them and meets them. The gospel critiques culture, especially this culture of consumption that is based on "do what feels good" and "find a need and fill it." Faith must serve a higher purpose than self-satisfaction.

The chief danger in a "receiver" orientation is that the receiver gets regarded as a "consumer" or as a "market," not as a child of God in desperate need of the divine touch. New paradigm leaders build communities of faith out of a love for Christ and people, not as an advertising medium for Christ.

11. Art Your Life, Art Your Church

Expect repeated "art attacks" in postmodern culture, as there is a new appreciation of aesthetics and art as a spiritual condition of human existence. People are now even wearing art, as the distinction between art and clothing is collapsing in "low" (look at sweaters) as well as "high" fashion.

The evidence for the arting of living is more than just the astonishing and burgeoning number of art galleries, art collectors, art schools, and artists, not to mention a flourishing art market. John Naisbitt's estimate that more and more of leisure time will shift to the arts until by the year 2000 the arts will have overtaken sports as society's number one leisure activity[47] is somewhat beside the point. Art is no longer something one goes to museums to see or concert halls to hear; art is not some commodity or activity. Art is the soul's orientation to life. Art is something that comes to you and shapes your life. "Cultured" is no longer something one learns to be or get, but a doorway to the soul that is hinged a certain way, screening out parts of life and letting in others.

The evidence can also be seen in the way auctions and art shows have replaced Studio 54 as the happenings of the 1990s. From Sotheby's (New York City) to Great Gatsby's or Red Baron's (Atlanta), these "auctions" come replete with buffets, bands, dancing, and drawings. They seem more like parties and extravaganzas than anything else.

In the modern era the arts were demoted in favor of the sciences and other industrial and military spheres of endeavor. Now even theologians (e.g., John Macquarrie[48]) are proposing that theology works better as an art than as the "science" or "history" it often became in the modern era. Those who actually do theology are the true artists and artisans—those who create not only for pleasure but for use.[49]

The Kantian divorce between art and act is ending. It is harder and harder to find even in the art community those who will whisper what the modern era shouted: "art for art's sake," that art has no social responsibility, that art is answerable only to itself, that nothing should limit unrestricted self-expression. Even artists themselves are beginning to admit that something is awry when one can have the finest of sculpture and the most regressive of social values.

Rilke claimed that the fundamental meaning of art was "You must change your life." Art draws us out of ourselves and into a transcending and transfiguring vision. Art in the postmodern era will be less a solo expression of individual creativity than an individual participation in the divine unfoldment through the life of a community.[50]

> *The artist is not a special kind of person,*
> *but every person is a special kind of artist.*
>
> COOMARASWAMY

New paradigm communities of faith will find ways to make the arts sacred once again. The church was once a great patron of the arts. The postmodern church will find ways to bring art back to everyday places and everyday life. Some will have "artists-in-residence" like St. John the Divine (New York City). But even more postmodern, some will boast studios and fine arts centers where the many artistries of their members are celebrated and displayed.

New paradigm churches will be patrons of the real art world where people art their lives and artists evolve their gifts, not the private art world that revolves around "art stars," art markets, and careerism. New paradigm believers will conceive and construct their lives as they would paint a picture or mold a piece of pottery—from an aesthetic rather than an engineering perspective.

Life is the greatest art form—especially life lived in community.

DesignerQuakes

SocioQuake 4: *Egonomics*

The economy now is the consciousness of postmodern culture. "Egonomics," or what Popcorn calls a "nicer narcissism now," is:

the other half of the "I Deserve It" syndrome. Where in Small Indulgences the emphasis is on "Deserve," in Egonomics, the "I" takes center stage. . . . Everybody just wants a little attention, a little recognition of the no-one's-quite-like-me-self.[1]

The word *flash* has lost its pejorative connotations in the nineties. People are tired of the "plague of sameness." They want to fill their lives with forms and fashions of beauty, however flashy, that fit them personally. Johnny Carson's mass audience (and mass appeal) has gone the way of General Motors' "general" motor. Yet at the same time, in typical postmodern fashion, the customized and individuated quickly get swept up into a mainstream popular culture.

What goes "in"—button-downing, line-toeing, cubby-holing, coffee-breaking, clock-watching, time-keeping behavior—is not nearly as watched or valued as what comes "out." Postmodernism is maverick-friendly. Identity no longer grows easily in potted soil with roots in class, nation, region, race, or workstations. Identity emerges more readily from a "Miami-Vice" cuisinart mix of narrative, music video, fashion events, image and economics. "Egonomics" makes style a central theme of postmodern culture.

In the modern era, form and style were mere decorative matters, secondary to content. John Locke, following Aristotle, identified "rhetorical ornament" and metaphors not with the communication of information but with the production of pleasure. As the poet Wallace Stevens said on more than one occasion, we care about a writer's "way of saying it" only after we decide the writer "has something to say." Or in more classical ways of putting it, "form follows function." Style was at best a test of thought.

In the postmodern era, by contrast, there is nothing "mere" about form and style.[2] One no longer gets one's hair cut (Churchill used to direct his barber, "Get on with it"). We get our hair styled, even bringing in outside resources if the ones at hand are insufficient. Ferrero Rocher boosted its share of the British chocolate market by doing nothing more than wrapping its undistinguished brown blobs in gold foil.

The philosopher Alfred North Whitehead anticipated this world in which style becomes the "ultimate morality of the mind." Style is not an adjunct, a decorative apparatus, but the expression of a governing, controlling life-choice, the orientation of an entire life-project. Indeed, a new relationship has emerged between ornamentation and structure, style and subject, in which subject has itself become a way of seeing things—a "style" if you will. Philosopher Humberto Maturana's classic 1959 essay "What the Frog's Eye Tells the Frog's Brain" repivoted the philosophy of biology around cognition at the cellular level.[3]

The novel *The Bonfire of the Vanities* (1988) is an example of style journalism or what Tom Wolfe calls "plutography." Other writers are pioneering what may come to be known as designer writing. Postmodern novelist Fay Weldon admits to three priorities in writing, in this order:

1. form
2. style
3. content

Beginning with Ronald Reagan, the same case can be made about the primacy of pattern over substance in politics.

Identity is now secured and settled by style—from monogrammed underwear to ergonomic Dustbusters to shrink-to-fit presidents. The media no longer cover elections; they are the election, and in postmodern elections what matters is not the style of politics but the "politics of style"[4] (how else can one explain the aphasia presidencies of "leaner, keener, meaner" Reagan and "kinder, gentler" Bush?). Skin and style gets chosen over blood and bones in a postmodern culture enamored with life's surfaces, albeit unsatisfied out of life's depths.

Management has already shifted from a "decision" science to a "design" science, where the idea is to design results, not make decisions that will lead to results. Quality and price now must vie with product design and image management as keys to market share. Design is now "what makes you fall in love with a product" says John Zoccai, the designer who came up with the airpump in the Reebok basketball sneaker that now boasts hundreds of millions in sales. Science is giving way to design in the decisions that people are making.

What is USAmerica's number one export? It is image and style. For the first time in history, a single civilization's images and poses, its values and culture are dominating the imagination of the entire world, straining and too often superseding indigenous life-styles.[5] Although international popular culture is increasingly heterogeneous, USAmerican myths still set the pace. There now is designer everything: designer scuba diving costumes, designer sardines. Pierre Cardin, who endorses both of these, has a total of 840 designer endorsements.

For postmoderns the expression of the self is style. Job satisfaction comes not from a job well done so much as from the style of doing a job. Giving themselves over to a variety of self-regarding experiments, busters in particular are as interested in a life-style as they are in a livelihood or even a life. It is a career, not a job; a style, not work that busters are after. Busters want, not what they say they want, but the looks of what they say they want. Power is not what influences others or gets them to do something. "Power" is not so much what is being looked for as style because style is what enables people to act effectively, to lead others, and to behave for the common good.

And everyone is searching for their unique style. Hence "egonomics." In

ONLY THE BAKERS OF PEPPERIDGE FARM COULD PACK SO MUCH SCRUMPTIOUS PERSONALITY INTO CLASSICALLY AMERICAN COOKIES. . . . THEY ADDED A HEAPING MEASURE OF SIMPLE FUSS AND BOTHER. THAT MEANT MAKING EACH COOKIE ONE OF A KIND, WITH AN INDIVIDUAL PERSONALITY ALL ITS OWN. SO THEY GAVE THEM RUGGED, IRREGULAR SHAPES, JUST AS IF SOMEONE HAD LOVINGLY SHAPED EACH COOKIE BY HAND.

PEPPERIDGE FARM LABEL
FOR "NANTUCKET" CHOCOLATE CHUNK COOKIES

modern society there was centralization and standardization. Postmoderns are suspicious of centralized or standardized anythings. They are especially tired of the plague of terminal trendiness. Indeed the latest trend is not to follow the

97

trends. Nonconformity has become the new conformity. No one wants to be known for having conventional tastes and standard ambitions. The postmodern fear of being ordinary reigns.

In the 1990s conformity is the big bugbear. The youth rebellion of the sixties continues in the consumer revolution in the malls where radical is chic. "Don't do what everyone else is doing" is the new egonomic style. Find your own personal style—resist convention, don't buy into the system, walk on the "wild" (a favorite nineties word) side. "The commodification of dissent," writes Tom Frank, "is the great ideological innovation of our time." The commercialization of nonconformism has become the "universal theme of American culture, the preeminent motif of the age."[6]

This explains why it is increasingly difficult for people to buy anything "off the rack." It is not just youth culture that chooses items that promote an image and expresses a personal sense of style. Everyone is on the prowl for distinctive outfits that are tailored to individual tastes and interests. The move is from mass consumption to individuated consumption; from "Fordism" to "post-Fordism." British sociologist John Urry summarizes the major features of "post-Fordist consumption" as follows:

> Consumption rather than production dominate as consumer expenditure further increases as a proportion of national income; new forms of credit permitting consumer expenditure to rise, so producing high levels of indebtedness; almost all aspects of social life become commodified, even charity; much greater differentiation of purchasing patterns by different market segments; greater volatility of consumer preferences; the growth of a consumers movement and the "politicizing" of consumption; reaction of consumers against being as part of a "mass" and the need for producers to be much more consumer-driven, especially in the case of service industries and those publicly owned; the development of many more products each of which has a shorter life; the emergence of new kinds of commodity which are more specialized and based on raw materials that imply non-mass forms of production ("natural" products for example).[7]

FaithQuake 4:
DesignerQuakes

1. Tagging

The creation by churches of a distinct identity for themselves in the form of a "tag"—a stylized signature or logo unique to each community of faith. There is an old saying: "God never leaves identical fingerprints." God is a creator of diversity and a respecter of individuality; the variety of biological life forms is constantly increasing. God works on and with each of us uniquely. God touches each church differently. God doesn't expect patterned responses. Every church and every pastor should give off a distinct style. Design-rich communities of faith are variety-generating churches.[8]

> *The world is not especially rare in good ideas and good emotions; it is rare in good expressions.*
> WILLA CATHER

Using the technical language of communications, the French scholar Pierre Babin characterizes the transition from a print being to an electronic being in this way: "We come to faith more through the ground than through the figure." Or using more accessible language, "The door by which we enter is not reason but longing, not the strictness of concepts but the 'look.' "[9] This makes the need for a distinct style all the more important, for something that sets a church apart from the crowd and builds an ever-growing base of loyalty. Design considerations in business cost only 2 percent of total overhead, but their effect is enormous.

A model example is the Peabody Hotel in Memphis and their resident ducks. There is basically nothing special about the hotel except those elevator-riding, lobby-waddling, fountain-swimming ducks. But those ducks have established an identity for this hotel—evident in everything from its stationary to its restaurant that makes the Peabody one of the landmarks of Memphis. Every church needs some duckies.

Scott Gross's book *Positively Outrageous Service* (1991) gives another example of how churches should consider doing some things that are outlandish, preposterous, even wild. One restaurant owner offers free meals to everyone one night a month. The restaurant picks a traditional slow time (Monday or Tuesday), but instead of handing the customer a bill, they are handed a thank-you letter from the owner. The results? Bigger turnouts other nights. Colonial Hills Church in San Antonio tagged itself by offering free childcare on Friday night—an outrageous and courageous program that reaped huge dividends for the church.[10]

One thing cannot be forgotten for "tagging" to work: the owner must be out front on those nights, mingling face-to-face with the customers. The "tag" is nothing unless it is attached to a face. In Paul Valery's inimitable way of putting it, you can't get drunk on a bottle's label. But postmoderns won't even pick up the bottle without an attractive label.

For rationalist institutions that have grown allergic to even the mildest metaphors, a call for new logos, signage, slogans, even clothing (T-shirts, ties, etc.) will come as something of a shock. Some preachers who are using slogans effectively include Jeremiah Wright ("Unashamedly black and unapologetically Christian"), Donald W. Morgan ("The exciting place on Sunday morning"), Cecil Williams ("You come to church to practice; you leave the church to preach"), Rick Warren ("This church is not measured by its seating capacity, but by its sending capacity").

In music there are inversions, palindromes, and so on. Bach was a master at turning musical phrases inside out like a sock, and we have enjoyed wearing these socks for centuries. It is time to do the same in writing and in other forms of communication. Preachers should not be afraid to deck up their ideas, deck out their discourses in word-playing, word-patterning, word-punning styles. Not since Horatio Alger's alliterative heroes and alliterative titles has it been so hard for people to resist an alliterative temptation.

2. Dress Is Address

Style is a moral issue, a medium without which messages cannot be delivered. This is why the "Dress-is-Address" faithquake is more than "looking the part" or "putting on a pretty face" or "dressing for success" or "the clothes making the person"—as in Eisenhower's short military jacket that the entire army eventually adopted and named the "Ike Jacket," or in the Douglas MacArthur image of sun glasses, corn cob pipe, gold braided hat, and tieless khaki uniform.

Style of dress in the modern era was more of a fashion statement than a theological one, a declaration at best of a self-consciousness or self-confidence. For example, Martin Lloyd-Jones believed that Christians should be "spiritually well-dressed" or else people could say, "Funny, you don't look Christian."

> You and I are to be such that as we walk up and down the streets of life, people will be struck and attracted. You have seen them turn and look at a well-dressed person. Well, it is something like that. They should be struck by us, and look at us, and think, "What is this person? I have never seen anybody quite like this before! What perfection! What balance! How everything fits together! How graceful!" That is the kind of people we can be and the kind of people that we must be.[11]

In contrast, the postmodern intimacies connecting aesthetics and religious faith make style less a fashion statement than a performance art and political message, a medium of unselfconscious public communication, a language with its own grammar, syntax, and vocabulary.[12] Postmoderns don't wear clothes anymore. They wear costumes.

George Barna puts this faithquake in bold terms. The "successful" church was "more than just an occasional experience; it was a *lifestyle*."[13] In theological terms, style communicates whether and where the gospel is "gracing" lives or whether/where there is a "dis-gracing" of the gospel. Faith and life-style are no longer cause and effect.

Aesthetic sense and judgment are critical to the life of faith. Christians ought to have style. One postmodern theologian has even made the case for bad taste being a moral liability—a "docudrama" of sinfulness, if you will; or as he puts it, "a mark of depravity as well as deprivation."[14] If God is ultimate Beauty, and taste the ability to see the beautiful, then good taste is of utmost theological significance. Just as graffiti artists purchase space with their bold styles and artistic flairs like advertisers purchase space with money,[15] how postmoderns dress affects how they look, feel, and connect with others. Who we are is partially determined by how we look—by our signifiers.

> *My friend, how do you come to be here without wedding clothes?*
>
> MATTHEW 22:12 (REB)

In classical terms there are four basic characteristics of good design: (1) unity; (2) variety; (3) balance; (4) harmony. It is less significant what one's personal or communal style is than that one have a style, one's style be a natural part of who one is, and that one's style be distinctively one's own according to the above criteria. A barbarous style, a reign of taste that is sheik and cheap, reflects base tastes and debased life-styles. Similarly a bland style, a judgment of taste that is boring and unvital, reflects dis-ease with and rejection of a peacock society that abounds in colorful fashions and padded plumages.

Who is watching over and watching out for your church's aesthetics? Watch your aesthetics!

3. A New Me-We Physics of the Self

One of the chief characteristics of postmodern culture is that opposites become two-in-one forces that move together. Just as tribalism and globalism move in tandem in postmodern culture (or "alternative" and "mainstream" as suggested above), so in this case the "egonomic" socioquake is becoming more individual and more communal at the same time. The importance of the individual (leadership) is being stressed at the same time the importance of the many (teamwork) is celebrated.

The paradox of the collective singular ("We the people") is at the heart of faithquake 4. People want to "be me" at the same time they know they can't be "me" without a "we" that doesn't exclude a larger "them." This new me/we awareness Danah Zohar calls *The Quantum Self* (1992). As an indication of the amount of collaboration required by the human genome project, as close to a quest for the Holy Grail as the postmodern era is likely to see, it took thirty-five laboratories working together to sequence one baker's-yeast chromosome. The article detailing the research had 147 authors.

The mature emergence of one's talents, abilities, and creativities best takes place within relationships and associations, not outside them. Paul brought together these dual whole/part directions powerfully in his letter to the Corinthians: "Now you are the body of Christ, and each one of you is a part of it" (1 Cor. 12:27 NIV). Or as a new country and western song puts the need for more than one head if we are to see around the corner or get around any problem: "What will I do with me without you." Churches that think of themselves as organic systems rather than organizational systems are even beginning to talk of the Bible as "The Book of Relationships."

> ## TWO HEADS, FOUR EYES.
> ### IGBO PROVERB

In the modern era individuals came to prefer the sound of their own voice above all others, and to be proud of the preference. Indeed, the crowning achievement of the modern era may have been the emergence of the sense of selfhood, which could not have been possible without the separation of individual identity from nature and from the group. But as sacredness became located in the individual, the capacity for intimacy with one's self ("self-sufficiency") was accented over the capacity for intimacy with others. What a wise woman in Gloucester County, Virginia, said about a neighborhood boy, weak-witted from inbreeding—"He too close kin to hisself"[16]—could be said of too many moderns who took a good thing too far and lived "self"-contained lives.

D. H. Lawrence once described the essential American soul as "hard, isolated, stoic, and a killer." Autonomous individualism defined the American dream: "do your own thing"; "be the best you can be"; "don't tread on me." Driven dippy and drippy by narcissism, late moderns became skilled at "autonomy competency,"[17] while being absolutely bereft of skills at being part of a larger whole and without the relational skills necessary for community consciousness and community competency. No wonder moderns feel so cut off and alone: from one another, from nature, from God. The individualism that became virtually pathological in the eighties was, in the terms of Kate Pullinger's novel *Where Does Kissing End?* (1992), a kind of "emotional vampirism."

> *We're all in this alone.*
> LILY TOMLIN

Few have understood better the consequences on the church of this modern doctrine of individualism than missiologist George Hunter. In his *How to Reach Secular People*, he distinguishes between the "chaplaincy" model of ministry and the "apostolic" model. In the "chaplaincy" model, people look to the church as their family's private chapel, and to the pastor as their own personal, private chaplain. Hunter estimates that at least eight out of ten churches operate out of a chaplaincy model, which is characterized by these four assumptions: (1) primary ministry takes place inside the church, not outside in the world; (2) the main object of ministry is believers, not nonbelievers; (3) ministry is the preserve of the clergy, not the laity; (4) the validity of ministry is measured not by redeemed lives or changed communities but by vocational satisfactions of the clergy. Apostolic communities of faith stand these assumptions on their head: ministry is a lay-led movement albeit educated and empowered by clergy, a movement directed outward to the world and non-Christians, which measures its effectiveness in terms of changed lives and communities.[18]

The new egonomic "me-ness," or what Joanna Macy calls "the greening of the self,"[19] is a reaction against the modern doctrine of individualism and this "chaplaincy" model. Before exploring postmodernism's appetite for closer relationships and a more "relational" or "ecological" self, it is worth a few paragraphs to understand fully what is meant by "individualism."

Individualism is perhaps best defined as the notion that the person ends with skin. The fence of skin keeps me in here and you out there. So much of what we take for granted is based on this new modern metaphor of "the skin-encapsulated ego" (Alan Watts), the I-am-in-here-you-are-out-there sense of self we operate with in our daily lives. The development of market individualists that comprises what we know today as "consumerism"—sovereign individuals (the imperial self) reaping rewards and exercising rights without account or accountability—was actually set into motion by the very people who opposed materialism and outlined the symbiotic possibilities between the individual and the community. We are now in a state of hedonism—the cult of self—that made consumerism possible[20] even in the church, where members think of themselves less as members ("What contribution can I make?") than as consumers ("What's in it for me?"), buying services from the church.

Yet the modern era, which gave birth to this I-am-in-here-you-are-out-there individual, portended a solution to how the twin forces of individualization and communalization might work together. John Calvin, while contending that the priesthood of believers means each person is gifted with special graces and functions, at the same time insisted that these gifts exist not for private use or self-interest or individual sake, but for the well-being of the community. Individual gifts are to be "transferred" to the "common edification of the church."[21] Calvin wrote:

> The "communion of saints," . . . though usually omitted by ancient writers, must not be overlooked, as it admirably expresses the quality of the church; just as if it had been said, that saints are united in the fellowship of Christ on this condition, that all the blessings which God bestows upon them are mutually communicated to each other. This, however, is not incompatible with a diversity of graces, for we know that the gifts of the Spirit are variously distributed.[22]

In the modern era, "The Green" is where this happened. "The Village Green" was the grassy field or commons in the center of New England towns that stood as its heart, the place that was owned by all and that reminded everyone that the community existed for the common good of all, not the private good of a few. The identification of the individual with the community is the basis for an essentially public freedom.

> *One is only human because of others, with others, for others.*
> AFRICAN PROVERB

The individual will still be and should be important in postmodern culture. Our global marketplace makes the individual the controlling center of the economic universe and the key to collective wealth. But with a "high" doctrine of the individual must come a "high" doctrine of the community. One cannot "go it alone," even in birth. Many a "singleton" is actually a surviving twin. Among a small portion of early detected twin pregnancies, only one infant develops and is born, while the other is reabsorbed by the mother's body.

In France the term *revolution* was not officially used until the autumn of 1790, fifteen months after "The French Revolution" had broken out. Postmoderns are in the midst of a similar, yet unnamed transformation that is inventing a new future for the blend of individuality and community, something different than anything with which we are currently familiar. The modern era found that individualistic and community values are not easily reconcilable. The postmodern era will not so much try to "reconcile" them as to "synergize" them.

It is the historic postmodern challenge to build a form of community no one has ever lived in—not a disembodied communitarian cipher of an ideal community, but a flesh-in-blood, feuding-and-bigoted real community that can simultaneously promote the individual and the community, and can develop an individuality nurtured by life-in-community where the individual is the conscience of the community, and the community is the incubator of the individual.

This new life of individual-in-community will be based on at least three great holographic principles:

1. We are all parts of a whole.[23]
2. The whole is present in every part, as in a hologram.[24]
3. All parts are interconnected.[25]

When holograms are cut in two or diminished, the whole is not lost. What is lost is some resolution. The image becomes blurrier and blurrier. So it is with the image of God in us as we become more and more separated from one another. In the words of His Holiness the Dalai Lama, "Within the context of our new interdependence, self-interest clearly lies in considering the interest of others."[26]

Compassion . . . is a keen awareness of the interdependence of all these living beings, which are all part of one another and all involved in one another.

THOMAS MERTON

4. A New Me

What are the signs of a postmodern "egonomic" individuality? This question is being answered in a strange way and from a strange source: the largest as well as oldest living creature on planet Earth.

It is not a blue whale, or a giant Redwood tree, but a fungus—an underground blob, also known as *Armillaria bulbosa*, a mass of subterranean cytoplasm that feeds off rotting organic matter and tree roots. It is estimated to be between 1,500 and 10,000 years old and somewhere between 100 and 1,000 tons.[27] This fungus lies beneath 37 acres of woodland in Crystal Falls, Michigan, a small-town (population 2,000) in northern Michigan near the Wisconsin-Michigan border that is coming to terms with its new-found identity through mushroom burgers, fungus fudge, Mushroom Festivals, and T-shirts that proclaim "A Humongous Fungus is Amungus: A. bulbosa."[28]

The village of Crystal Falls is also having to gear up for the inevitable Fungus Wars, as the state of Washington has challenged Michigan's megamold pride of place with *Armillaria ostoyae*, a fungus allegedly spread over 1,500 acres beneath the forest slopes of Mount Adams. Without genetic proof of their claim, the newest challenger is a 160-acre clump of aspen, 165 miles south of Salt Lake City. Forty-seven thousand stems derive from the root of a single plant, which weighs an estimated 13.2 million pounds, or 60 times bigger than Michigan's fungus and 33 times bigger than a blue whale. Since the Crystal Falls fungus is still the oldest, 1,500 years of age, its claim to pride of place in the postmodern inventory of metaphors remains unsurpassed.[29]

The fungal world is now seen as something entirely different from the plant or animal kingdoms. Multicellular life is divided into three kingdoms: plant, animal, fungi. As opposed to the plant (redwood) and animal (whale) kingdoms, fungal mycelia do not respect defined boundaries. Their growth patterns (in Michigan's case, eight inches per year) are not predetermined, but unpredictable.

When gourmets gather and devour the delicious "honey mushroom" of A. *bulbosa*, they may be startled to discover they are actually gobbling up the fungus's reproductive organs. Mushrooms are how fungi reproduce.[30] Mushrooms are to fungi what individuals are to communities. An "individual" mushroom is not an isolated outcropping or autonomous entity or widely scattered, discrete organism. A population of individual mushrooms are the means by which the networks of foraging tube-like hyphae that make up fungal mycelia retain their identity and continuity.

Stephen Jay Gould suggests that "this underground fungal mat" is forcing us "to wrestle with the vital biological (and philosophical) question of proper definitions for individuality." Traditionally, an individual has been defined in terms of "bounded entities with definable form." In this organism, however, the mushrooms "are only the visible fruiting bodies of an underground totality."[31]

Perhaps it would be better to look at people as more like fungi and less like plants and animals (whales, orangutans, roses, etc.) with set boundaries.[32] At least the metaphor gets us seeing "self" as a part of rather than apart from the Earth. Or as John Seed, director of the Rainforest Information Center in Australia, puts it: "I try to remember that it's not me, John Seed, trying to protect the rainforest. Rather, I am part of the rainforest protecting itself. I am that part of the rainforest recently emerged into human thinking."[33]

Since "individuals" have already been insulted by comparing them to fungi, let's add to the insult by the parable of spit and snot.

There is an ancient riddle: "What is it that the rich man puts in his pocket and the poor man throws away?" The answer, of course, is "snot."[34] There is another ancient riddle from mountain culture about how to treat rich people that my grandfather taught me: "Never spit upwards. It will always fall back in your face."

What is it that keeps your and my spit and snot from insulting everyone we meet? Simply two square yards of skin which cover our bodies. Skin for us is separating tissue, a covering that keeps me in here and you out there. It protects and separates us. An individual ends in the skin, as in Fred Allen's description of one individual in particular: "He was so small that it was a waste of skin."

The truth is that skin puts us in touch with one another. More bridge than barrier,[35] it is one of our bodies' most marvelous information processing systems. To keep these connections and informations fresh and alive, we shed our skin all the time. Eighty percent of dust in our homes is shed skin. Robert Frost gave us this fundamental spiritual principle about life, "You have to live by shedding"[36]—shedding illusions, shedding dead wood, shedding false notions and habits, and shedding skin.

As long as our body fluids stay inside our two yards of skin, they are healthy and clean. But once they leave the boundaries of our bodies, they become filthy and foul. Take spit or saliva. We are finding out much new information about saliva. We now know that introverts appear to salivate more than extroverts do. We now know that inside the human mouth more than 200 species of life (bacterial) claim residency. And we now know that 95 percent of all cavities are caused by a bacterial infection that takes place only during the twelve months following the eruption of baby teeth. The source of the infection? The mother's saliva.[37]

But there is one fact that hasn't changed. Saliva in the mouth is natural. In the hand or air, saliva is gross. Those who demonstrated in the sixties in Mississippi tell of meeting an eighth-grade black girl named Thelma who was the first African American in the local public school. Her teacher made her stand until everybody else had been seated. As she stood there in her clean, starched dress, the other youngsters walked past her place. One at a time they spit on her chair, making a puddle of saliva in which her teacher told her to sit, pretty dress and all.[38]

There is a proverb popular among the Akans of Ghana: "One does not spit and put it on the tongue." Or "How can one spit on the floor and put it back on one's tongue?" Try this little experiment. Spit on your hand and look at it. What is the difference between the spit in your hand and the spit in your mouth? Only the fact that it has left the boundary of your body. Now put the spit back in your mouth. Having trouble?

Try another experiment. Get a glass of water. Spit into that glass. Now drink the water. Having trouble? You drink from a glass and swallow spit all at the same time all the time. But try drinking from a glass into which you have spit.

The trouble we are having with all this saliva and spit is what we must get over if we are to have a new understanding of individuality. In the same way spittle had always been a symbol of enmity and derision but became with Christ a symbol of grace and healing (John 9:6; Mark 7:33), and was even used in the baptismal rites at Rome and Milan, so perhaps it is in the image of spit and saliva that postmoderns will come to see that the hyper-doctrine of individualism, which cursed so much of the modern era, can be turned into a blessing. Is this not the scandal of the gospel? The curse of being hanged on a tree was transformed into the very symbol of forgiveness and salvation. What is in life most cursed and hateful can become the greatest instrument for redemption and blessing.

Or take another body fluid that, as long as it stays within this "wall of flesh" is fine but as soon as it leaves the boundary of the body becomes foul: urine. Andres Serrano's *Piss Christ*,[39] which submerged a religious symbol in a body fluid, created a controversy like few works of "art" in history because of our discomfort with our bodies. How many heard these spiritual dimensions to Serrano's work? In medicine today urine is a means of ascertaining truth. Urine checks reveal what is happening inside our bodies. Urine readings tell us whether there is present alcohol, drugs, diseases, and infections. Urine tests tell the truth. A crucifix in urine may be a plea for the church to return to the true meaning of the cross.[40]

In the larger talk about community and the specific communitarian movement, it is well not to forget that a sense of self and of individuality is not inconsequential. How could the ordinary men of Germany's Reserve Police Battalion 101 become killers overnight? How could they follow orders to shoot and kill over 38,000 Jewish women, children, and elderly people between July 1942 and November 1943, and send another 45,000 men to the gas chambers at Treblinka? One study argues that what distinguished the 80 percent who pulled the trigger from the 20 per cent who refused was group identity and belongingness. "To break ranks and step out, to adopt overtly nonconformist behavior, was simply beyond most of the men. It was easier for them to shoot."[41]

Connections are the medium of more than social life. Attachments are the medium of a mature self, a complex psyche that can change and develop over time only because it can "get outside its own skin" and enter into relationships with others. The "me" is its relationships. The essence of the "new me" is "a self among, not a self apart."[42]

5. A New We

The covenant God made with Israel was not with individuals, but with a community of people. The modern era's individualized reading of biblical texts (especially Paul) make it difficult for us to appreciate the communal nature of the Christian vision of the life of faith; or in the "pc" clichés of postmodern culture, the "weness" of "wellness."

There is a craving for community and the common good, a need to establish communal identities, that are taking the Western world by storm. Robert Bellah's classic *Habits of the Heart* (1985), its successor volume *The Good Society* (1991), and Robert Wuthnow's recent *Acts of Compassion* (1991) are clarion calls for the church to offer a new sense of community and to restore a communal "memory" among the USAmerican people. Will the church stand as an alternative to modernity's individualizing forces, or will it continue to be part of the problem?

The problem with all of these "calls," however, is that the communal "memory" Bellah, Wuthnow, and others invoke and celebrate is hatched in a very nasty WASP's nest. As Paul Leinberger and Bruce Tucker point out in *The New Individualists* (1991), will "going back" and reappropriating tradition work when that past was so homogeneous and hierarchical and the future so multicultural and decentered?[43] Future forms of community taking shape as part of "the third democratic transformation" (political scientist Robert Dahl's phrase), many of which we have yet to conceive, may emerge more from the adhocracies and networks we are forging now than from our "republican" past.

Lyle Schaller has discovered that "the word *community* has now surpassed the word *first* when choosing the name for a new congregation."[44] What might be some signs of a truly postmodern "egonomic" community in nature as well as in name? Six components seem especially crucial: (a) stories, (b) singing and laughter, (c) innovation, (d) cooperation, (e) new informality, (f) table culture.

A. Tell Me the Stories: Without a story, one is without a self, and without a community. Story is the beginning and continuum of community, for it is by adding voice upon voice to story upon story that communities are built. In fact, a "narrative culture" is perhaps the most succinct definition of a "community."

The push to narrate is as strong if not stronger than it ever has been. Stories function in postmodern culture where "propositional truths" once functioned in modern culture. The development of a moral life depends on one's capacity to hear and tell significant stories.[45]

Paul Ricoeur has done more than most to show us why we "narratate" our lives and how these stories, myths, parables, and genres work. Parables, he argues, disorient us in order to reorient. For a culture that has lost its way, or as Dante would put it, a culture for which "the straight way was lost," stories take us home by the only way possible—through the labyrinth of metaphor and parable. Dante's direction, called "the conscious return . . . to the Center," is a coming to consciousness that "is not a discovery of some new thing; it is a long and painful return to that which has always been."[46]

> *YOU DON'T HAVE ANYTHING*
>
> *IF YOU DON'T HAVE THE STORIES.*
>
> LESLIE MARMON SILKO

In postmodern culture it is TV that sculpts our individual and communal identities. Television generates the mythology, and gives people the stories and images by which they live, die, and understand their lives. Unfortunately, the medium is not conveying the message, at least not the message of the gospel.

A prime reason for this is because, for the church, the road less traveled is the road traveled. The road less traveled by religious leaders is the road being traveled by the culture: the electronic highway. The church seems to have the notion that the more impressive the medium, the more impoverished the message. The more congested the highway, the more reason to find the forgotten routes. Let Robert Frost take the road less traveled. The mission of the church is to be where the people are, to take the road best traveled.

To accomplish its mission, religious leadership will use media to tell the stories of the faith: creative leaders of the future will develop media literacy. To get any message heard, they must be visually literate "media viewers" and "media doers." They must create their own films, videos, audios, and multimedia projects to become active producers of multimedia stories. Communities that will reach twenty-first century culture for Christ will have as part of their staff full-time media directors, as part of their facilities, television studios and postproduction facilities. They will also be routinely using the radio and television for both advertising and broadcasting, as only 300 to 500 of USAmerica's 350,000 churches are now doing according to Lyle E. Schaller.

Storytelling has been defined as "the symbolic transformation of experience into meaning."[47] The church needs postmodern storytellers who will see themselves as "wordsmiths" and "imagesmiths" or what I call gardeners of words (and word-processors); storytellers as "image builders" or what I call gardeners of images (and gardeners of omni-media); storytellers as "world builders" or what I call gardeners of a new world that is struggling to be born through our stories: "This is my story, this is my song."

Faith is opened up to a postmodern culture through the imaginational more than the rational, the symbolic more than the dogmatic, through images more than through "points." In Pierre Babin's words, "Do you want to express the gospel today? Use symbolic language. That was Jesus' language, and it is the dominant language of the media today. It adds modulation to abstract words. It is the best way of putting thought on show."[48]

B. Music, myth, and mirth: A mission statement for postmodern communities would read very simply: we have a screw loose, we have a death wish, and we have a sense of humor.

To have a screw loose means that we are open to walking on the wild side of life, where the winds from the God of Holy Surprises blow and sing.

To have a death wish means we are less into climbing ladders and clutching crowns than we are into bearing and lifting crosses and rolling away stones.[49] One gains life by losing it. The death wish may also mean that we are not trying to "survive" but that some other movement or congregation may come along that is more responsibly or effectively delivering the gospel to our culture. An example of this attitude is Willow Creek. When asked who they will minister to after their target audience passes by, they respond, "Someone else. We did our job."

> *Imagination was given to man to compensate him for what he is not. A sense of humor was provided to console him for what he is.*
>
> HORACE WALPOLE

Since the devil never laughs, a sense of humor is the best weapon in the fight against evil. "One of the greatest weapons of all is laughter, a gift for fun, a sense of play which is sadly missing from the grownup world," Madeleine L'Engle has written as she calls for Christians "to take ourselves seriously enough to take ourselves lightly."[50] In fact, the urban reformer Jacob Riis once suggested that a "professional humorist ought to be attached to every reform movement, to keep it from making itself ridiculous by either too great solemnity or too much conceit."[51] Laughter lightens every load. New paradigm leaders will learn to be at once light-hearted and deeply serious.

On an island off the southeast coast of France, in the famous Abbey of Lérins, stands a twelfth century sculpture with the title *Christ souriant,* which translates as "The Smiling Christ." It portrays Jesus on the cross the moment of his death—his eyes closed, his head tilted to the right, and on his lips a smile.[52] It is this sense of connectedness between myth and mirth that is bringing a spirit of celebration back into religious life. The year 1992 may have been a turning point in the life of one United Methodist Conference. Bishop Edwin C. Boulton adjourned the East Ohio annual conference, meeting at Lakeside, Ohio, to the gazebo by the lake. There awaiting the delegates was a dance band playing big band music as the bishop and his wife led the annual conference in an afternoon of dancing on the boardwalk.

C. and D. Innovation and Cooperation: It may be helpful to analyze how both function together in postmodern communities by reviewing a study of what happens to hometown retailers and downtown businesses when a Wal-Mart or K-Mart come to town. The researchers found that the local businesses can actually flourish when discount store chains plop themselves down on the scene, but only if two features are present: (1) innovation and (2) cooperation.

Innovation is essential because the presence of a discount store creates a totally new environment. Nothing can ever be the same again. If change is seen as a friend, not an enemy, and adjustments are made in light of the new environment, major benefits can accrue from spillover effects of increase in retail traffic, need for new and complementary products and services, and so on. For example, if a town already has a general apparel store, switch to maternity or big/tall or children's clothing.

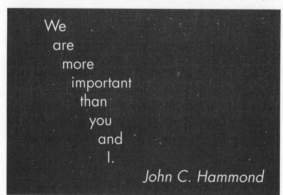

We
are
more
important
than
you
and
I.

John C. Hammond

Cooperation and joint strategies by merchants and community leaders can lead to a new conception of one's store as a part of a shopping district rather than a solitary business. Strategies like extended hours, uniform signage, promotional activities, and better parking work only if done in teamwork with other merchants. They don't work as a single strategy.

With a spirit of innovation and cooperation in place, the coming to town of a K-mart or Wal-mart can actually be a "catalyst" for increased economic vitality of a small town. The authors conclude their study with this observation: "The real enemy facing rural merchants is an unwillingness to change."[53]

Scientists are even presenting in direct contradiction to neo-Darwinism the controversial thesis that cooperation rather than competition is the key to survival. In other words they are turning Darwin on his head and shaking him hard. Teamwork, not competitive edge or advantage, drives evolutionary diversity.

Evidence for this comes from microbiologists who have identified the emergence of eukaryotes. An advanced two-part cell that was formed as a result of symbiotic partnerships among bacteria, this constituted "a leap in evolutionary complexity far greater than any that has occurred since."[54] All life we know of today—from zebras to zucchini—developed from such cooperative ventures. It is not divide-and-conquer, competitive strategies that win the day. Rather it is cooperative, holistic, teamwork ventures that constitute the grain of the universe. Authoritarian attitudes and structures need to give way to team spirit in every area of life for safety and survival sake—even in those unlikely spaces like airplane cockpits where the consequences of human error are so disastrous.[55]

E. New Informality: The need to feel "at home" at church extends to what people wear. In fact, a "dressing up" for church is part of establishment religion's problem. Mark Twain's icy commendation of "a good man in the worst sense of the word" describes vividly a picture-perfect church that puts on the ritz spiritually, its eyebrows arched constantly in niceties of moral judgments, its shampooed spirits intolerant of any uncleanliness of body or misshapenness of mind or disheveledness of spirit. The para-messages of the body—its gestures, its clothing, its energy—constitute a language that needs no translation.

We "dress up" spiritually as well as physically when we go to church. And our "dressing up" becomes a "dressing down" on others, whom we make to feel like a lion in a den of Daniels. We starch our souls in as stiff and staid a finery as our bodies, and wonder why the world mocks the church's smug and stuffy moralism, its unrelieved tone of solemn unction—the flatulent moralizing of a fashionplate faith.

This is one of the reasons why twelve-step programs work: they create nurturing, come-just-as-you-are communities that accept people for who they are, without pretense, without feigning "goodness," without putting on any "airs," only putting one's worst foot forward in an honest appraisal of oneself—"I am an alcoholic . . . Lord, have mercy on me a sinner." In the words of historian William Irwin Thompson, "The sacred is greater than the sacerdotal. The

113

Pharisees keep up their costumes and are careful with whom they associate, but Jesus travels with whores and tramps."[56]

> *It is never the object of confession, at least in the Catholic tradition, to present oneself as a likeable character. One seeks not admiration but forgiveness.*
>
> ANTHONY BURGESS

Postmodern culture puts on no airs; it is characterized by a new informality that "dresses down," not up. Tight-collared shirts and high-heeled shoes are mercifully going out of fashion in the workplace. Nothing arch or archaizing is "in." Casual, comfort, and chambray are the new "dress for success" dress codes. A recent survey finds that 38 percent of 500 companies surveyed have switched to more casual attire at work in the past five years, with 67 percent allowing casual dress at least occasionally.[57] Indeed, when wearing more formal wear outside the office, the suits and dresses worn are more flamboyant, more colorful, more baggy and slack, with shirt and tie usually arguing.

In fact, the new conventional wisdom (partly inspired by Sam Walton in his baseball cap, hunting clothes and pickup truck, and by "the worst-dressed billionaire in history" Bill Gates) is that a company culture that is buttoned up—that insists on suits and ties and wingtip shoes—is a company wedded to old chain-of-command ways of doing business and a company lucky to be in place much less in one piece ten years from now. By contrast, a company culture that is open-collar—that has lightened up its style with tennis-sneakers and skorts—most likely has also loosened up its structures, and can expect to be soaring into new heights of creativity and productivity in ten years. A similar theory could be propounded about churches.

The real issue, of course, is not what fibers people drape over their bodies, but what spirits they bear in their hearts. Florida may well be the most informal place in USAmerica on Sunday morning, as boosters are leading the march of this new informality. But no generation is as judgmental today as the booster generation, whether or not they wear their "Sunday morning best" to church or not.

For example, I preached at a supposedly new paradigm boomer church in the desert Southwest where a member of my staff accompanying me was the only one present that morning wearing a tie. He was made to feel just as uncomfortable for his dressy self as someone showing up in jeans and a Batman T-shirt would feel walking into an "impression management" First Church.

Indeed, after the service I was accosted for bringing a member of the "suits" with me, for invading their fellowship with the "suits" look, and for obstructing their worship with oppressive memories and hurts. The real issue is not what one wears to church, but whether the church is filled with an atmosphere of openness and acceptance where people can feel free to wear whatever they feel freest worshiping in.

> We have always had two or three Rocks of Gibraltar we could count on: the church, the bank, and the law. We can't count on any of these now. No wonder we are frustrated and awfully gloomy.
> Cultural historian Ray Brown

The come-just-as-you-are church knows the theological meaning of the word *grace*, the secular word *acceptance*. After all, is there anyone righteous among us? No, not one. Anyone around who is unmixed good? Not anyone I know. There is an old story about the gangster who rushed into a saloon shooting right and left and yelling, "All right, you dirty, lousy, SOB's, I'll give you ten seconds to get out of here. I'm robbing this place." Immediately the customers all fled in a hail of bullets—all except for one man who stood by the bar calmly finishing his drink. "Well?" said the gangster, waving his smoking gun. "Well," remarked the one remaining man, "there certainly were a lot of them, weren't there!"[58]

We are, all of us, "factions": both saints and sinners at the same time. Church is the time to accent facts (the latter) over fictions (the former). Ambrose Bierce defined saint as "a dead sinner, revised and edited." My favorite definition of saint, however, is the one that calls saints nothing but sinners who go on trying.

Which church will it be, the church of telling lies or lives? The world is hungry for communities where the warmth of spirit shines through for those who are "trying"; where the watchwords of the God being worshiped as well as the worshipers themselves are "see how he loved [them]" (John 11:35) and "he loved them to the end" (John 13:1); where what is being preached is not a work ethic, not a culture ethic, not a success ethic, not a moral ethic, but a gospel ethic, which says in verbal and nonverbal ways that (1) there is nothing you can do to make God love you less and (2) there is nothing you can do to make God love you more. As Emerson would put it, "the world will make a beaten path to the door" of that church—"That's the place for me"—and even beat down any door that stands in their way of getting to a place where people put on love gloves every time they speak your name or shake your hand, however you look.

F. Table Culture: The Greek word *koinonia* means more than "fellowship." It means basically a shared life, an "all togetherness" that expresses itself differently in every generation through new forms of togetherness, especially around tables. Ardie Kendig-Higgins calls her church "a dating church," by which she means a church where its members court one another, "consciously date one another" through activities, adventures, parties, and eating together.[59] For energy levels to be maintained, there needs to be constant dating and romance. Romance is as important to keeping a church alive as it is vital to keeping marriages alive. And around a table is where much of that romance takes place.

Jesus' ministry was characterized by what scholars call "fellowship meals." The Last Supper was the last of this series of "fellowship meals." Biblical scholar James D. G. Dunn wonders whether the transformation of the common "Last Supper" into the ritual act of "The Eucharist" and its separation from the context of an actual meal table in the home hosted by the head of the "house church" did not "mark the loss of a dimension of fellowship, common participation which was a central feature of Christian beginnings."[60] Can we bring back the "Lord's Supper" as a community celebration, not simply an ecclesiastical performance?

Jesus' world seemed overpeopled with outcasts. Jesus' table fellowship with real-life lowlifes outraged the pious among the people of his day, as Luke reports (15:1-2). An authentic biblical table culture will similarly outrage the pious of our day, especially when the church starts imitating Jesus and "throws parties" for those not yet "worthy" of having parties "thrown" for them—postmodern equivalents of Jesus' staple of table companions (adulterers, swindlers, prostitutes, peddlers, tax-collectors, donkey-drivers, shepherds, tanners, excise-men, etc.).

The new paradigm church will find every excuse conceivable to have a party: baptisms, confirmations, baby showers, graduations, anniversaries, holy days, and so on. When people are moving into a new house, why not form a human chain from moving van to house, celebrating the empty truck with a mountain of pizzas? At New Year's Eve, integrate into the Love Feast/Watchnight Service slides of the church's communal life and memories during the past twelve months. Or during Lent why not put on "St. Peter Pastry Parties." No Christian will get past the Pearly Gates without knowing how to make St. Peter tested and approved homemade bread or "hot-cross buns."

6. Easy-Believism

G. K. Chesterton once observed that when people stop believing in religion, they do not believe in nothing, they believe in everything. In the medieval period people believed in the authority of religion. In the modern period people believed in the authority of science. George Bernard Shaw was perceptive when he wrote that the average modern person is about as credulous as was the average person in the Middle Ages. The only difference is the object of their credulity.

Today people are spiritually credulous. This is one reason why the term *secular* does not apply to postmodern culture and why secularization theory was the hula hoop of sociology. Secular means "not concerned with or devoted to religion" (*Oxford English Dictionary*). Postmodern culture abounds in alternative spiritualities and diffuse religiosity. In the words of Popcorn, "We're bonding together against isolation; in groups that bring us together for reasons from personal to political. Cult religious and associated fringe groups are up; there are at least 40 percent more listed religious groups than a decade ago."[61]

One is now as likely to hear Eddie Murphy delve into a deep spiritual discussion on the Arsenio Hall show as to watch Billy Graham conduct a crusade. One is as likely to read Michael Jackson announce that the purpose of life is "to ignite the spark of divinity in us and give meaning to our lives"[62] as to read Robert Schuller to help us think more positively.

We've gone in one generation from "God is dead" to "you are God." We've switched from wondering whether God can be found in "the secular city" to seeking "the god within" through spiritual practices. Literary critic Harold Bloom says USAmerica is a dangerously "religion-soaked, even religion-mad society."[63] One mathematician and physicist, Peter Russell, even argues that the world is moving toward a "spiritual supernova," which he labels a "white hole in time."[64]

The modern era bred doubt. Its burning question was God's existence. It could not imagine how anyone with any brains could be a believer. The postmodern era breeds superstition. Its burning question is God's presence. Our problem today is not doubt and disbelief, but false belief. People believe anything and everything, whether the tall tale or the bold lie: Gaia and Green Man; NEO therapy (Never Ending Orgasm) and SETI-ology (the search for extraterrestrial intelligence); male bonding wild-man workshops; Breatharians (California group who believes we can survive without food or drink if only we'd breathe properly) and Searchers (they hold weekly out of body experiences). One University of North Carolina study found that almost one out of ten Southerners thinks Elvis is still alive.[65]

Busters can act like cynical nonbelievers in anything, but they are finding the "spiritual" willy-nilly, even on roller coasters. " 'The Beast' . . . is a religious experience," says Paul Ruben, former twentysomething editor of *Roller-Coaster!* magazine. "You find God [there]."[66] Some busters are finding God in the disintegration of our social and economic order, which they cheer on while singing the REM song "It's the end of the world as we know it and I feel fine." With every counterfeit spirituality comes added testimony to the failures of organized religion to deliver the goods, the biblical goods of good news.

This historical moment, to the surprise of rationalists and positivists, is one of deep spiritual hungerings and religious resurfacings, if anything a time of "easy-believism"—and who is not constantly amazed at what people nowadays *do* believe? "With the exception of anything my mom and dad said, I believed everything" is how humorist/journalist P. J. O'Rourke summarizes our spiritual state.[67] The prevalent spiritual state of easy-believism yields a gaga gospel where people in this "spiritually famished time" (*Newsweek*) are open to anything and everything. Indeed, it seems at times as if we are living in a day when some people will believe anything so long as it is not in the Bible. How ironic that the modern era, which set about to destroy ignorance and superstition and belief and flirted with "credicide"— the belief in nothing and the deep suspicion of all beliefs—ends up this way.

> *Why did the idea of the congregation degenerate into the idea of the local club? It was a perfectly natural development. The majority of people didn't believe in Christianity at all. They commonly thought of it as a device for safeguarding their private prejudices. . . . their private prejudices were public enough to enable them to form a club for their common protection against the gospel.*
>
> GEDDES MACGREGOR

7. Economics

Who is the poorest person in the world? Uncle Sam. Do you know anyone else in debt by 4 trillion dollars?

This comedy routine suddenly becomes unfunny when it is remembered whom the joke is on—every man, woman, and child in USAmerica, now in debt almost $40,000 each because of one profligate Uncle.

There are two economies: the market economy and the household economy (of family, friends, neighbors, church). The church knows the first exists. But it doesn't understand market economics. The church understands the second intuitively, but doesn't know that household economics exists. This real economy of human needs and services, of caring and compassion, is in need of rebuilding. Religious leaders must come to see themselves as social investment brokers, matching human resources and social capital with needs and opportunities.

> *Our lives have become a hell not because money is too important to us, but because . . . it is not important enough.*
>
> JACOB NEEDLEMAN

An understanding of how wealth works in the emerging global economy is absolutely essential. Postmodern culture is at base an economic paradigm. Postmodern humans are a species of *Homo economicus*. The language, rituals, and symbols of "economism," which the *Oxford English Dictionary* defines as that which "imposes the primacy of economic causes or factors as the main source of cultural meanings and values," dominate our everyday lives. In the words of *Time* magazine's peek into the century ahead, "economics will rule over the twenty-first century. All the big questions confronting the world in the century ahead are basically economic."[68]

The collapse of virtually all communist economies reveals two important insights. First, the critique of capitalism and the market model by Karl Marx has some insightful things to teach us. Louis de Bernières's third novel begins with a parable of "the greatest feat of advertising in modern history": the worldwide conquest of capitalism has moved into space, where it has made a billboard of the moon, which the world's most powerful soft-drink company has painted red except for its name, which beams through space for all to see.[69] While Marx's analysis of the wrongs of capitalism may be more or less right, the way to deal with capitalism's flaws is not through a socialized or centrally managed economy but through a guided market economics. Representative democracy and economic freedom are the pivotal political and economic pluralisms around which postmodern life will flow.

Second, what will dominate political discourse in postmodernism's "cybernetic economy" (Albert Bressand) are the concerns of economic pluralism, not political pluralism. Although economic pluralism is interdependent on political pluralism and social pluralism, it is a geo-economic era in which we live. Investment capital has displaced diplomacy and weaponry. Geo-economics, especially in its emerging trinity of economic groupings (European, Asian, and American), is turning geo-politics into a backstreet phenomenon. Political lobbyists can no longer afford to focus on the executive, legislative, and judicial branches of government. The new battleground is international and economic. Decisions made in the board rooms of multinational companies and across negotiating tables in international trade agreements have greater force than anything that happens on Capitol Hill.[70]

It should not be as hard as it is for the church to understand all this and start thinking of itself in economic terms, especially that part of the church known as the Protestant Reformation, which has bequeathed to western history the cultural linking of piety and economic activity. We have long known there are economic consequences to religious belief. So why are the economies of the local church so dated? It is not just the churches' "economic justice ministry" that is such an anachronism.[71]

Virtually every time the church deals with economic matters it does so anachronistically. Offering plates are not the antiques of the future, but the antiques of today. They are designed for a cash culture in a day when money is electronic impulses, and when what is important to a person can be identified quickly by what is automatically withdrawn from their checking account. Indeed, studies have demonstrated that people spend 23 percent more when they buy with credit cards than when they buy with cash.[72] How many churches do you know that encourage automatic monthly withdrawals from checking accounts or credit cards? Yet it's the fastest way to increase the budget.

And what about that budget? Actually, budgets work no better than diets do. Bob Schwartz's book *Why Diets Don't Work* (1992) gives four rules for going off diets which would help churches to get off being controlled by budgets:

1. Eat when you're hungry.
2. Eat exactly what your body wants.
3. Eat each bite consciously.
4. Stop when your body has had enough.

Every church and every pastor should have "enough" to enable them to do the mission of God in their place, but no more than that. But instead of proclaiming a theology of enoughness, the church is too busy reveling in its low salaries (If you pay peanuts, you get monkeys), attacking money and wealth, and taking cheap shots at economic exchanges like shopping.

The church's problem is not money. As the late Joseph Campbell put it, money is nothing more, or less, than congealed energy. Money has tremendous power: to energize for good, or to energize for evil. Rather than clergy being so busy attacking money and the moneyed, perhaps they would be better served to see how they themselves could become more "wealthy" in the fullest sense of that term—even standing in the tradition of Amos, the well-off member of the Judahite gentry, whose extensive education and considerable wealth enabled him to risk a prophetic ministry that still resounds today.[73]

Similarly, the problem is not shopping itself. Our weekly tours of shopping malls are not necessarily a postmodern homage to our "stations of the crass." How else are we going to clothe ourselves and feed ourselves and house ourselves? Indeed, the stimulation of self-reliance and communal empowerment through the purchasing of products made by Third World craft communities is proving to be of more significance than anyone imagined. Peruvian rugs, Mayan patchwork quilts, native American jewelry are all indispensable for the social and economic development of impoverished communities here and around the world, especially when such shopping is done through alternative trade organizations (ATOs) that are sensitive to social and economic justice.

Wealth is more than money or consumption. Wealth is the mix of land, labor, and learning—all of which are increasingly defined in electronic and musical categories: *Homo economicus musicalis*. The hierarchies of the nation-state are being recontextualized into a new hierarchy of global electronic music and global electronic economies. Our economic thinking must go beyond monetary processes to include human and planetary needs. Conventional economics is not strictly speaking "economics" but "chrematistics," or the art of making money. The church must learn and lead an "ecological economics" that brings all the resources of the Earth into musical relationships.[74]

Ironically, it is some of USAmerica's most conservative churches as well as ethnic traditions that are proving to be the most nontraditional and innovative in their economic thinking. For example, the African American community is coming to realize the power of economics faster than almost anyone else. Pastor Buster Soares has been a prophet in his own community in his adamance that African American leadership move "the movement" from its fixation on civil rights to economic development and empowerment.

Many black churches, which have been since their inception both spiritual and economic forces in their neighborhoods, have heard the words even if they haven't always acknowledged them or publicly applauded Soares himself.

The shift to a service-dominated economy may change all this. Detroit's Hartford Memorial Baptist Church, where Charles Adams and his people bought an eight-block bombed out area of the "War Zone" and turned it into a thriving complex that includes small shops and fast food restaurants (including McDonald's)[75] is one example of the black church thinking economics: acquiring property, building housing, providing venture capital and technical assistance for small businesses, starting financial institutions, job training, and so on. Some of the most creative advances in community development corporations (CDCs)—by now there are over 2,000 of these nonprofit, locally run corporations, with 320,000 housing units built nationwide in the past five years, more by far than the federal government—are being pioneered in the African American community.

8. Beware the Warps of Wraps

There can be a warping effect of wrapping. Form affects content. Wraps warp contents if one is not careful. People's lives warp and tremble under the strain of tight wrapping, especially when the wraps do not fit the contour of the subject.

Sometimes wraps conceal emptiness. The package is attractively tied, all neatly merchandised, but no merchandise of any intellectual or theological substance can be found inside anywhere. Some have even suggested this explains why postmoderns give such attention to architecture as an art form ("a magnificently articulated skin, body to be supplied by someone else"), why sets of leather-bound books adorn home libraries and pastoral studies, as well as why the most sophisticated "popular" television genre is the talk and interview show ("the faces and the issues come and go, but the format is always the same").[76] The ever-present danger of the medium trivializing the message was graphically portrayed by a teenager's T-shirt, which emblazoned the oval logo of Ford Motor Company over the words, "Have you considered the Lord . . . lately?"

> "Guide to the Six Best Novels to Be Seen Reading in 1992"
>
> ESSAY TITLE IN TATLER MAGAZINE

One of the greatest threats of postmodern culture is its disjoining of information and values, data and meaning.[77] Stuart Ewen has done the most to warn postmoderns about the divorce of image and meaning that accompanies the politics of style. In the "perpetual play of images," history can be seriously perverted by the confusion and interchangeability of "material values" and those "values of mind and spirit" that build freedom and justice and peace.[78] "Face values" and surface images must never become a substitute for "the real thing."

When style replaces identity, there ensues a fathomless shallowness. The postmodern world quickly becomes "The Land of Lost Content."

WorkQuakes

SocioQuake 5: *Cashing Out*

The trouble with the rat-race is that even if you win, you're still a rat.

LILY TOMLIN

People who have everything but who actually have nothing are coming to see their lives as facing the wrong way. Fertile in goods, barren of good works, the chase of go-getters, power-couples, and mover-and-shakers is turning around, doing a radical U-turn (the literal meaning of the Greek *metanoia*), or what is called in Japan "U-turn gensho." In America the U-turn phenomenon is called cashing out or increasingly downshifting.

For USAmericans U-turning, cashing out, and downshifting mean jumping off the rat race, seeking refuge from high-income, high-stress life-styles, and living with values more oriented toward personal contentment and communion than material consumption or professional achievement. No matter how socially sanctioned the addictions to fame, wealth, and power have become, increasing numbers of people are reevaluating the high cost of life energy expended while running on these tracks.

Urban dwellers around the world are giving up high salaries and fast lanes for the high life and slow living of small towns, rural areas, sea resorts, and mountain villages. As two "ex-yuppies" put it, "We're less interested in keeping up with the Joneses and more interested in having time for our families. We've decided that perhaps we'd rather be 'well-rounded' than 'highly-sharp-

INOPEM ME COPIA FECIT

PLENTY HAS MADE ME

POOR.

LATIN PROVERB

ened.' "[1] The prizes of consumerist societies—the doohickeys, gazingus pins, and other valueless objects—are no longer worth their prices.

According to Faith Popcorn, cashing out is not "copping out or dropping out or selling out. It's cashing in the career chips you've been stacking up all these years, and going somewhere else to work at something you want to do, the way you want to do it."[2] Of course, partly we are being forced to slim down our borrowing-and-acquiring life-styles because of economics. As we have moved from an "industrial" economy to a "service" economy, low-paying service "Mcjobs" will account for 75 percent of all jobs by 1995. Most Americans are two paychecks away from homelessness. "Wallet fasts" have become as much necessities of economics as ethics.

There are fewer and fewer jobs requiring college degrees—to be precise 165,000 fewer new jobs a year on average than between 1984 and 1990, when one million degrees were awarded on average each year. During these seven years 20 percent of all college graduates ended up in jobs that did not require degrees. Between now and 2005, the total is expected to reach 30 percent or almost one out of three.[3] The economic necessity of two incomes has created changes in social structures and living patterns that are yet dimly understood by demographers and sociologists.

But the larger issue is that people are left high and dry after having squeezed out substitutes for God in sex, success, and career ladders. They sense that existence is more than the sum of bodily functions and malfunctions. They wake up one day and discover that life has whizzed past them. They awaken to the fact that they have never lived their life—they've only lounged with life, or lunched with life, but never really lived life. They realize that their problems center not in what they don't have, but in what they are doing with what they do have.

Americans aren't asking what they want next, but what they want most.

MONEY MAGAZINE

Whether "cocoon cashed-out" or "country cashed-out," the trend is quality over quantity.[4] People are going "back to the future," back to family, friends, old-fashioned values, old-timey living, and God. Hollywood even did a whole movie on this socioquake. Rent *Curly Sue*. GOP polls, in testing how important family-values-caring is to voters, discovered to everyone's surprise that, when voters are asked to describe their greatest objective in life, fully 56 percent say a closer relationship with God.[5] The signs and codes of the cashing-out "semiosphere" are all around us.

Evidence 1: People wear flannel shirts and hiking boots, sleep in flannel sheets, watch *Northern Exposure*, buy home tool kits, and listen to country music. Popcorn says gardening clothes are now the number one look, replacing jogging suits. The more an outdoors culture we become, the more people will take to wearing hats again.

An unheralded but significant phenomenon of the nineties is the return of the small farmer and "exurban farming." Too small to be tracked by the census, "nonfarms" are ringing megacities as part-time farmers are taking to the soil as much for spiritual and mental and physical cultivation as for financial betterment. When there is an economic component, it is in the form of specialty items such as organic vegetables, herbs, and exotic foods. Homestead Farm in the Washington, D.C., area caters to city customers who enjoy the drive into the Maryland countryside where they can personally pick fruits, berries, and vegetables that will grace the family table that very day.[6]

Evidence 2: Long before the *New York Times* announced "The western is back" in the summer of 1991, Popcorn "brailled" the reemergence of western images and themes in American culture. If any aspect of our national heritage can claim to be "the official American ideology," as the late historian Warren Susman observed, it is "westering." The new interest in rural and western symbols—cowboy clothes, Southwest art, ranch culture—is about as strong in Europe as in USAmerica. Suzuki motorbikes didn't sell in Europe until a new ad campaighn portrayed them as "aluminum ponies, steeds for urban Euro-cowboys."[7]

Country singer Garth Brooks sold more albums in the early 1990s than any other musician. The culture that started down a rocky road musically in the 1950s has now discovered country roads—and made them rocky. Country music has virtually replaced rock as the number 1 sound in USAmerica. The great American cowboy is riding back into our consciousness at the same time the actual cowboy is riding off into the sunset. (The number of ranchers has dropped by nearly half since the 1960s; the average age of ranchers is now 59.) If you want to find a "cowboy," you're more likely to find one in an airport than on the range.

In the religious arena, while the over-all music industry doubled its revenues between 1980 and 1990, gospel music tripled its growth from $180 million to $500 million in recording sales. Any guesses which, of all the kinds of gospel music, had the highest percentage of increase? Southern gospel, a blend of country and folk, which now has its own twenty-four-hour satellite radio network called REACH. Take a listen sometime to Garrison Keillor's 1992 Carnegie Hall Concert with "The Hopeful Gospel Quartet" (Sony Music Entertainment).

Evidence 3: "The Folking of America" makes heroes of folksy Garrison Keillor, Robert Fulghum, Willard Scott, Charles Kuralt, Joe Garagiola, William Least Heat-Moon (*Blue Highways, PrairyEarth*), even H. Ross Perot, whose phenomenal candidacy for President had the appeal it did more because of his homespun old-fashionedness than because of his outsiderhood. A similar case could be made for Clinton's sax appeal among the baby boomers.

I myself started watching the *Today* show when Garagiola returned, partly because where else are you going to hear the host of a slick TV show tell you down-home, "bless-my-whiskers" stories like this one about visiting a drugstore.

> From the shelves I selected a bottle of Extra Strength Tylenol, twelve ounces of Kaopectate, an elastic knee support, a supply of corn plasters, some Dristan, a vaporizer, a remedy for sore gums, and a tube of Preparation H. I took all that stuff to the counter where they rung it up on the register and bagged it. Then, as the clerk handed me my purchases, I couldn't believe my ears when I heard him say, "Have a nice day!"[8]

Evidence 4: Where is the number one place USAmericans want to live? Small towns. When the *Times Literary Supplement* asked writers to describe the ideal city, one response they received was this: "The ideal city must be the one that's quickest to get out of."[9] The "fifth migration" in USAmerican history (the fourth, 1950–1970, was from the cities to the suburbs) is people rushing to escape the artless suburbs and the crime-ridden, career-driven cities for the safe streetscapes of small towns and the bucolic roofscapes of rural areas. Visitors to Disneyland and Disney World spend less time on rides than they do wandering along Main Street, USA, and "getting the civic kicks that they cannot get at home"[10] at the multinational urban centers of Epcot.

In 1989 Gallup Poll asked USAmericans where they would most like to live. Thirty-four percent chose a small town; 24 percent a suburb; 22 percent a

---

The Bronx? No Thonx.

OGDEN NASH

---

farm or rural area; only 19 percent a city. People are willing to pay big bucks to live in the few historic small towns that still remain—for example, Marblehead, Massachusetts; Princeton, New Jersey; Acworth, Georgia; Oak Park, Illinois; Manchester, New Hampshire; Alexandria, Virginia; Sonoma, California; Nob Hill/Northwest, Oregon. What is the fastest appreciating real estate in the country? Small communities that are two hours away from major cities. Laments like this one from die-hard urbanists—"It is no good telling people to go and live in the wide open plains of Canada or the Far West because, even if forcibly transported, the moment your back was turned they would drive, march, or crawl back to the nearest metropolis. You can't blame them: nature is a horrible thing to happen to anybody"[11]—are noticeable precisely because of their rarity.

There is even a parish-Planet movement (others call it the "one life-one home" movement, others bioregionalism[12]) that encourages people to claim one community as one's parish (it may or may not be the home of one's birth or childhood), settle down there for life, bond with the land and neighbors until ready to die protecting it, live within its carrying capacity, and make the future for planet Earth better because of one's efforts. Newburgh, Indiana, a quaint small town on the Ohio River, prides itself in being the place "Where we hang our hearts." If the modern era created "displaced" persons, the postmodern era is creating "placed" persons.

The age of mobility is coming to a close. Americans are increasingly staying put and settling down. In the first 3,187 days he was governor of New York State, Mario Cuomo spent a mere 36 nights away from the executive mansion.[13] Postmoderns are putting down roots; they are showing commitment to a culture of place and a sense of place, from which derives a sense of self. They are practicing low-impact living. Wendell Berry has convinced the busters, at least, that if you don't know where you are, you can't know who you are. Or in the words of the late novelist, Wallace Stegner, people today are realizing that it is high time they started "looking around" instead of always "looking ahead."[14]

The urbs are in trouble—urban blight is matched only by suburban plight—creating a new demographic phenomenon which has been dubbed "penturbia," the fifth major geographical and social living pattern in American history.[15] But first the old urbs of urban and suburban.

A baby will be born sometime around the turn of the millennium that will tip the balance of the world's population from rural to urban for the first time in history. In the United States, 73 percent of the population is already urbanized.

The world is moving from nation state to city state, with internationalized megacities boasting their own traditions, museums, sports teams, distinct governments, and "foreign policies." Cities are here to stay, but what state those cities will be in is uncertain.

This is why a 9 November 1991 article in *Newsweek* can pose the question: "Are cities obsolete?"[16] Cities are not healthy. They are not wholesome. They are not ecologically viable. They are built on an unsustainable economic base, and they are not human scale. Indeed, modern cities were designed not for people but for commerce and corporate life, especially the world's megacities of 10 to 12 million inhabitants. But the fear of urban living, at least as people currently understand "city life," is growing and cannot be reversed.

Some scholars are even talking of the "Lebanonization" of America's cities into burned out and blighted war zones from which black professionals are leaving as fast as whites. Even the corporate world is fleeing downtown cities for USAmerica's 200 "edge cities," cocooned communities and exurban business centers on suburbia's fringe that portend the shape of "urban" life in the twenty-first century.[17]

Architecture, the most public of all the art, took the lead in shaping the modern Western world. It is now taking a lead in giving form and substance to the postmodern, multicultural world dawning around us. The official triumvers of high architectural modernism were Walter Gropius, Le Corbusier, and Mies van der Rohe. The guiding principles of modernist architecture were logic, utility, and efficiency. The simplified lines and pure forms announced modern design's desire to break away from the classical and traditional styles of the past. In the classic formulation of architect Louis Kahn, "What do the materials want to be?" What modern materials of steel and glass and stone wanted to be became the cathedrals of commerce—the modern skyscraper— and the temples of consumerism—the horizontal skyscraper known as the mall.

I never talk to brokers or analysts. . . . Wall Street is the only place the people ride to in a Rolls Royce to get advice from those who take the subway.

FINANCIER WARREN BUFFETT

The church was not a bystander in modernism's celebration of the cathedrals of the industrial age. The United Brethren in Christ built the first "sky scraper" in Dayton, a building that dominated the skyline of this "All-American" midwestern city for decades. Is there anything in our homes or offices that resembles the outline of the classic Miesian skyscraper?

How about a featureless filing cabinet. A filing-cabinet life is precisely what the modern era foisted on its rank and file, who are continually ranked and filed all the way up the bureaucratic line. Or as author and publisher Clifton Fadiman puts it caustically, for most moderns life became "a search for the proper manila envelope in which to get themselves filed." Prince Charles has lambasted the way in which modern architecture did not so much reflect "the spirit of the age" as succeed in creating an "age without spirit."[18]

The design and the doctrine of these skyscrapers, which future historians will see as nothing more than clerical factories, taught moderns to choose their box, to "find your niche," to figure out how they "fit in" and "play your part," to learn their "job description" and to follow a "chain of command." Only in this way could cubicled, partitioned moderns climb the line-management ladder of success. What was the "reward" for those who endured daily rammings in and out of their cubicled apartments to their cubicled cars to their cubicled offices? One day, if moderns compliantly stayed put in their cubbyholes until told to come out, a few of them might get filed in a "top drawer" office at the top of a glass box or "God-Box" (the nickname for 475 Riverside Drive, New York City, the old headquarters of establishment Protestantism).

To a generation committed to "out-of-the-box" thinking and stand-out living, to busters more interested in fitting together than fitting in, the chorus of the 1960s Malvina Reynolds' song "Little Boxes" sticks in the craw of the soul.

> Little boxes on the hillside
> . . . .
> And they all look just the same.

In postmodern architecture, the question is not "What do the materials want to be?" but "What does the land want to be?" or "What does the space want to be?" Postmodern artists and designers like James Hubbell, Tom Alberts, Peter Calthorpe, Day Charoudi (MIT), Sim Van der Tyn (UC Berkeley) and the husband-wife team of Andres Duany and Elizabeth Plater-Zyberk are less interested in dropping skyscrapers on postage stamp lots or plopping boxes on mountains than in helping the land come to consciousness in a physical space. They imagine everything they design and build as alive and able to help us become more alive and whole.

The high-rise buildings of modernity will give way to more ecological designs friendlier to the land, even new forms of alive "earthen vessels" that come out of the earth rather than are forced on it, buildings that generate energy by their generating community. Admittedly, the soft rhythmic lines of these "earthen vessels" will take some getting used to, as the right angles and straight lines of modern architecture give way to more organic designs and curvilinear constructions. Buildings that are living, breathing organisms will replace the sealed walls of buildings with layered "bioskin" (see the work of horticulturalist Anna Edey), or glass windows with a "cloud gel" (see Day Charoudi's work) that turns opaque or transparent depending on the light and temperature.

Indeed, the best hope for the cities of the world is not making them more urban but making them more small town. In architecture and landscape design the movement is away from the giant glass boxes of Miesian modernism to the small-town architecture and the multicultural architecture of "neo-traditionalism" or "small-town thinking." Urban planners and community organizers call it the "eco-city" or "urban ecology" movement.

Postmodern living is also expressed in the eco-village movement, which brings together the best of the old-fashioned comforts of traditional villages and the best of modern cities. Eco-villages are cooperative communities that live in harmony with nature by growing their own food, generating their own energy, treating their own wastes and yet linked electronically to the rest of the world.[19]

Whatever name it goes by, at base it is an attempt to make the city more healthy and liveable by bringing back townscapes to urban places and by making streetscapes look and feel more like small-town America. It does this by rebuilding urban areas, not by destroying all the familiar and traditional landmarks, but by bringing back the old while bringing on the green spaces, pocket gardens, community parks, river corridors, alleyways, tree-lined boulevards, wide porches, and facing swings.[20]

For example: The Osaka Business Park in Japan is a model for twenty-first century urban development, based on the Japanese garden concept of "Karesansui," a method created during the Muromachi golden age of art and culture. The new Boston Artery, a portion of which is scheduled to open in 1994, will spell the end of the old urban freeway. It will be the last project of the interstate highway system, the end of the thirty-eight-year, $129 billion urban interstate freeway era.[21]

Another example: Urban Design Associates Architects (UDA) of Pittsburgh worked with citizens groups in Richmond, Virginia, to rebuild the Randolph neighborhood in ways that respected past traditions while reflecting a denser, diverse mix of income groups, ages, cultures, and housing types. "Our basic battle cry was 'build neighborhoods with streets and front yards and back yards and porches' " states the UDA principal about their efforts to reestablish at Randolph the "past glory" of traditional community.[22]

Another example: The community development plan for Church Square in Cleveland brings back the "mixed use" town planning in which the village center and all the essential services are within walking distance—homes, post office, town hall, corner groceries, restaurants, and Main Street shops and offices. The small-town concept fosters a feeling of community partly because nothing is farther than a quarter mile from anything else.

The enemy of cities has not been real-estate agents or developers, but misguided urban planners, traffic engineers, and zoning boards. It is the cold rationality of today's linear, Euclidian zoning codes that segregate into homogeneous "class ghettoes" rich and poor, old and young, housing from commerce and industry. Everything is ordered, classified, tidy and neat only in "heritage" cities like Old Sturbridge Village (Massachusetts) and Genesee Country Museum (Mumford, New York), and these are without inhabitants, only visitors.

> The logic of history requires gardens in our cities, a pastoral landscape aesthetic in our suburbs, and unadulterated wilderness for retreat. We have precious few of these.
>
> AMERICAN LAND FORUM PRESIDENT
> CHARLES E. LITTLE

As Jane Jacobs pointed out in her classic *The Death and Life of Great American Cities* (1961), the isolated, self-contained, homogeneous ghettoes and "dead spaces" of cities are gifts to the world of rationalist planners and zoners. What the small town did once, and new urban villages are trying to do now, is bring all these back together in a blend, as neighborhoods become communities. The megacity then becomes a collection of squares (small villages and microcultures) rather than super-blocks.

The small-town architectural movement would design urban villages or eco-communities wherein nothing is done that disrespects the whole, where people with diverse income levels live close together, and where everyone lives harmoniously with nature, working within the limits imposed on us by nature. In Mobile, Alabama, the city constructed office and residential buildings around their giant live oaks rather than remove their trees. The rural, small-town seat of North Carolina's poorest county, Columbia (Tyrrell County), is partnering with foundations and federal agencies in making a greenway for the new Pocosin Lakes National Wildlife Refuge the centerpiece of their economic development plans.

The Jerusalem Talmud declares that no one should live in a city that does not have green gardens. Cities must have green belts around them, green spaces and green corridors, to make them habitable for humans. The "new vil-

133

lage greens" and "town squares" of the late modern era, shopping malls, are all privately owned and heavily "secured." Few things vanished faster in the modern era than public space. As goes public space, many are arguing, so goes democracy.[23]

This is not to suggest that the churches should abandon the cities. On an urbanized planet, with one in two people living in cities (by 2000 some say three out of four people will live in cities—in 1900 the figure was one in 20), God may be calling more not fewer Christians to live in the city as a prophetic witness or pastoral ministry, something that Floyd McClung calls "servant residency."[24]

After moving in 1973 as international executive director of Youth With a Mission (YWM) to Amsterdam, the "sex capital of Europe," McClung, his wife and two children (ages five and seven) decided in 1980 to take up "servant residency" in the heart of Amsterdam's world-renowned red-light district amid the porn shops and sex clubs and child pornography and hard drug users and AIDS infestation. The family's love for the city has meant that they have no regrets. But their move was clearly an act of crossbearing sacrifice that was entered into only after much prayer and discernment.

Suburbia is fast becoming as troublesome as urban America. At the very moment USAmerica is almost the first suburban-majority nation in human history (the 1990 census revealed that nearly as many Americans now live in suburbs as live in cities, small towns, and rural areas combined), and at the very moment politicians are telling us the power is shifting from the cities to the suburbs, the truth is that USAmericans are realizing that suburbia, the California dream that the boosters generation gave the world, is becoming obsolete.

One former mayor even advocates in a new book that the suburbs be abolished completely, though he would do so for the sake of the city.[25] In the words of Tom Sine, "Boosters are the pacesetters of the kind of extravagant, luxurious living that is fundamentally out of touch with the kind of world we live in. This is the generation who has defined what the good life in America looks like—and increasingly its dream is being called into question."[26] The moment the suburbs became the norm, more and more USAmericans are realizing that the norm was a nightmare. Why?

First, suburbs are ugly, ugly, ugly.

> Have you ever noticed how often new housing developments are named after what they have destroyed? There are no trees on the grounds of the "Oak Grove Condominiums." The eagles have flown from the "Eagle's Nest," and you can't see the lake from "Lake View Apartments" because other buildings now block the view. Rarely does the new creation incorporate and honor the old setting.

Sadly, the name is often only a tombstone commemorating the beauty that previously existed.[27]

Largely a creation of government policies, suburbs are what Ada Louise Huxtable characterized as the "slurbs." Where the original suburban dream was a bucolic setting, where a modern version of gentleman farming could be played out on rural estates, or at least half-acre lots, the dream soon became a nightmare of postage-stamp, back-to-back, half-million dollar Tudor houses ("McMansions") with turquoise pools. Where if neighbors had wanted to talk to neighbors, which was seldom, they could have easier leaned out a bedroom window than leaned over a backyard fence. One recent book documents the loss of shared purpose and sense of connectedness in one simple statistic: Fully 72 percent of 2,000 USAmericans interviewed did not know the people living next door. Two-thirds never got involved in community activities.[28]

FaithQuake 5:
WorkQuakes

1. Dump Dumbbell Living

Modern suburbs are one of the most environmentally destructive ways of life ever imagined by the human species. Suburbs were not built for people. They were built for cars. In the words of Andres Duany and Elizabeth Plater-Zyberk, from suburban living "it is quite easy to conclude that the single most important constitutional principle is that cars must be happy."[29]

Suburbia has become an autocracy where car is king, and commuter polluters the obedient subjects. It is the car that enables a growing service industry to live in the suburbs and travel to the center city each day to provide the social kindling for FIRE (Finance, Insurance, Real Estate).[30] Historians will one day look on the low-density but high-traffic of suburban development and shake their heads incomprehensibly.

> *Pedestrians are people on their way to or from their cars.*
>
> LA saying

According to architects of Duany and Plater-Zyberk, "the chief defect of the suburbs is not so much aesthetic as the fact that as civic environments they

135

simply do not work."[31] This is why suburban sprawl-and-mall living has become such a dumbbell existence. Picture a set of dumbbells, with work at one end, home at the other, and the connecting line a "strip" of asphalt on which a motorist spends one's life. Indeed, suburban living is a multiple dumbbell existence as the mall, the school, and the church were connected to the home by ribbons of asphalt. One study of Orlando, Florida, estimates that the average single-family house makes thirteen car trips a day. Suburban middle-class, middle-age sprawl is bad for everything and everyone, especially women. A suburban mother's lot in life, Peter De Vries once commented, is to deliver children—obstetrically once and by car forever after. The vast freeway system separated neighborhoods into class enclaves until today it is much easier to get to the proverbial "other side of the tracks" than to cross a major freeway.

The average vehicle speed in London today is roughly the same as it was in the Middle Ages—how's that for progress?[32] In Seattle police have already caught a half dozen stolen cars by chasing them down on bicycles. Gridlock is evidence of our "cultural cholesterol," the hardening of our social

> *AND THE WIND SHALL SAY: "HERE WERE DECENT GODLESS PEOPLE:*
>
> *THEIR ONLY MONUMENT THE ASPHALT ROAD AND A THOUSAND LOST GOLF BALLS."*
>
> T. S. ELIOT, *The Rock*

arteries that is blocking our flow of living, and jamming and damning our creative energies. No bypass operation, whether more streets or more bridges, more tunnels or mass transit, will change our basic problem: our fat, glutinous life-styles. We are literally exhausting ourselves to death. Cars trap lead in the blood, noise in the ears, poisons in the lungs, children in the house, housewives in bedroom communities, and garbage in the garden. Cars have become too expensive in every way—even economically: cars cost a buck-a-mile to drive, or if gas were priced to cover its true costs, it would be $20.00 a gallon.[33]

2. Retrieve the Small Town

For these reasons, and more, the newest trends in postmodern living are the re-creation of the old-fashioned small town and the back-to-the-land or "penturbian" vision.

This new demographic phenomenon of penturbanite living has people returning to the rural countryside and wilderness areas in celebration of community, conservation, family togetherness, frugality, and land-nurturance. Actually, the penturbanite vision is more a return to the early nineteenth-century Jeffersonian ideal of suburban living,[34] which sought to ground democracy in rural property ownership.

"The new town, the old ways" is the motto of architects Elizabeth Plater-Zyberk and Andres Duany, who have been called by Vincent Scully, the dean of American architectural historians, "the most interesting young architects practicing today." The two of them have participated in forty "small town" suburban projects nationwide. One of these, the celebrated Seaside on the Florida panhandle, was the putting into practice of the postmodern development formulas elaborated by another husband-wife team, theoreticians Leon Krier and Rita Wolff. It has been honored as the best new development of the eighties by *Time* magazine.[35]

True, not everything is wonderful and good about small town living. Postmoderns must be careful not to romanticize traditional communities and bathe in nostalgia when talking about "community." Small towns have their own demons: too many like-minded people coming together; too much common ground; repressiveness of originality; cultural claustrophobia; Anglo-Saxon ethnic supremacy. There is an old saying: "there is no substitute for a strong conscience unless you happen to live in a small town." Georgia *Advocate* editor Mark Westmoreland notes from experience that "The great thing about living in a small town is that everyone knows you; the terrible thing about living in a small town is that everyone knows you."[36] The reigning form of social control in small towns is what sociologists call "public secrets" (meaning gossip, backbiting, etc.). Tightly woven communities create their own unique snags.

But that the small community and family integrally and synergistically function together is one of those staples of human society. What Lewis Mumford called archetypically "the neolithic village"[37] models the way forward for a world that must create new pedestrian communities. People who care about one another, talking about one another's experiences and problems, can even sanctify "gossip" into a holy thing[38] that strengthens the communal fabric.

What a tremendous moment in history for churches to be on the breaking edge of this change, especially oldline denominations whose majority of churches are in small towns across America. In fact, Ray Kroc purposely placed his golden arches near steeples, enabling more than half the USAmerican population to live within a three-minute drive of a McDonald's. Candidate Bill Clinton's patented proletarian bus trips through small-town America in the summer of 1992 helped him convey a new vision of America that harked back to the myth of a sitting-on-the-front-porch heritage and yoked it to a high-tech future. A variety of voices have called for more "porches," a connecting zone that bridged in the past the private individual and the public citizen.[39]

137

People are moving to small towns because of atmosphere, lower taxes, smaller more responsive and safer school districts, and so on. There is assumed in "rurbanization" and small town migration that small towns have services that people are used to in the urbs. Urbanites and suburbanites aren't going places where there aren't good doctors, good hospitals, good schools, good day cares, good libraries, good church school programs, and so on.

They also aren't going places where there isn't a positive answer to the question "Is this a friendly place to live?"—which too many times can be answered differently for natives than for newcomers. Small towns and small-town churches must be prepared to change, especially to become more "small town," if they are to benefit from the urb exodus. They would do well to join the Small Town Institute and contribute to its bimonthly magazine *Small Town*. It would also help if small-town churches came to see themselves as area churches and programmed for area-wide residents.

The church can also help small towns get themselves prepared to withstand the pressure from newly arrived urban romantics to transform rural towns into neosuburbs with wider highways, paved roads, more fast food outlets, and so on. The problem with people fleeing back to the land is that it can be bad for the land. When they settle in, some of the very things that attracted them there in the first place are the first to be destroyed. Former *Harrowsmith Country Life* editor Thomas Rawls warns in his book *Small Places* how these newcomers have enough money to so change the community that "the next generation of natives can't afford to live in their hometowns."[40]

Finally, the race issue must be addressed in small towns. For one thing, some of those leading this exodus of the urbs are "buppies"—black urban professionals. Even though the churches remain a stronghold of segregation—the work force, schools, the military, even neighborhoods are more integrated than the churches—small-town and rural churches are more segregated than urban churches. What also makes it imperative for churches in small towns to face the race issue is that part of the motivation behind the urbs exodus is racial.

One may live in small-town or rural areas, but the electronic revolution has made everyone a part of a national culture, and increasingly a global Euro-Disneyfied culture. Yet the contemporary reemergence of regional culture can be a form of resistance to the homogenizing forces of a globalized economy, as Pierre Clavel's study of "opposition planning" in Appalachia suggests.[41]

3. Facilitate Electronic Life-styles

The church can help design and authenticate new electronic life-styles and modes of family living for its people. Today 5.5 million Americans have given new meaning to the word *homework*—they are working now full-time out of offices in their homes or "hoffices" as these "electronic cottages" (predicted in

Alvin Toffler's *The Third Wave*) are increasingly called. Imagine the doctor's home with office attached. It is the image of the future, as the American Home Business Association predicts 20.7 million full-time home-based businesses ("Dataden"? "Laptopia"?) by 1995.[42]

The computers and communications technology of electronic culture gives people the freedom to choose where to live, and to live in two places at once. Homes can be hooked up to a worldwide network of communications, a global nervous system comprised of smart houses, smart cards, smart automobiles, and smart telephones and computers. The next hurdle? To get rid of "keyboards" through voice activated inputs and surgically implanted headphones.

The self-employed contracting and telecommuting of these postmodern electronic cottages bring benefits and bring problems. There is more family time—but twenty-four hours a day, and what changes in family living? There is better day care for single parents—but what about productivity? There is more control over schedule—but what about increased isolation and loss of benefits like health care and sick time, which are increasingly prohibitive?

Nevertheless, the benefits of electronic life-styles are enormous. Self-employed contracting is a retrieval of the great American tradition of family businesses. Indeed, 95 percent of all businesses in this country are family owned and operated, featuring employees that are typically relatives. In self-employed contracting there can be closely knit personal, caring relationships that stimulate communal ambitions for the good of everyone.

**Is there a McDonald's in heaven?
A child's inquiry to the pastor**

---

4. Don't Work at It, Play at It

Work is the characteristic form in which modernity has chosen to define our social and personal identity. Hegel worked on his *Logic* manuscript on his honeymoon in 1811. We used to "play tennis." Now we "work on our backhand."[43] The modern period found romance in work rather than in life or in community.

Just as the "work ethic" was a driving force in the creation of modern societies, so a "play ethic" will be a driving force in postmodern cultures. The postmodern era is a leisure age. Hans-Georg Gadamer identifies the "mode of being of play" as critical to living in truth. Far from "play" as something one does, play is more a state of being than doing, a state of aesthetic consciousness; far from frivolity, even silliness, play "contains its own, even sacred, seriousness."[44]

139

The modern era deified work, which in its initial form was a curse.[45] Work was not part of God's original design for Adam, who was instructed to "tend and till"—that is, conserve and create the garden; to live a life that perpetuates itself and surpasses itself. In preindustrial cultures, the need to work to survive was limited to three hours a day. Technology is returning us to the savannah; the fifteen-hour workweek is almost within reach for those with their buns in the butter, especially the intellectuals who have leisure time for playful reflection and think that they deserve pay for it.

The scriptures call us to garden, not to work, and especially not to a workaholism that collapses "work" into "paid employment" and the quest for "Job Charming." The scriptures also call us to rest ("keep" the Sabbath) and play. Play is rooted in grace, while work is rooted in works. In the words of Robert DeRopp, "Seek, above all, for a game worth playing. Play as if your life and sanity depend on it. (They *do* depend on it.)"[46]

Clearly, the modernist conception of "work" as a unitary, unremitting *beruf* or "calling," as Martin Luther formulated it, is inadequate for the postmodern information age where everything is mobile and multiple. Theologian Miroslav Volf has written an extremely helpful probing of a more postmodern, or what he terms a "pneumatological" view of work based on the multiple "gifts" one receives and exercises.[47] That makes work a plural noun, not a unitary pronoun. But most suggestive of all is the call by James Robertson in Britain's Fred Bloom Memorial Lectures for the creation of an "ownwork society," a transformation of the dominant form of work from employment to ownwork.

> Ownwork is an activity which is purposeful and important, and which people organize and control for themselves. It may be either paid or unpaid. It is done by people as individuals and household members; it is done by groups of people working together; and it is done by people, who live in a particular locality, working locally to meet local needs. For the individual and the household, ownwork may mean self-employment, essential household and family activities, productive leisure activities such as do-it-yourself or growing some of one's own food, and participation in voluntary work. For groups of people, ownwork may mean working together as partners, perhaps in a community enterprise or a cooperative, or in a multitude of other activities with social, economic, environmental, scientific or other purposes in which they have a personal interest and to which they attach personal importance. For localities, the significance of ownwork is that it contributes to local self-reliance, an increased local capacity to meet local needs by local work, and a reduction of dependence on outside employers and suppliers.[48]

For work to continue to be a meaningful activity, it needs the kind of revisionist refinement like that provided by Charles Handy's five-fold classification of work: "wage work" (under an employer), "fee work" (more entrepreneurial offering ones services to customers or clients), "study work" (keeping up in an information age requires sustained endeavor), "home work" (chores such as cooking and cleaning), and "gift work" (for the community or friends).[49]

The need to give up modern conceptions of work applies even and especially to marriage. The replacement of romance with relationship has meant that marriage has become more and more "work"—"relationships take work"—and less and less "fun." Comedian George Burns, when asked by Barbara Walters why his marriage to Gracie Allen had worked so well and lasted so long, replied immediately, "We didn't work at it."

Marriage is better defined as play than work. Postmoderns already have enough work to do. Postmoderns don't need more jobs. They need more joy. They need more play. They need more romance. The way to better marriages and tighter embraces is less "working it through" than "playing it through" and "romancing it through." Love can't be manufactured from "working" at something. This is one reason why the word *netweave* has replaced *network* throughout this book.

Popcorn herself doesn't call what she does at BrainReserve work. "It's really playing," she says.[50]

5. No Benefit of Clergy

There are three vigilante groups that are right now beginning to wreak vengeance in a variety of ways for the church's disregard of them and the church's "distancing" of God:[51] the laity, the marginal, and young adults.

A fellow newsman always said that Damon Runyon was the kind of man who "will throw a drowning man both ends of the rope."[52] The church has thrown both ends of the rope to these three groups for too long. Now they have come back to town with their own ropes and with other things on their mind. An early warning signal is always monetary giving patterns. Giving to churches and religious organizations topped $67.6 billion in 1991. This was a $6.8 billion increase over 1990 statistics, which amounts to an inflation-adjusted growth of 2 percent. This giving to religion, however, accounted for 54.2 percent of total giving in 1991, which stayed the same as the 1990 figures. In other words, people are increasing their giving to religious groups in smaller proportion than their giving to other benevolent causes. Early indications of 1992 patterns of giving show an acceleration in that trend.

In terms of the laity, tensions are building up among the baptized ministers. They are getting restless, and are wresting from the clergy the franchise they believe Christ gave them when he established the church.

The issues that rise to the top of the church's agenda are by and large not those of the people. The church is ruled by a clerical minority that carries on

141

about institutional matters of deep interest to the clerical minority (ordination issues, language of the liturgy, etc.) rather than the true concerns of most church members. With 99 percent of the majority immobilized by a 1 percent minority, it is only a matter of time before a massive uprising takes place: a lay liberation movement[53] that protests feeling cut off from decision-making and being denied access to theological debate.

In some ways the last thing the church needs is simply another liberation movement. But "lay liberation" in one sense encompasses all other liberation movements. One of the most insidious distinctions ever developed by the church is this class distinction between clergy and laity—or in secular terms that really mean what we say, the professional and the amateur. The clerical era of the church is apparently nearing an end as the people of God reject the class separation. Many church members think it is time to deemphasize clergy as well as "dechurch." The driving force of the church must be the "laity," not the "clergy." The pastoral leadership of baptized ministers is missing in the oldline church today.[54]

The resentment that is building against clergy is almost at the point it was in Luke's parable of the good Samaritan, where the priest and Levite are exactly the opposite of what good neighbors should be. Here is but one of many recent calls for disposing of the professional class of the church: "Could it be that clergy are neither necessary nor, in the long run, good for church? Is it possible that one of the best things that could happen to the church would be for the clergy to resign and take secular jobs?"[55]

An ending to the clergy reign does not dispute the body's right and need to have diversities of ministries, or varieties of order, or even hierarchical "offices." If a community is to be in mission and ministry, it needs a variety of leaders making a variety of contributions and offering a variety of gifts. It belongs to the economy of the church to distinguish between elders and deacons, bishops and archbishops. In contrast, the distinction between clergy and laity is extrinsic to the faith and alien to the life of the church.

No clerical offices or ordination rites were asserted in the early church. Second Testament Pentecostal scholar Gordon D. Fee, observing the Bible's surprisingly "relaxed attitude toward church structures and leadership" given our heavy investment in these issues, contends that "leadership in the New Testament people of God is never seen as outside or above the people themselves, but simply as a part of the whole, essential to its well-being, but governed by the same set of 'rules.' They are not 'set apart' by 'ordination'; rather their gifts are part of the Spirit's work among the whole people."[56]

In fact, there is remarkable consensus among biblical scholars about the lack of biblical consensus over "church structures" and "governance." What can be said with confidence amounts to two statements: first, that there is no "revealed" or "once-for-all-time" model; and second, the Christian biblical model of governance structures is not one of "clergy" and "laity" with the former exercising authority and responsibility over the latter, but a community of faith in which some "servants of the farm" (1 Cor. 3:5-9) work as part of the whole on behalf of the whole, preparing the whole church for ministry and mission in the world.

We are to call no one "rabbi" or "father" or "master," Jesus said, because "you have one teacher and you are all brothers and sisters" (Matt. 23:8-12; cf. Mark 10:42-44). Or to turn to Christiaan Beker's work, "there is no hierarchical division in the worship service between cultic officials and a passive laity. . . . Instead of uniformity or passive dependence on 'the minister,' there is mutuality in service and leadership."[57] Princeton exegete James D. G. Dunn makes an emphatic declaration that priests did not exist in the first century. The word *priest* "is never used in the New Testament to describe a group of Christians to distinguish them from other Christians." In fact, according to Dunn's exegesis of the book of Hebrews, the Christian religion breaks with Judaism precisely at this point: Christians don't set apart an order of priests within its ranks.[58] The words of F. R. Barry summarize the issue: "In the Bible, the *Clêros* means the *Laos*—the Lord's portion—that is, the people of God."[59]

The postmodern church apparently will not tolerate the beloved "benefit of clergy." "Benefit of clergy" was a privilege claimed by the medieval church as part of its overall claim to immunity from secular interference. The medieval courts granted to all tonsured clergy exemption from trial for felony in a secular court. In the fourteenth century benefit of clergy was allowed to all who could read, as proven by reading a particular verse in the Psalms called "The Neck Verse" (usually Psalm 51:1, so-called because presumably reading it "saved one's neck"). The privilege was abolished in America by an Act of Congress in 1790, and in England in 1827. Until that time, statutes that were passed and designed against invasion by this exemption expressly declared that their operation was "without benefit of clergy." The postmodern church is too anti-institutional and disestablishment to operate for the "benefit of clergy."

By the time of Clement (see 1 Clem.40.5) and Ignatius and Hippolytus the categories of priest and laity were making a comeback, and by the end of the fourth century the forces were well at work to make believers objects of priestcraft rather than subjects of priesthood.[60] But the current forms of distinction between clergy and laity are a residue of medieval Christendom, forms which were actually enhanced by the acute clericalism, both Protestant and Catholic, of the Reformation. "The clericalism of the Word," one historian rightly notes, "is every bit as radical as . . . any clericalism of the sacraments had ever been in Catholicism."[61]

143

In spite of all the Reformation talk about the "priesthood of all believers," priesthood remained a special province of the professionals. The Reformers opened up the Bible to the laity, but did not open up the ministry to the laity. Given the class resentment concerning the clergy, it is only a matter of time before the postmodern church will place ministry into the hands of the people, to the same extent that the modern church placed the Scriptures into the hands of the people. A populist postmodernism will stay in much better ideological standing than a populist modernism ever did.

The modernist thrust toward specialization, as well as the controlling mechanistic, organizational metaphors of the Enlightenment, gave to the church a caste of "professionals" and "hierarchies" whose job it was to run the church. The church is not a machine that needs specialists who will grease its parts and manage its operation for it to function smoothly. The church is an organism on a pilgrimage, a living body that needs all of its parts to work efficiently and harmoniously. When one part is sick, the whole body suffers.

This is not to excuse laity from getting the church into this unhealthy condition. Laity in many cases headed the Faustian negotiations with "clergy" that issued in a pact straight from hell: "If you do our ministry for us, we'll pay you. (Not well, by the way, but we'll pay you.)" Laity thought they were getting the bargain end of the deal by paying "professionals" to do and direct the work of ministry for them: "Let's pay the pastor to do it." But such sentiments were encouraged by modernity's elitist, anti-populist bias, or as some have dubbed it, modernity's "cult of the cultivated."

Postmodernism's hostility to elitism could not be farther from the modern era when the masses were, in religion as in art and literature, always wrong. The modern world worked toward the exclusion of vernacular faith from the church, and the clerical elite have been quick to decry the vulgarization of theology that "popular piety" occasions. The masses were taught to hold in awe those who can speak Greek and Hebrew; they were not taught to hold in awe the average five-year old in Athens or Jerusalem who also knows Greek or Hebrew.

"Going into ministry" has come to mean "getting ordained," or keeping ministry within the club. It is expected of laity to lay there—laity are the sheep and clergy the shepherd—or in the words of a Roman Catholic book on the laity: "The church bureaucracy has successfully convinced its pew-sitters that their role in the kingdom is to pray, pay and obey—mostly pay."[62]

This distinction between do-it-all clergy and do-nothing laity is evaporating in favor of new definitions of shared ministries and full-time ministry. Soon only two categories of leadership will be discussed in the church—"baptized ministers" and "ordained ministers." In fact, if one is interested in actually doing ministry, one shouldn't get ordained. Ordination authorizes a baptized minister to educate and train other baptized ministers in the art and science of ministry.

All Christians are ministers. Some Christians are baptized ministers and others are ordained ministers. Everyone has a ministry. Everyone has a mission. As a minister, one attends to the community of faith. As a missionary, one attends to the world. Ordained ministers of the church have no other role or function than to attend to the health and vitality of the other ministers and missionaries. Or as Paul puts it, some have been given gifts "for the equipping of the saints for their work of ministry" (Eph. 4:12).

Those who have been "ordained" are not set off as part of a different caste, or a special class raised above everyone else. Those "ordained" are no different from everyone else in church, a sinner saved by grace, with no greater privileges other than perhaps being exposed to greater temptations than everyone else. The role of the minister is not service to the church, or managing the structures of the institution, but service to the world. The role of the ordained minister is to loosen up and lighten up the church to let that happen. Ordained ministers have a church-centered ministry. Ministers have a world-oriented ministry.

Moses' father-in-law was named Jethro. He may have been history's first "leadership consultant." In Exodus 18:13-27 Moses "was kept busy from morning till night" tending to the needs of the Israelites and refereeing their disputes. Jethro said to him:

> Why are you doing this all alone? . . . You are not doing this right. You will wear yourself out and these people as well. . . . You should choose some capable [people] and appoint them as leaders of the people. (GNB)

Jethro's word is still waiting to be heard.

CHAPTER SIX

AgeQuakes

SocioQuake 6: *Down-Aging*

I s senescence on its way to obsolescence? This is now a serious question, being asked across the world of science and medicine.[1]

Age—along with gender, race, and class—stands as a major distinguishing feature in USAmerican culture and church life.[2] The graying of the human species has become a mass phenomenon in the postmodern era. The number of Americans over 65 has doubled since 1950, from 18 million in 1965 to 30 million today, 35 million by 2000, 39 million by 2010, and 51 million in 2020. By the year 2025, Americans over age 65 will outnumber teenagers by more than two to one.

For the first time in American history, the number of American elders now outnumbers American teenagers. During the sixties and seventies, the 65-plus age group grew more than twice as fast as the whole population; the 75 plus category is the fastest rising of all. It is not uncommon to find estimates that the median age will eventually reach 50. Programs supporting the aged absorb 27 percent of the federal budget (about the same if not more than the Pentagon).[3]

These are but some of the demographic changes and statistics behind a new coming to terms with coming of age, a phenomenon Popcorn calls "Down-aging." In her words, "down-aging" is "the refusal to be bound by traditional age limitations . . . redefining down what appropriate age-behavior is for your age."[4] Down-aging means that when people are told to "Act your age!" the age they act is getting younger and younger.[5]

The postmodern era has established what I call "A New Prime," a new age-standard for "the prime of life." How old will you be when you wake up one day and realize there is no longer an older generation? People over 50 think "old age" starts later and later. In 1985 it was 71; now it's 79, says the *Wall*

147

Street Journal. Those surveyed used to feel 11 years younger than they were. Now they feel 15 years younger. Old age simply hasn't arrived yet for many people. Popcorn notes the nice irony that "the same baby-boom bunch that once said 'Don't trust anyone over thirty,' now says with equal militance, 'Life begins at forty.'"[6]

> "Don't trust anyone over 30," though it has been good to plastic surgeons, is not a credo to grow old by.
>
> TED CONOVER

There is no area where more oldthink ideas need to be donated to the postmodern garage sale than this one of "aging," especially if a new "class struggle" is to be averted, a "class struggle" not between economic classes but between age classes. Let's start at the beginning.

Someone once said that the human body, with proper care, will last a lifetime. But how long is a lifetime? Contrary to conventional Christian thinking, postmoderns have not expired with biblical promptness when they reach "four-score years and ten." The biological barrier for the human body is more like six-score years plus or minus ten. While some researchers argue that "inborn limits" will make life expectancy impossible beyond 85, the trend is now the other way. Some scientists believe it could reach 150 years, and others like Richard Cutler, a biophysicist and lifespan specialist at the National Institute on Aging (NIA), pushes it to 200, 300, or more. "The final proof is not in, but I see no limit to our life span," he argues.[7]

In other words, it now appears conservatively that God designed the human body structurally and spiritually to last 120-130 years,[8] which is a metaphorical way of saying, a long time. The advanced ages of biblical figures like Moses (120 years) and Abraham (175 years) may be saying more to us than we think. By the way, according to one legend the "secret" of long life was given to Abraham by an angel: "Eat yogurt." There are even some biblical scholars who suspect the "milk" in the phrase "milk and honey" referred to yogurt—not the low fat refrigerated Yoplait kind, but the kind of milk that is clabbered by drifting bacteria.[9]

Of all the people who have lived to age 65 in the history of the world, more than half are alive today. USAmerica's 55 percent rise in average life expectancy since 1900—a rise of 27 years from 47 to 75 pushed upward by antibiotics and maternity care—nearly equals the gain achieved in all the previous 3000 years. The fastest growing group of USAmericans are the centenarians, which according to Census Bureau statistics numbered but a few thousand in 1950, but will reach over 100,000 by the year 2000 and over a million by 2080. The odds against living to be 100, according to a 1987 National Institute of Aging report, "have dropped from 400 to 1 for people born in 1879 to a mere 87 to 1 for those born in 1980."[10] A child born in 1992, some experts are saying, can anticipate a life expectancy of 90.

When Moses died at 120 (a number repeatedly used as a metaphor for old age), the Bible says "He was clear of vision and full of vigor." The gift of longevity is more importantly seen in qualitative rather than quantitative terms. "We're at a turning point in history," declares Richard L. Sprott, associate director of the biology program for the Institute on Aging in Bethesda, Maryland. Research into molecular mechanisms of life is creating a revolutionary paradigm shift in understanding aging and the possibilities of old age.

Aging is now seen medically as something not inevitable, but manageable, even to a degree reversible. In fact, most of the physical problems associated with "aging" are now seen as preventable. It is not inevitable that parents become children to their children. Daniel Rudman, a professor of medicine at the medical College of Wisconsin, alert to the fact that aging involves a drop in naturally occurring growth hormone levels, performed a study in 1990 of elderly men that demonstrates how genetically engineered human growth hormones (hGH) can actually reverse the aging process—skin becomes taut, muscles harden, fat melts away, organs return to youthful stamina and vigor.[11]

Even without expensive ($14,000 a year) hGH doses, people can already alter their aging rates by their diets (low-fat and one-third reduction of daily calorie intake), their exercises, their intake of antioxidant supplementation, and so on. A 1992 University of Michigan study found a veritable "Fountain of Youth" elixir called GSH (glutathione) which is found in high levels among healthy older people and in low levels among those who die young. The major sources of GSH are cabbage, cauliflower, and broccoli (though whether GSH is available simply by eating these vegetables has yet to be proved). Through simple life-style changes, such as high-roughage, low-protein cuisines[12], people can "age-proof" their bodies. Studies have shown that IQs can actually rise with age, and that many intellectual functions keep on improving with age. Older adults are able to learn as quickly and as easily as younger persons in most situations.[13] Declining mental agility is less a consequence of aging than a sign of disease processes such as hypertension,[14] stroke, Huntington's, Alzheimer's, or Parkinson's diseases. The more active older people are, the better their brain functions, which leads some brain researchers to suspect that exercise slows or prevents the mental decline long associated with the aging process.

Although the majority of memory researchers currently believe that aging brings with it decreasing speeds in processing information and decreasing skills in encoding information (by age 30, the brain begins to lose thousands of neurons a day, until by the time we reach 80 our brain weighs about 7 percent less than it did in our prime), there are significant and growing numbers of scientists who dispute the "tip of the tongue" syndrome much less the inevitability of memory loss. Seventy-year-olds and eighty-year-olds routinely outscore and outperform their grandchildren on memory tests, and the average seventy-year-old performs as well overall on memory tests as do 25-30 percent of twenty-year-olds.[15]

The point of all this is not to turn back the clock, to fool Mother Nature or stop Father Time. "We're not going to make old people young again," says endocrinologist S. Mitchell Harman at the National Institute on Aging. "However, we may be able to make their bodies more like young people's bodies."[16] Only 26 percent of those 65 to 74 have any health complaints, according to the Census Bureau. The point is to be able to live "younger longer," not live "older longer." George Roth, chief of molecular physiology and genetics at the NIA, insists that their goal is "not to add years to life but life to years."[17] Or as another gerontologist puts it, the object of research is to help people "die young as late as possible."[18]

FaithQuake 6: *AgeQuakes*

1. Third Agers' Coming of Age: USAmerican society is becoming more age irrelevant while at the same time age is of increasing importance. Age remains a primary organizing principle of the kinds of roles and rewards people are permitted. This makes it imperative that Christians embrace new and at times paradoxical ways of approaching life and conceiving the weathering of a human being, specifically less in linear fashion and more in terms of spiral patterns of human existence.

Postmoderns have been gifted with the joy of fulfillment and creativity spanning almost a century—a gift our predecessors of a hundred, even fifty years ago would have not even comprehended. The age-grading concept of the Third Age (*le troisieme age*)[19] seems ideally suited to the postmodern era. According to this theory life is periodized into four stages, preparation, responsibility, fulfillment, and decline; the first three each spanning twenty to thirty years, the fourth stage, lasting three to four years, can occur in any age. There is wholeness in each age, new chances, new creativities, new challenges in each age. In each one of these stages, we are in the process of aging; doing many different things in the course of a long life (90 plus years).

Our mission as disciples of Jesus Christ is to make sure that no one is kept from embracing each one of these ages for reasons of income, occupational class, infirmity, gender, or race. The excitement of diversity is to bring the three ages together—quick studies, hard workers, and old hands—to make a difference in the world. The church can develop "turning-point ministries" or what I prefer to call molting ministries to help people move with enthusiasm and integrity from one age to the next.

The First Age: Lasting twenty-five to thirty years, this is a period of biological development, education, and preparation. The question of the First Age is "What school do you go to?" First Agers are taking longer to grow up. They are postponing economic independence, marriage, maturity, and so on as they get educated for ten careers (IBM now tells its employees that they can expect four career changes in their lifetimes) if not educated for life. They are adding more and more initials to their names: B.A., B.S., and as higher education has gotten higher and higher, M.D., J.D., M.Div., M.B.A., Ph.D. They are also, through travel and studies abroad, receiving an understanding and appreciation of the many cultures and people with whom we share this ever-shrinking globe. The motto of First Agers seems to be: adulthood can wait.

> *You don't raise kids. You raise carrots. You sponsor kids.*
>
> JESS LAIR

The automobile made possible First Agers' separation from parents and the development of a distinct First Agers' subculture that is divided into three parts: childhood, adolescence (youth), and "twentysomething." Generally this is a great time to be alive, a great age—though First Agers feel both pampered and neglected at the same time; pampered with things, neglected with time. The biggest First Age problem has also become its deadliest problem: the chaos of an emerging sexual identity and those surging, gurgling hormones that wreak such havoc with one's mental, physical, and spiritual equilibrium. First Agers are more at risk than any other age, partly because puberty is coming sooner and sooner (there is a pill to keep puberty out of single digits for

151

females), while marriage and economic independence are arriving later (late twenties, early thirties). Twenty years is a long time to "just say no" without tremendous support systems in place all around you, support systems that the oldline church has steadfastly refused to provide its young people.[20]

The Second Age: If the question of the First Age is "Where do you go to school?" the question of the Second Age is "What do you do for a living?" or "Where do you work?" This is a period of independence and responsibility and busyness—making babies, parenting children, paying bills, paying off accumulated debts incurred from First Age, saving up for the Third Age, often deferring dreams and suppressing secret longings about life in the process. The stretch in between the First Age and the Third Age is also the most socially complicated.

The Second Age is the time of life most filled with productive work, social activity, and parental responsibilities. Second Agers can now parent children at any point in this thirty-year expanse. Women in their fifties, using in vitro fertilization (IVF) techniques, can now give birth as easily and effortlessly as much younger women. In fact, there are some who argue that there is no obvious age limit to IVF pregnancies.[21]

It is also a time of life filled with utter exhaustion and stress, especially the last half of this age and its mid-life crises, whether menopause or viropause. This is the age-group the church wants to work the hardest, and this is the age-group that has the greatest difficulty adjusting their "timestyles" to provide the volunteer time and resources to do the work of the church. It is the group with the least discretionary time, and even possibly the least discretionary money. The invitation of Jesus to those who are "weary and heavy laden" is felt by this group as bringing them not relief and rest from the weight around their necks, but more weight, more work.

The Third Age: For the first time in human history, a new era of human evolution, a new phase of life, is now possible: The Third Age. This new culture that we call the world of the "senior citizen" can be the period of deepest personal fulfillment, highest creativity, and perhaps the longest and most productive period of our lives—witness Ronald Reagan.

The fastest growing segment of American society is the Third Age. We are spending roughly one third of our lives in this period when, according to some anonymous doggerel:

> Of late I appear
> to have reached that stage
> when people look old
> who are only my age.

Life's greatest contributions and discoveries can be made in the Third Age. The future will see scores of new Third Age institutions like SCORE (Senior Corps of Retired Executives), Elder Hostel, and so on. We are now seeing two generations "retired" (people in their sixties and seventies, with parent or parents still around), and will soon see three generations "retired" in five-generation families. The "graying" components of a community are its greatest strengths, not weaknesses.

Like the saguaro cactus, which doesn't begin sprouting its first arm until after age sixty, the Third Age can be when we grow to our fullest stature as a human being. The National Center for Health Statistics reports that almost 66 percent of USAmericans aged 75 to 84 report that their health was excellent, very good, or good; 23 percent replied fair, and only 11 percent poor.[22]

> *People in the third age should be the glue of society, not its ashes.*
>
> ### Director of Fordham University's Third Age Center, MONSIGNOR CHARLES FAHEY

As western novelist Larry McMurtry explores in his most recent book *The Evening Star* (1992), the Third Age can also be a highly sensual time of life, when sex is most rich, plentiful, and satisfying.[23] Indeed, one Chicago study found that the happiest people in USAmerica are married couples who have frequent sex after sixty. It had been thought that frequency of intercourse declines with age. But then along comes *The Janus Report on Sexual Behavior* (1993), which professes to have proof that older people are having sex as often as teenagers, with more men over sixty-five reporting sex a few times a week than men aged eighteen to twenty-six.[24]

Whatever the statistics, a sexually exciting seventh, eighth, and ninth decades of life with lots of lovemaking is now the norm for the Third Age. One study found that 81 percent of women were sexually active in their 60s and 65 percent sexually active at age 70 and above; among men 91 percent were sexually active in their 60s and 79 percent sexually active after age 69. Seventy-five percent of the flaccidity problems men face are physiologically induced. "Smoking, diabetes, hypertension, elevated cholesterol—without a doubt, those are the four erection busters" claims a University of Chicago urologist.[25] In fact, the *Harvard Health Letter* points out how "partners over 60 may have an unprecedented opportunity to become biologically and emotionally in synch."

A man's tendency to reach orgasm more slowly is well suited to the longer time a woman needs to become aroused. Birth control hassles are finally over, children are no longer likely to burst into the bedroom at inopportune moments, and both partners have a lot more time than they used to. Despite what mere youngsters may think, elderly women fully retain their capacity for multiple orgasms and older men can have an orgasm without attaining an erection.[26]

The Fourth Age: This stage is when we take life seriously, which isn't possible until we take death seriously. In the Fourth Age we face our mortality. We become painfully aware we are running out of days. The Fourth Age, which can occur in the First, Second, or Third Ages, is when life begins to lose grip and ground. USAmericans with disabilities, whose life expectancy on average is thirteen more years after the onset of the disability, are forced to take death seriously at a much earlier age.

In the Fourth Age the conjunction of aging and disease does apply, as its inception inaugurates a period of serious physical decline before death. In the words of the Yaqui proverb, "Death is always following us, but it doesn't always turn on the headlights." On average, by age seventy-five the number of cells in the human body has declined by as much as 30 percent. Sometime or other this process takes its toll on one or more major systems,[27] and the headlights get turned on.

The Fourth Age today occupies on average three to four years, which, interestingly enough, is the same span of time spent on the brink of the grave in previous centuries. In the postmodern world, soldiers must know when and how to fade away. The frontier of the Fourth Age lies in the new possibilities of "squaring off the curve," to use the language of gerontology. Through a lifestyle of total wellness, there is the opportunity to live life to the fullest throughout an exhilarating and extended Third Age and then die suddenly in a mercifully short Fourth Age.

The major spiritual challenges of the Fourth Age are testamentary acts: divesting all one's accumulations, investing in the future as faithful trustees of creation, choreographing one's death, and the like. The Fourth Age is a period of lightening up for the resurrection journey, returning to the nakedness with which one enters and exits the world. The Fourth Age is not without its consolations. Perhaps in no age does one gets one's own way more than in this one (as anyone who has attended a parent in the Fourth Age can attest).

2. Don't Throw Out the Wrinkles

People are now spending an average of twenty-three years in retirement. Unprecedented! According to an Ohio University psychologist, everyone's best chances of having an annual income of $1 million or more will arrive when we're between eighty and eighty-nine years old.

Not too long ago an average worker spent an average of 100,000 hours or fifty years on the job. It will soon be just 50,000 hours, or twenty-five years in a "job." What will people at their creative, working peaks do with that 50,000 hours? Use their stability, experience and knowledge selfishly, sitting out a third of their lives in retirement centers or motor homes? Or use it to the glory of God—learning new skills and developing parts of themselves so that they can leave this world better than when they found it?

Redefine *retirement*: The concept of retirement, as it developed since the 1960s, is an obscene and vulgar concept.[28] It is based on giving persons in their later years societal permission to go whoring after youthfulness and to regress to an adolescent state of existence. In fact, a case could be made for Florida, not California, as the most hedonistic state in the U.S. In "adult" communities like Sun City Center, Florida, and Sun City, Arizona, there are R-rated living arrangements that exclude grandchildren and even children over fifty from buying or renting in the settlement.

> *I never read in the Bible where God retired anybody.*
>
> BILLY GRAHAM

The Sun Belt is not the only area where seniors are "retiring." Illinois, Pennsylvania, Ohio, New York, and Michigan are expected to have over one million elderly residents by 2010. The truth is that throughout USAmerica, there are millions of retired people still kicking, but very few of them raising much dust. The final curtain has fallen on their life long before their death. The only way "retirement" is salvageable is through the triumph of the concept of re-tiring (retreading; getting a new grip on life) over retiring. Name something in nature that "retires"? Name someone in the Bible who retired? Does God ever retire?

The "Retired Christian Syndrome" that emits the sound—"We had our turn; now its their (i.e., the younger generation's) turn"—needs to be heard for what it is: wolves' words in sheep's clothing, the have-it-all hedonist cry of "I'm spending my children's inheritance." Among church members from eighteen to sixty-four years of age, 45 to 56 percent claim to be "volunteering." Among church members over sixty-five, only 38 percent claim to be "volunteering." Among nonmembers under 65 the figures are 28 to 37 percent, and over 65, 26 percent. Church members were found to be 50 percent more likely to volunteer than nonmembers.[29]

To overcome this lack of volunteering, churches might consider the possibility of integrating nonintensive health-care facilities and "retirement" communities into their spatial complex.

155

3. Netweave The Third Age with The Third Sector

When Alexis de Tocqueville visited USAmerica in the 1830s, he was most impressed not with the nation's political or governmental sector (today: one federal, fifty state, and eighty thousand local government entities). Nor did the nation's commercial or economic sector (today: fifteen million commercial entities, both above and underground) inspire his greatest praise. What struck him the most about his travels across this nation was the tradition of "The Third Sector": a web of voluntary societies (today: several million) primarily created by religious associations that are dedicated to independent action on behalf of the public needs and social betterment.[30] De Tocqueville unveiled in the nineteenth century a mysterious trinitarian interdependence between religious traditions, voluntary associations, and democratic institutions that his twentieth-century successors Robert Bellah and Robert Wuthnow have confirmed in more scientific fashion.

"The Third Sector" or as sociologists prefer "The Independent" or "Nonprofit Sector" is currently made up of a vast array of societies ranging from educational institutions (universities, public and private schools) to hospitals, museums, libraries, orchestras, and mutual aid groups (e.g., Alcoholics Anonymous). Religion has been the primary force behind the establishment of "public spaces" and "free zones" (Max Stackhouse) in the nonprofit sector, although in the modern era the primary agency for social betterment became less and less the church and more and more the state.

The state take-over of large portions of "The Third Sector," with the American service state now at least three times as large as the whole Soviet economy,[31] is an experiment that has failed. The visible hand of the state as a social engineer and ethical arbiter has no better grip of the problems than the visible hand of the state did organizing people's economic lives. In fact, sociologist Virginia A. Hodgkinson argues:

> Community formation in the future may be even more reliant on voluntary religious associations than they were in the past. If a new progressive movement ushers in the twenty-first century, its birthplace will not be in political parties or government but in the local congregations and adjutant religious organizations of America.[32]

There are two dangers in talking about the role of the church in "The Third Sector": the first is claiming too much (as in the Fundamentalist Right), the second is claiming too little (as in the eclectic New Age gnosticism of urban intellectuals) for the church. What is not claiming too much is the fact that the more religious the persons, the more likely those persons are to be community leaders, volunteers involved in improving a community's quality of life, and philanthropists with their money and time.

Indeed, it is "realistic" to claim that faith communities will lead the way in netweaving with others to help "The Third Sector" out of its double bind: it can't keep going as it is, but it seems impossible to change. Or as pollsters quote USAmericans as saying, government programs are abject failures, but people still want to expand them.[33] Voluntary collective strategies of action are a crucial counterpoint to institutionalized forms of power and authority.[34]

At the same time, it is equally a sociological "reality" that, again in Virginia Hodgkinsons's words, "there has been no substantial increase in per capita giving and volunteering in America over the past thirty years; in some denominations, there has been a decline. The reason for this decline seems to be the declining emphasis on the part of denominations to transmit the tradition of charity and stewardship and a concomitant failure to train clergy in the importance of this tradition,"[35] as well as a failure to treat volunteers with the same respect as professionals.

Hodgkinson calls for "stewardship" to be taught by seminaries and religious traditions so that faith communities will come alive and flower in the already exotic undergrowth of grassroots movements with grassroots activisms for community service. Habitat for Humanity is a model of the possibilities of multinational and multidenominational alliances, in this case for the sake of housing and home ownership.

4. Deal in Time Dollars

A new economic system is being born in "The Third Sector" that will work wonders for the church. Sometimes called "service credits," at other times "care shares," Ralph Nader calls it "Time Dollars."[36] This barter currency is the native currency of the church.

Time Dollars work like this: you purchase quality child care by house-cleaning or lawn-mowing. You pay a medical bill by volunteer work for the doctor's charity-of-choice. You buy an insurance policy by committing yourself to providing legal counsel for the poor, or by teaching an adult literacy class for a specified number of years.

Time Dollars is a new economics for a new volunteerism and citizen activism. Barter networks are springing up all over the country. In 1992, there were more than 500 barter clearinghouses in USAmerica and Canada. They did $6.4 billion in business, a 9.3 percent increase over the previous year's volume. The "Local Economic Trading System" (LETS) is a computer-mediated barter system where one can trade fishing lessons for fish fries. A real-life example? A Chicago florist provided flowers to a hotel in a swap for several rooms, which he then turned over to a local trucking business that had agreed to do on-the-road advertising for his shop. All three companies in the transaction belong to the same bartering clearinghouse.[37]

The church needs to join community agencies, schools, local hospitals, and community colleges that are already administering some 3,000 serious Time Dollars volunteers, the majority of whom are over 60. The investment in Time Dollars does more than address people's needs. In Ralph Nader's words: "When strangers start acting like neighbors, and neighbors start acting like extended family, communities are reinvigorated."[38]

Boosters are the biggest potential volunteer corps available to the church. One survey revealed that the person most likely to be working for peace and justice in the world is your grandmother, although the survey mentioned above also shows that Third Agers in the church are not as likely to volunteer as First Agers or Second Agers.

I preached in one church where, just before the sermon, the chair of one of the boards making a fund-raising pitch for the new building campaign announced that she had been planning on taking an early retirement that year and donating a lot of her new time to her church. But she realized that the church needed her money right now more than it needed her time, so she had decided to be a different kind of "volunteer" for the church: she would postpone retirement and volunteer her working time to the church, thereby donating one year's salary to the church's building program. The much lamented "graying" of our churches may be the salvation of our world.

Volunteering may also be the salvation of elders themselves. In his new book *Give to Live: How Giving Can Change Your Life* (1991), Douglas M. Lawson reviews studies that demonstrate that giving to others provides health benefits. In fact, those who performed regular volunteer work had death rates two-and-one-half times lower than those who did not volunteer.

5. Grammy Rewards

"Think Grandparent" is the motto of the Foundation for Grandparenting. It would make a great motto for new paradigm communities of faith. A new appreciation for the "grand" side of eldering, and the establishment of what psychiatrist Arthur Kornhaber calls "a new grandparental identity" is an imperative postmodern missional task.[39]

> *I PLAN TO GET VERY ACTIVE IN THE GRANDCHILD BUSINESS.*
>
> PRESIDENT GEORGE BUSH IN HIS CONCESSION SPEECH

"Grandparents" is a sociological category invented in the modern era, especially in New England. This is the first generation of grandparents to know most of its grandkids, to live to see their grand offspring. What a gift! A couple hundred years ago most males mar-

158

ried in their late twenties and died in their early fifties. Today, in Britain, one grandparent in five sees a child or grandchild daily. Between one-half and two-thirds see one weekly or more.[40]

The roles grandparents can play in the lives of young people are numerous: historian, mentor, role model, wizard, seer, sage, angel, nurturer, patron, part-ner, to mention only a few.[41] Having grandparents around boosts children's IQ and self-esteem. Research studies consistently show that infants and children raised with father or mother plus grandparents develop far better emotionally and intellectually, as do the parents themselves. Parents are good at spending "time around kids"; grandparents good at spending "time with kids" (there is a big difference between "time around kids" and "time with kids"—30 percent of kids report their first sexual act in their own house while one or both parents are at home). If Bernie and Bobbie Siegel are right in their conviction that there are "only two significant issues in the world today . . . the preservation of the planet in its physical sense, and the raising of children who are loved,"[42] then grandparenting may have arrived on the sociological scene just in time to save us all.

One of the dangerous effects of television against which the church must alarm and arm itself is television's elimination of "play between parents and children in about 70 percent of the American homes." Also endangered in the wake of television are table-talk and "grandmother tales."[43]

6. Don't Be Afraid of the Child in You

Let the child in you out. Those things that keep us young and childlike are available at every age (creativity, curiosity, risk-taking, etc.). We have older people in us and younger people in us at every age. When we attack or ridicule older people, we are attacking and ridiculing the older people in ourselves. Similarly, when we attack and ridicule the "younger generation," we are negating and ridiculing the younger people in us as well.[44]

Adults can commit child abuse on themselves. The children's book illustra-tor, writer, stage and costume designer Maurice Sendak laments how in post-modern society "growing up means you have passed the divide from live

> *Anyone who forsakes the child he was is already too old for poetry.*
>
> STANLEY KUNITZ

human being into moron." The goal of "civilizing" institutions like schools and churches is almost to wipe out the child. One emerges in adulthood "a zombie—dumb as asparagus" with only "fragments" of childhood still intact. Yet Sendak has proved in his own artistry that "the more society crushes the child, the more it emerges in destructive adult behavior."[45]

How many times have you seen adults acting like kids in restaurants and other public places—holding balloons, playing games, "acting up"? Joe Killian calls this "the circus of the soul." Faith Popcorn reveals that half of the Halloween costume business is now for grown-ups; it was only 10 percent ten years ago. More money is now spent on recreation than on clothing.[46] In many markets "Sesame Street" has so many adult viewers it is moving to 7 in the evening. Increasing numbers of adults are going on their own to FAO Schwarz and Disney World, not to speak of grown-up toy stores like The Sharper Image, as we are stockpiling our suburban cribs with teddy bear playthings and blanket securities.

There are some "ghosts" of childhood that we need to drive from our hearts and homes, to be sure. But at least in this case, the words of the bumper sticker—"It's never too late to have a happy childhood"—are wiser than the words of the poet—"We always live our childhood again."[47] One can find playmates even in adulthood. This is the reason for the success of books like John Javna's *Cool Tricks! A Grown-Up's Guide to All the Neat Things You Never Learned to Do as a Kid*—like walk the dog with a yo-yo, blow human-sized soap bubbles, make shadow-figures on the wall, shoot marbles.[48]

The "inner child" is the vogue today, and the archetype of the child so dominates therapeutic thinking that some suspect it is responsible for psychology's lack of theoretical imagination. The psychotherapy trade, which the head of the Jung Institute, James Hillman, points out is a "large business," always needs, as does any big business "new raw material such as abuse, trauma, childhood molestation," and so on.[49] The point of letting the child in us come out is not to go backwards ("if you're looking backward, you're not looking around" Hillman warns[50]), but to press forward in life as a tree presses forth from an acorn without losing the innocence, the wonder, and the joy of that nubbed state of existence.

7. Embrace the Child Outside You

What is an adult?

A child puffed with age.

FRENCH WRITER
SIMONE DE BEAUVOIR

Let it in. The obsessions of psychotherapy with the "inner child" and "personal growth" betray a world more oriented on self than others, argue James Hillman and Michael Ventura in their *We've Had a Hundred Years of Psychotherapy*. It is time the "outer child" was lauded as well as the "inner child." The child must be treated as a responsible and highly valued member of society, and of the church.

Postmodern culture is profoundly hostile to children, and promises to get more so. Children constitute the poorest class of USAmerican society, with one-fourth living below the poverty line. Already the home life of many children has become a house-of-horrors—from the loneliness, indeed homelessness of latchkey freedoms to the fearful silences of behind-closed-door abuses. The church can be a primary oasis of support and love, a primary haven of refuge and peace for children.

One New Jersey church recently announced in the paper its "Second Annual All-Church Banquet . . . No children under 12, please." Alas, all too many Christians don't include children, whether consciously or unconsciously, in their "all-church" thinking. Have you ever seen a sandbox in a sanctuary? Who will be the first church to include an entrance door for children as well as adults, something the magical children's store Imaginarium has done all over the world to entice children into its consumerist paradise?

The Church of the Nazarene has a model quality children's ministry that combines the best features of a club and the scouts. Called The Nazarene Caravan Ministry, it includes weekly get-togethers, membership standards, special uniforms and badges, group signs and pledges, advancements and awards. A holistic, noncompetitive approach to faith development, children are helped to grow physically, mentally, socially, and spiritually.

Postmodern children must be seen and be treated as trusted and serious contributors to the well-being of the church and the world.

8. Move From Aging to Saging

What if we viewed aging less in terms of our body and more in terms of our mind and spirit and soul? Depending on our degree of dotage, or degree of gerontophobia, we back into aging. We view aging in terms of our bodies—scraggly necks, multiple chins, belly rolls, false teeth, balding hairlines, bulging waistlines, cottage-cheese thighs, crows'-feet laugh-lines, and barnacles on the birthday suit, and beta amyloid deposits on the brain. As Tom Wakefield puts it in *Lot's Wife*, "Bits that had previously stuck out had now shrunk."[51] Or in Robert Frost's way of putting the question of the Third Age: "What to make of a diminished thing?"

But it is as morally arrogant (i.e., ageist) to associate the Third Age with disease and death as it is wrong (i.e., racist) to think of blacks as inferior or wrong (i.e., sexist) to think of women as subordinate to men. Ironically, in some earlier cultures death was more naturally associated with children or mothers than with seniors, since few people lived to old age and many children and mothers died in the childbirthing, childrearing process.

Awaiting discovery by the church is the native American tradition of Wisdomkeepers. Also known as "eldering," elders are approached in aboriginal cultures as sources of knowledge and healing because of their life experiences, as well as resources upon which one draws for leadership and power in moving into the future. What respect accrues to old people in America today is patronizing and kindly—at best it grants them attention because they are walking history books not because they are part of the contemporary social and intellectual hot spots of energy for decision-making. Sage and seasoned elders can be the most creative members of society.[52]

God has so fixed it that our body's decline is balanced by our soul's maturation; moving through "body time" and "soul time" may be inversely proportional. Our bodies peak physically during the early twenties, although some believe the peak takes place at puberty. Our minds and spirits peak physically late in life, and ideally at the moment of death. In other words, the less creative and beautiful our body gets, the more creative, or as the Puritans would say, the more "perfect" and beautiful our soul can become. Or as Helen Stout wrote in a Seattle workshop on aging for her seventy-nineth birthday, "My paintings grow smaller, my dance steps slower, my words more and faster, my thoughts and dreams richer."[53]

In adolescence and early adulthood the body is at its best; but the mind and spirit have a long way to go. The confusion of childhood and the cruelty of adolescence is well-known by every parent. At the First Age spiritual maturity is rudimentary at best. The most characteristic feature of adolescence is the "know-it-all" attitude, which only attests to the intellectual immaturity of this unpleasant stage. One comic speech writer said that in the Renaissance, one man could possess the sum total of human knowledge; in the present, it takes two teenagers and a cab driver. The First Age is not the age most likely to elicit the words every parent wants to say: "This is my beloved son / daughter, in whom I am well pleased."

When we move from aging to saging, people in the Third Age will become the pathfinders for social change, not the doorkeepers for social control. We will look to Third Agers for leadership, inspired by their love of learning, their concern for others, their spiritual outlook, their wisdom about the ways of the world, and their hope.

9. Be Post-nuclear

Accept and program for a new spectrum of family relationships—increasingly known as the "matrix family"—that removes from normative status the child-centered nuclear family and replaces it with a multigenerational household and complex of relationships that bind people together by blood and duty as well as friendship and circumstance.

The "nuclear family" is an invention and aberration of modernity, especially

of the 1950s. The "nuclear family" is one of the strongest progenitors and pro-
tectors of patriarchy. It is extended families that undercut the patriarchal
model. Stephanie Coontz whose work *The Way We Never Were* is about how
Americans mythologize the traditional family: "Contrary to popular opinion,
'Leave It to Beaver' was not a documentary."[54]

In 1958, the number of homes in America where the husband was the
"breadwinner," the wife the "homemaker" and "child-rearer" was 72 percent.
In 1990 it was 7 percent. Two incomes are now almost an economic necessity. The church has been largely unresponsive to the latch-key kid syndrome. When programs are proposed for "Parents Night Out," or for after-
school tutoring sessions, many churches seem more concerned about their
carpets than their children. Churches that respond to post-nuclear culture
will offer low-cost child care, reaching out to youth through ministries of ath-
letics and recreation, elder hostel equivalent programming, or twenty-four
hour day care.

10. Venerate Croning and "Spiritual Eldering"

Increase religious programming and respect for elders, especially women
elders. The church is already undergoing a paradigm shift with respect to
women's leadership. What did the Roman Catholic surgeon say to a patient
who happened to be a United Methodist bishop? "Wait until I tell my priest
that I operated on a bishop and removed her ovaries!"

But the larger issue here is more than women's leadership. Women's wisdom, the wisdom of "old crones," is vital to the continuing health of the
church, and of the globe. Much of traditional women's knowledge (i.e., "old
wives' tales") is disappearing which could provide wells of wisdom on a variety
of issues, including but not especially domestic ones.[55] The croning tradition
needs to be preserved in tandem with the political and economic rise of
women to positions of authority and power.

Rabbi Zalman Schachter has coined the term "spiritual eldering" to describe
the process of harvesting one's lifetime of experience and offering it to the
next generation as "elder wisdom." Rabbi Schachter explains it in his workshops like this:

> When you are working on a computer, sometimes you type a whole page and
> then the power goes out. If you have not saved your work to disk, it is all lost. A
> lifetime asks the same questions, "Are you saved?" You must write into the
> global awareness what it is you have accumulated in your lifetime and who you
> have become.[56]

The church must ask its women "Are you saved?" and then help them be
saved. The church is positioned to do this partly because of the growing

163

importance of organized religion to those in the Third Age. One Harris poll found that 71 percent of people over sixty-five found religion "very important," compared with only 49 percent of other adults. The church can do much to counteract the culture where men tend to gain power as they age, while women lose power—this is one of the reasons why older men "get the nubile young bodies, and older women tend to get dumped."[57]

11. The Hidden Hungry

Help Third-Agers and beyond become more nutritionally conscious. Women and children are especially at risk when it comes to malnutrition, especially in two-thirds of the world countries. Malnutrition is one of the biggest threats to Third-Agers and especially to Fourth-Agers.

While 12 percent of people older than sixty-five now live below the poverty level (as compared to 35 percent in 1959), 20 percent are at risk of malnutrition or are the "hidden hungry." The reasons why this is so are complex: isolation (empty dinner tables aren't conducive to food), poverty (when it's a choice between food or medicine and rent, the food goes before the medication), multiple medications induce nausea or diminished appetites, disease, physical limitations (shopping, cooking), tooth and mouth problems, and so on. Churches and synagogues can help address every one of these factors through advocacy, education, and wellness programs that might include parish nurses.

If the church is to speak in the voice of postmodern culture but out of the voice of eternity, it must exercise its lungs in the service of some new constituencies. The Women's Abuse Center estimates that four million men "violently attack or abuse women" whom they date or live with.

Postmodern culture is becoming more accessible to the disabled at the same time it invalidates the invalid like never before, even to the point of seeing those with severe "disabilities" as a "wrongful life" or as a "category mistake," as philosophers are wont to call those ideas that have no right to exist. There is a new form of Western exploitation of the poor: the increasing profiteering in human body parts that is making the world's poor a major donor source for body replacement parts. These are but a few of the moral questions the church must do more than gnaw on in the future, like a dog worrying a bone.

12. Seventh-Generation Decision-Making

Dietrich Bonhoeffer once said that the only real ethical question is how shall the next generation live? New paradigm communities of faith will enlarge their sense of community to include heirs and forebears. They will forge a new sense of partnership among the living, the dead, and the unborn.

We need to integrate the native American ethic whereby we can see our-

> IN OUR EVERY DELIBERA-TION, WE MUST CONSIDER THE IMPACT OF OUR DECISIONS ON THE NEXT SEVEN GENERATIONS.
>
> FROM THE GREAT LAW OF THE SIX NATION IROQUOIS CONFEDERACY

selves as good "heirs" of past generations as well as good "ancestors" of future generations. Some Native American traditions refrain from making an important decision until they gauge its impact on "the seventh generation."

Earliest Christianity is known for its close sense of dead and alive living together. Indeed, one of its most persistent adaptations is the combining of the place of worship and place of burial; the faithful buried its members close to the church or under it, where the living would be reminded by the dead that the majority of the church lies underground, that the church is not composed only of its living members. The church even built some of its most glorious chapels to honor and house its dead, not just serve the living. For sanitary reasons as well as cultural romanticism, in the nineteenth century the dead were isolated from the living—first in rural cemeteries, then in lawn park cemeteries, then in memorial parks, where we remembered them, but didn't relate to them or comingle with them. Perhaps it is time for a change, especially with the numbers of those being cremated.

We living must come to see ourselves as existing in community with the dead and unborn. The decisions we make affect them, and they have something to say and light to shed about what we are doing and where we are going. Postmoderns need to feel the weight of their absent presence. In postmodern culture, progress will be defined from the perspective of the dead and unborn as well as the living.

13. Not Everything You Can Do, I Can Do, Much Less Do Better

Aging is a complex process shaped by a mixture of genetic and environmental factors. A lot of who we are and will be, what we can do and can't do, is decided either before birth or at birth. Some people are given at conception a "tall candle," others a "medium candle," and still others a very "tiny candle."

Those with a "tall candle" can eat vats of fried foods, inhale tons of nicotine, and drink truckloads of scotch, and live to be one hundred. Those with a "tiny candle" can abstain from alcohol, eat vegetarian, and breathe mountain air and still kick the bucket at fifty-seven. Each additional inch in height over

5'4" carries with it a corresponding decline in life expectancy of 1.2 years, according to one Ohio study.

The church can help people come to terms and make peace with the candle they have been given, and to live within those limits. Contrary to the endless gushings of "If I could do it, you can do it too" motivational best-sellers, it is not true that "Everything you can do, I can do better" (as my brothers and I used to chant tauntingly at one another). The Egyptians learned this lesson the hard way as they tried to follow the Israelites through the parted waters. Not everything some of us can do, all of us can do—period, much less better.

CHAPTER SEVEN

ColorQuakes

SocioQuake 7: *99 Lives*

*I*n his autobiography, the composer John Cage tells of a counterpoint class at UCLA under the great master Arnold Schoenberg.

Schoenberg sent everybody to the blackboard. We were to solve a particular problem he had given and to turn around when finished so that he could check on the correctness of the solution. I did as directed. He said, "That's good. Now find another solution." I did. He said, "Another." Again I found one. Again he said, "Another." And so on. Finally, I said, "There are no more solutions." He said, "What is the principle underlying all of the solutions?"[1]

Multiplicity is the postmodern force behind what Popcorn calls "99 Lives," her megametaphor for this cubistic phenomenon of multiple-sidedness, the "crazy ambition to be as many people as we could possibly be."[2] No postmodern is purely one thing. No postmodern only does one thing.

If the modern era tended to chew more than it bit off, the postmodern era bites off more than it chews. Multiplicity is not so much a phenomenon of the rare "genius" (Jakob Ludwig Felix Mendelssohn was a gymnast, chess-player, translator, linguist, draftsman, painter, travel writer, teacher, administrator, conductor, violinist, organist, pianist, musicologist) as it has become an accomplishment and obsession of the many.

From the postmodern perspective, every singularity is a community of singularities. Every single day is a community of days lived in one—the "work day," the "home day," the "traffic-commute day," the "devotional day," the "school day." The question is not, How did you spend your day? but rather, How did you spend your days-within-a-day? Even further, How did you spend your days-within-your-days-within-a-day? In sum, are you making each moment happen?

167

Similarly, every self is a community of selves, not a unity and continuity of one "centered" self. "True to oneself! Which self?" Katherine Mansfield wrote in her diary.[3] Postmodern thought has turned with a vengeance against Enlightenment notions of a fixed center toward which we strive, or a single central self.[4] To have "many sides" to one's personality is today a compliment. A decade ago it was an indictment, causing other people to wonder "Who's the real you?" An "integrated" self has pulled together the multitude of selves into a we/me.

The Greek *persona* means "mask." A personality is a plurality of masks, not a single one. Notice our language when we say "She has a together personality"; or "He's not very together." Our very self is both individual and communal. Part of mental health is getting to know and understand one's inner cast of characters, some pleasant, some not so pleasant. Or as Stephen Dedalus puts it in James Joyce's *Ulysses* (1922), "We walk through ourselves, meeting robbers, ghosts, giants, old men, young men, wives, widows, brothers-in-love. But always meeting ourselves."

A primary definition of mental illness is when the "personality" or community of characters breaks up and breaks down into persons, not a whole personality. A marvelous new Diane W. Middlebrook biography is out on poet Anne Sexton. Sexton killed herself after trying everything in life there is to try. Middlebrook describes Sexton's insanity in terms of her "singular, exclusive, one-track vision of the world," her sanity in terms of "the mobility of poetic language, words running off in all directions, multiplying significance, releasing the poet from a monolithic vision of herself."[5]

In one of the most important articles on the USAmerican self ever published, psychologists Hazel Markus and Paula Nurius present not a self but a set of possible-selves-along-with-a-now-self: "Possible selves represent individuals' ideas of what they might become, what they would like to become, and what they are *afraid* of becoming."[6] Likewise, in the multiple-drafts model of the mind, the brain unconsciously processes innumerable streams of information simultaneously, creating multiple and ever-changing interpretations of experience.[7] Intelligence is plural. No mind is singular.

To live life on many levels at once—the level of the personal, where one never judges or condemns but accepts and forgives and makes space; the level of the theological, where one critiques, celebrates and communifies a tradition embraced from the depths of one's being; the level of the ethical, where one discerns and discriminates choices based on values that emerge from the theological character that frames one's existence: this is postmodern living.

Indeed, one's ability to be and do two things at once, or to process more than one kind of information simultaneously, is now taken as evidence of one's mental maturity and health. (Can you walk and chew gum?) For example, any normal three-year-old child can walk and can unwrap a Tootsie Pop, but cannot do both at the same time. In contrast, any adult can walk and hold a conversation while unwrapping the candy.[8]

"Man does not live by bread alone." Multiplicity in living is at the heart of the Christian faith. Multiple foci are the norms, not the exceptions to a life of variety and unembarrassed multiplicity of vision. Italian writer Umberto Eco has captured this multiplicity in his definition of an intellectual as "someone who is interested in everything, and in nothing else."[9]

> IF YOU BRING FORTH WHAT IS WITHIN YOU, WHAT YOU BRING FORTH WILL SAVE YOU. IF YOU DO NOT BRING FORTH WHAT IS WITHIN YOU, WHAT YOU DO NOT BRING FORTH WILL DESTROY YOU.
>
> JESUS CHRIST

Postmodern culture wants to "Get it Together!" If each of us is a cast of characters, a composite of cultures and identities, the entire cast belongs in a single play, on a single stage.[10] Hence the perplexed fascination (Ted Peters calls it "Trinity talk"[11]) of many contemporary theologians like Jürgen Moltmann, Leonardo Boff, Robert Jenson, Catherine Mowry LaCugna, and Eberhard Jungel with the Trinity.

Christianity is a whole-in-one religion. Theology, Christology, and Pneumatology collapse into one. God is Whole: God is One. God is three-in-one and one-in-three. God is "all put together." As we become progressively more like God, we become more whole and more "put together."

We can be many things at once without violating the one who we are. We can do many things at once. Indeed we cannot do only one thing.[12] More and more people have multiple jobs, multiple families (one example is the "boomerang families"—adult kids who return to the family nest after college), multiple homes, and so on. To make ends meet in a world of moving ends, two-income households are now a virtual necessity. Instead of parents with one job and five kids, we now have parents with five jobs and one kid.

Popcorn rightfully frets about all this. We're faxing so frantically "the world's production of fax paper can't keep up. . . . We've lost that great playing-for-time excuse, 'It's in the mail.' We've lost those little 'grace notes of time' we used to have while we waited for the news to get from here to there."[13] What is the antidote to the stress of 99 lives? Popcorn calls it "streamlining." In business terms it is known as "cluster marketing."[14]

I call it "stacking." These are the multifunction activities or products that get two or three jobs done at once or allow you to get done two or three jobs at once: time-saving, time-efficient processes and products. This is why time management products are so highly coveted, with little regard for price. Hence the appeal of Stephanie Culp's *Streamlining Your Life: A 5-Point Plan for Uncomplicated Living*[15] or Ken Blanchard and Spencer Johnson's *One Minute Manager*.[16]

"Stacking" or "streamlining" or whatever name you give it is a key concept for the 1990s. After a 1980s addiction to acquiring more, in the 1990s, as we have seen, more is less. Stacking will affect every aspect of postmodern life: from the way people eat—sporadic dining, frequent snacking for energy, easier meals—to the way people pray—"flash prayers" that take advantage of the hundreds of opportunities a day for prayer[17]—to the way people worship—fast-paced, without dead spaces, with collections of cash "offerings" increasingly antiquated.

FaithQuake 7: *ColorQuakes*

1. Bash-Bury Committees: British scientist Barnett Cocks wrote in a 1973 issue of *New Scientist* words that have more meaning as the years pass: "A committee is a cul-de-sac down which ideas are lured and then quietly strangled." An English visitor was watching his first American football game. When asked how he liked what he saw, the Englishman said: "Not a bad sport, but they seem to have an excessive number of committee meetings."

The church has become mummified in red tape. Speak the word *committee* and people hear "bureaucracy." Exorcise every bureaucratic spirit you can get your hands on. When the wind behind the sails is lost, the sails are no good. A church dense with committees is a regatta of red tape that stands for unspiritual commitments, wasted time, unproductive hours, poor stewardship, and bored scribblings on the back of envelopes. A sign that came out of the woodwork and made its appearance on many church bulletin boards in the 1980s reads: "For God so loved the world that God didn't send a committee."

> *I'm sick of commissions.*
> HILLARY CLINTON

In my consulting work with churches, I was privileged to meet a senior partner in a law firm whose love for Jesus inspired her to donate half-time work each week to her church as its volunteer coordinator. With agony in her voice she announced to me that if her pastor, whom she loved dearly, did not come to the point where he could see that asking people to serve on committees was a death warrant to enthusiasm and discipleship, she was going to quit her "job" and redirect her efforts at helping the church to enter the new world. She demanded of me, "Doesn't anyone in the church see that asking people nowadays to serve on 'committees' is the kiss of death?"

> In every committee of twelve, one will love you and one will betray you.
>
> LYLE E. SCHALLER

The problem inherent in committee structures is revealed by the following simple mathematics. With only one other person to work with, one only has four combinations of signals—communications by mouth, body, gestures, and expressions—to process in intelligent decision-making. By the time the size of the committee gets to ten, the number of possible ways of people relating to one another are 5,110.

2 people	2 signals
3 people	9 signals
4 people	28 signals
5 people	75 signals
6 people	186 signals
7 people	441 signals
8 people	1,016 signals
9 people	2,295 signals
10 people	5,110 signals

Kirkpatrick Sale, who presents this chart, finishes it off with an aside: Does anyone "wonder that a committee of ten takes so long to achieve anything at all, and that's usually only when most of the participants are so worn down that they cease to participate or give off any signals whatsoever."[18]

As that English visitor saw so quickly, the committee system is fit for a football world—a world of time-outs and half-times and huddles. In the postmodern era, however, one has to run fast just to keep in place. It is more a hockey or basketball world, where substitutions are made on the run and where strategies are sent in while the play is still going on. God moves fast. In the words of Welsh priest and poet R. S. Thomas, "He is such a fast/God, always before us and/leaving as we arrive."[19]

Ever notice how it looks and sounds different in a bureaucracy—silent corridors, straight walks, formal exchanges, banging doors? Be known as the church that hates committees, that never even uses the word *committee* (it's easier said than done), and whose hallways (if you have to have them) don't replicate bureaucratic sounds and sights. Build a replacement system not on the principles of bureaucracies but adhocracies.

"Adhocracy" is a postmodern netweaving process that distances itself from the rationalism, technology, and bureaucracy of modernity.[20] Call them "task forces" or "focus groups" or "action groups" or "project teams" or "roundtables" or "team Tauruses" or whatever. The new paradigm replacement for committees is a small group that is light, fast on its feet, and is employed to venture one vision but empowered to disband once that vision has become flesh.

Get organic, where everything that is created or worked on is seen as a living, breathing organism. In an organic church, relationships are primary and structures secondary. The church became an inorganic world in the modern era. As Milton J Coalter, John M. Mulder and Louis B. Weeks have shown in *The Organizational Revolution* (1991), much of what we take for granted today in church administration—"departments," "directors," "specialist experts," "national boards," "goals and objectives"—are actually the church's adoption of modern business strategies in the late nineteenth and early twentieth centuries. This is the time when "the pastor's study" became "the pastor's office."

Organic ideas, bionomic understandings, will become some of the mega-metaphors of the postmodern era. An organic community can decentralize into looser, more responsive netweaves of organically-related units. Develop a town-meeting mentality, where issues of both local and global importance can be openly aired and communally decided. Just as in our internationalized, economized world, God's kingdom is transnational.

The challenge in transforming the institutional church is actually to deinstitutionalize it, deprofessionalize it, to radically alter it through the profound processes of organizational and structural transformation that come when the church is viewed as a bionomic entity or "organism" rather than an "organization," when adhocracy is promoted over bureaucracy, and when leadership teams and alliances are built. If the establishment churches can decenter themselves along less controlling and bureaucratic lines, their declining market and job share will level out.

2. Dechurch the Church's Body Life

Reduce the power of institutions; increase the power of the people.

The church knows better than most groups how to embrace a new Body Life for itself, one that is based not on bureaucratic structures and organizational metamodels but organic and democratic understandings of the Body of Christ, especially that "scarlet thread" of the blood of Jesus Christ that draws all the diverse organs together and sews them together into one Christbody community. Get rid of organizational charts, job descriptions, chains of command, centralized programs, long-range committees, five-year plans, and *Robert's Rules of Order*.

Decentralize and destructure church administration and redistribute decision-making power. Experiment with plural, decentralized, organic leadership models and non-authoritarian decision-making processes. This does not mean consensus, which actually stifles if not paralyzes movement (know anything good in history that has waited until "near unanimity" as one theologian defines *consensus*). Instead of consensus decision-making, try critical-mass decision making, which allows many different decisions to be made at the same time by various groups.[21]

Or try a decentralized "consensus" model in which consensus does not mean agreement but assent. In this model for everyone to assent to a decision or direction does not mean everyone agrees with it. It simply means everyone is "on board" and that small groups have the autonomy to act without central control.

The patron saint of the Body of Christ is not St. Robert. Nor is its method of decision making based on "majority rules." In the cry "We want Barabbas! We want Barabbas!" Jesus himself found out how dependable "majority rule" can be. New paradigm communities will bring as few issues to a vote as possible. Every vote that is not unanimous leaves some people not feeling "in" or "out" of favor. Furthermore, whenever something is voted on in the church, it is evidence that the church is being run on democratic political principles rather than on biblical and spiritual principles. The church can recover its ability to "put on the mind of Christ" through the workings of the Holy Spirit who distributes gifts of ministry in unpredictable fashion. For it is Christ who must rule his church, rather than the majority vote.

> *THE BORDERS OF OUR MINDS ARE EVER SHIFTING AND MANY MINDS CAN FLOW INTO ONE ANOTHER AND CREATE OR REVEAL A SINGLE MIND, A SINGLE ENERGY.*
>
> W. B. YEATS

Materials scientist Rustum Roy has even argued that it would behoove the social order as well as the church to return to the biblical use of the "lot" instead of the "ballot" in its selection of leaders. Aside from the "lot's" acknowledgment of God's use of chance as an agent in history, Roy argues, the "lot" protects democracy from the twin election evils of money and media.[22]

173

3. Walk Out-of-Step

Ants walk out of step with one another for the same reason human soldiers carrying wounded on stretchers walk out of step: the more legs on the ground, the more load that can be lifted and carried.

For the last five hundred years Western cultures walked lock step in tight formation with one another. Non-Western cultures were not allowed into the march, and while looking on from the sidelines were depreciated, demeaned, and sometimes destroyed as the attempt was to make other cultures over into the Western image.

The postmodern world now being born respects the many different ways of walking, and in fact recognizes that the weight of the future cannot be carried unless we learn to walk together out-of-step. The "decline of the West" and the last gaspings of unicultural USAmerica is a cultural transition that has birthed too much lamentation and too little appreciation of the way other cultures can teach us and transform us. Indeed, the mission "fields" have become the mission "forces" of the postmodern church.

Here are some of the results of a fill-in-the-blanks exercise I conducted with the trustees of the seminary. Under the assumption that it's easier to say what the future isn't than what it is, we did some counterfactual hypothesizing about the future. I proposed to them the statement "Whatever the future is, it isn't _____." They filled in the blank. Here are their responses:

Whatever the future is, it isn't white (i.e., "only vanilla flavors").
Whatever the future is, it isn't Western.
Whatever the future is, it isn't European.
Whatever the future is, it isn't Tom, Dick, and Harry. (It's more likely to be Hans, Hosea, and Hoshimoto; or Gretta, Monique, and Tashanda).
Whatever the future is, it isn't business as usual.
Whatever the future is, it isn't print oriented.
Whatever the future is, it isn't male-dominated.
Whatever the future is, it isn't tolerant of dogmatism.
Whatever the future is, it isn't "You ought!"
Whatever the future is, it isn't "Go West young man." (It's more likely to be "Go global.")

The world that is coming will leave the church no choice but to negotiate and navigate differences. We can celebrate our differences and uniquenesses in the same way the modern era celebrated unity and similarity. Gregory Bateson defines *difference* as the "differences that make a difference." The more the church lives out of oneness, the more differences matter and need to be sharpened. Whereas the Reformation was preoccupied with unifying behind that which set "Protestants" apart from Rome, postmodern Christians must learn to play as many notes, and sing as many parts, as they can on their common keyboard.

The church lost something unique when its congregations ceased singing in parts and began singing in unison. The postmodern church will teach itself to sing in parts once again. Monoculturalists sing in monotone. They can only

> ## I'll teach you differences.
> ### KENT IN *KING LEAR*

hit one note. It's time for the church to conduct a worldwide choir.

Postmoderns accept the permanence of pluralizing realities. The valuation of plurality over sameness, the coming together of the *plurus* around a common *unum* (which increasingly is being called "pluraformity"), the celebration of "them," the "other," and the "outsider," means that issues of pluralism and diversity are here to stay. The church will only flourish as it adjusts to the deference toward difference, and abandons patterns of living and thinking wherein "difference has become indifference."[23] *Vive la difference!*

This means Christians will learn to walk out-of-step with other persons and nations and cultural traditions. People can share the same space but live in different worlds and walk in different styles. The church proclaims that God was in Christ, "reconciling" the world. Will the church put its practice in line with its proclamation? Will the church be a truly reconciling community where people who differ can nonetheless accept one another even if not agree with one another?

To risk diversity is to raise democracy to an art form, and the doctrine of the trinity to new heights. It is important for residents of a post-Christian nation to pause at Jesus' exact instructions in his Great Commission (Matt. 28:19-20): "Go therefore and make disciples of all nations, baptizing them in the name of the Father and of the Son and of the Holy Spirit, and teaching them to obey everything that I have commanded you. And remember, I am with you always, to the end of the age." While the object of discipling is "nations" (*ta ethne*), the object of baptizing and teaching is "persons" (*autous*).

Evangelism is not my reproducing in you what faith in God looks like in me. Evangelism is calling others to a faith in which my way with God may not be God's way with you. There are many ways to experience the love of God and live the life of Christ. This is why trinitarian theology is already proving to be one of the most important aspects of the Christian tradition for the postmodern era. It is this doctrine that addresses the issue of the one and the many, the singular and the plural, the particular and the universal, the individual and the communal.

4. The Coloring of America

The chemical responsible for our skin and hair color is "melanin," one of the most stable and insoluble chemical compounds known to science. In fact, melanin lasts longer than perhaps any other biological molecule—it has been found in mummies, mammoths, and the ink of 150-million-year-old fossil squids. The issue of color will always be with us. It will not go away.

Jesus was not "color blind." No matter how heartwarming the story, when people talk of Jesus' "color blindness," the color everyone ends up seeing is usually more white than black. The challenge facing postmoderns is the nurturing of a crayon consciousness and learning to wear in public a "Jacob's coat" of many colors: shaping a common public culture out of diverse cultures of color. At Pentecost God created a multicultural, multinational, multipower, multilateral church. The Pentecost dream can be realized in the postmodern church if it learns to speak in many tongues.

> *All the colors of the world.*
>
> BENETTON SHIRTS

In the postmodern air there are many frequencies. Or in Paul's advice: "There is a variety of gifts but always the same Spirit; . . . working in all sorts of different ways in different people, it is the same God who is working in all of them. . . . All these [gifts] are the work of one and the same Spirit, who distributes different gifts to different people just as he chooses." (1 Cor. 12:4-5, 11 JB)

It is one thing to spout off statistics. For example, by the year 2000, one child in three will be from a nonwhite or Latino household. Jay Leno jokes about a man dressed up as Uncle Sam who can't linger to chat because he's on his way to open a new Toyota dealership.

It is another thing to see those statistics take over the breakfast table. For example, by 1992, more USAmericans ate tortillas for breakfast than bagels or biscuits or pita bread; more salsa is sold now than ketchup. The year 2056 is the magic date cited by sociologists as that moment when the majority of the USAmerican population will be nonEuropean, nonwhite. As it is now, Asians, Africans, and Hispanics make up one-fourth of the population.

We are all ethnics, every single one of us. We all are a people of color. We are not a melting pot described in Israel Zangwill's 1908 play *The Melting Pot*, a people melted together into homogeneous form through the fire of equality and freedom. "Since 1909 the Melting-Pot has itself suffered a certain meltdown," write Christopher Ricks and William L. Vance. "Assimilation has felt less and less distinguishable from a simulation."[24] We are especially not a "triple melting pot" (Will Herberg) of Protestant, Catholic, Jew, as we seemed to be in the 1950s. The modern era's "melting pot" has become a postmodern "pot of marbles" (Haddon Robinson's metaphor). At the same time the rubbing marbles can smooth and shine one another, they also can scrape and scratch one another.

For I dipped into the future, far as human eye
    could see,
Saw the Vision of the world, and all the wonder
    that would be;

Heard the heavens fill with shouting, and there
    rain'd a ghastly dew
From the nations' airy navies grappling in the
    central blue;

Till the war-drum throbb'd no longer, and the
    battle flags were furled
In the Parliament of Man, the Federation of the
    world.

ALFRED LORD TENNYSON
Locksley Hall

We are to be the color God made us. We are not to melt down or bleach out who we are, or become something we are not. One of the most reliable predictors of cancer in later years is sunburn.

Contrary to popular perception, the "melting pot" will continue to gurgle above the intermarriage burner, which will still often be set at "high." (The rate of interracial marriages is increasing dramatically.) But the failure of the integrationist vision in modern culture will continue to disappoint and frustrate many postmoderns as the increasing effect of reproductive technology is to make private memory and collective memory the same thing. Over and over again, studies have demonstrated that race shapes attitudes much more strongly than does income.[25]

Nor are we a "stew" (as the 1960s sometimes put it). Nor are we a "salad bowl" (the metaphor of the 1970s). Nor are we a "mosaic" (the metaphor of the 1980s), with various traditions stitched in place and separated by spans of yard or grout.

We are a stir fry. "We are living in the first half-century of human history," Charles Murray has written, "in which the races of mankind have tried to live side by side as equal participants in the same societies—geographically side by side, not just metaphorically."[26] The strength of USAmerica is that it is the continuing and contiguous creation of all the world's cultures. Indeed, it is the constant stirring and turning over of the ingredients that keeps USAmerica whole, fresh, and at the front. Yet, in the words of historian Carl Degler's essay "In Search of the Un-hyphenated American": "To tell the story of an ethnic or racial group living within the confines of the U.S. without reference to the whole of America is to truncate its identity as well as the identity of all other Americans."[27]

> *Any student I'm not prepared to learn from, I'm not prepared to teach.*
>
> HISTORIAN JAMES D. NELSON

Partly because of the power of popular culture and its evangelist television, there is the homogenization of cultures into a planetary consumer culture, a kind of generic humanity. Louis Menand, Professor of English at Queens College, has written about the ways in which the people of the United States are becoming less, not more, diverse. "What most of the 'identities' aspire to be . . . are not separate and rival realms of value, but different flavors in the same dish." De Tocqueville was among the first to notice this phenomenon: "the United States is a country in which people, permitted to say whatever they like, all somehow end up saying the same thing."[28]

In typical postmodernist fashion, however, there is also at the same time a particularization of political life characterized by militant religions, resurgent ethnicities, tribal identities. That is why in the minds of some conservatives mass "multi-culti" leads inevitably to separatism. It need not be. But the centrifugal forces of the coming century are likely to generate more ethnic tensions, forced migrations, "ethnic cleansings" (the current attempts at eradicating the Kurds, the Bosnians, the ethnic Burmans, and the Shiite Muslims is only the beginning), even massacres, urban riots, wars, and genocides. Thanks to the global devolution revolution, and especially the Soviet break-up, the new Pan-Islamic Federation stands ready to flex its nuclear-weaponry muscles. As we are learning from the African continent, intertribal conflicts can be as brutal and nightmarish as international wars. Ethnicity is most threatening when it comes to mean collective loyalties that exclude or kill others.

In USAmerica, we are entering a period of deep polarization, even "culture wars"[29] that are being declared by more than the paranoids and separatists. Bitter moral skirmishes over abortion, homosexuality, schools, art, and so on betray deep cultural clashings between diverse moral systems. It is entirely foreseeable that our inner cities may birth new civil wars over moral and economic cleavages. It is unlikely, but not unthinkable, that the "United States of America" in the twenty-first century could look more and more like an America-Herzegovina.

All this rubbing together and rubbing against each other could polish one another rather than fulfill Hobbes's nightmare of society as "the warre of all against all." But the church is poised to insist that people not support practices that they find morally offensive. And the church can help by finding ways to counterbalance the postmodern tendency for society to fragment into mutually unintelligible cultural enclaves. For example, The United Methodist Church is offering "United Methnic" camping adventures that bring together teens from various cultures for shared transcultural outdoor experiences.

5. Get Tribal and Get Global—Decentration

So much of postmodernism is an echo system, a company of contrasts. An awareness of the forces pulling the people of the Earth in diverse directions is one of the chief keys to understanding and navigating the postmodern phenomenon. The postmodern era will be an institutionally decentered society.

Instead of culture operating out of a fixed center, the center now cannot hold and is not holding. A collapsing center is giving way to a culture heading in a variety of opposing directions at the same time, often a dual movement (*itus, reditus*) without any need of reconciling the contradictions. Postmodern culture unites (reconciliation is one of the highest acts of human creativity) while at the same time it separates (releases and sets free forces and figures heretofore bound).

In this oxymoronic sensibility, opposition is both a kind of subject-matter in narrative as well as a kind of narrative itself.[30] The postmodern movement in two contrasting directions, this obsessive oxymoronism, frightens the church. It shouldn't. All texts are duplicitous. All truths conceal as much as they reveal. As every parent knows, love both unites and separates. The harmonious co-existence of incompatibles is a staple of existence. The world was created in a dual movement from God and to God, the eternal double truth of every church that seeks to bring word to flesh.

Once one understands that in postmodern culture all things have their unity in this opposing movement, this inherent doubleness, this distinguishing dual directionalism, one has found the key to living and moving and making a difference in this complex era. As we have seen over and over again in one faithquake after another, opposites attract and adhere. The Christian church had better be prepared at the same time to move within and without, to see itself as both exclusive and inclusive, to understand an information technology that is characterized by greater specialization and greater diversity, and to follow a Christ who is both the particularity of God's Israel and the universality of Israel's God.

> *For anything to be real it must be local.*
> G. K. CHESTERTON

When missiologist David Bosch argues that a missionary church is involved in a double movement of inculturation—"at once [an] inculturation of Christianity and [at the same time a] Christianitization of culture"[31]—he is assessing for the religious arena what historian Benjamin R. Barber, in a widely read article, characterizes for the world's economic and political spheres: the world's twin futures of retribalization and globalization, world glasnost and local gringostroika.

Barber calls these "Jihad vs. McWorld," as "the planet is precipitantly falling apart and coming together at the very same moment."[32] The institutions of the nation-state are decentering, "scattering" political power away from the macro level of the state towards local and regional levels as well as global structures. For example, the successful newspapers of the twenty-first century will be both the USA Today's of the world, "The nation's newspaper," and the Parsons Advocate's of the world, "The only newspaper written for and by the people of Tucker County, West Virginia." The forces of integration and disintegration operate in tandem; we are becoming more and more "world citizens" and "tribal citizens" all at the same time; the world is becoming more "at home" and "abroad" at once. The "nationalism" modernity brought with it belongs to the past, a retrogressive and atavistic force in postmodernity. Its replacements are a more severe "downward" tribalism and a more genteel "sideway" globalism.

To get tribal does not mean to exclude other peoples. To be a member of a tribe is not to exclude membership in other tribes: indeed multitribalisms are the future. The new tribalism gives us the search for membership in a single tribe and embraces multiple identities and multiple tribes. The postmodern world is becoming more One World and Many Worlds at the same time.

The new globalism and the new tribalism go together. In the latter, there is a taking seriously of other people's traditions and cultures, learning from them and learning to live with them. In many of the discussions about "multiculturalism," however, what has been missing is the recognition that the new global world is an economic world, not a political world. Economics has replaced politics as the power paradigm. Instead of political confrontation, one now has economic confrontation and competition. The future to a new multicultural globalism is through geo-economics, not geo-politics.

Michael Walzer notes how the new tribalism—while it brings a positive commitment to one's own history, culture, and identity—also brings with it a parochialism and cultural supremacy that is negative and permanently disfiguring, as the many tribal wars around the world right now attest. The new tribalism is bankrupt if it does not differ from a simple revival of the old premodern tribalism. Postmoderns must find meaning and identity in multiple tribes:

> The self . . . is capable of division and even thrives on it. Under conditions of security . . . I will identify myself with more than one tribe. I will be an American, a Jew, an Easterner, an intellectual, a professor. Imagine a similar multiplication of identities around the world, and the world begins to look like a less dangerous place. When identities are multiplied, passions are divided.[33]

The new tribalism is violent if it also fails to differ from the old in its embrace of the earth and all earthlings. That is why it simply won't do to replace "patriotism" with "humatriotism" as some are suggesting.

The decentration of society "downward and sideways" is matched by a "decentration of self" (James Fowler's phrase) or what others dub "deselfing"—emptying and giving up of self after the lonely journeys of the boomer self ethic. As we saw in faithquake 4, people feel a need to be part of a larger community, a more intimate family. But when one lives together in community, one gives up something to live in them. You can't be a member of a tribe or community and not give up something. There is in community living some inevitable restrictions of choices. Yet a different order of self-fulfillment comes out of life lived in community than takes place in a life lived exclusively for self.

6. Can You Keep Open House, and Be At Home Away-From-Home?

The postmodern church will keep open house for all sorts and conditions of beliefs, so long as when they come in they help with the housework.

This will be one of the chief ways the household of the Christian faith keeps clean in the future—the brushing away of one's own dirt and grime that is accomplished through this open house with other religions. Tom Ogletree calls this a "hermeneutics of hospitality," which he defines as "to welcome strange and unfamiliar meanings into our own awareness, perhaps to be shaken by them, but in no case to be left unchanged."[34] To keep open-house means to welcome the good and the true and the beautiful from whatever houses they proceed, even to the point of putting one's views and life-style at risk.

Theologian Hans Küng has provided a charter for open-house experiences in his elucidation of three great principles: (1) a world ethic is requisite for human society to continue; (2) peace among the nations is impossible without peace among the religions of the nations; (3) there can be no peace among the religions without dialogue among the religions.[35] The conversation must begin with a "trialogue" among the three Abrahamic missionary religions (Jews,[36] Christians, and Muslims)—hence Küng's projected trilogy *The Religious Situation in Our Time*—and then a dialogue among the Abrahamic religions with Eastern religions.

> *I DO NOT WANT MY HOUSE TO BE WALLED ON ALL SIDES AND THE WINDOWS STUFFED. I WANT THE CULTURES OF ALL LANDS TO BE BLOWN ABOUT MY HOUSE AS FREELY AS POSSIBLE, BUT I REFUSE TO BE BLOWN OFF MY FEET BY ANY OF THEM.*
>
> MOHANDAS KARAMCHAND GANDHI

There are some religions that one simply doesn't let in the house. In fact, there are some religions that are downright mean and destructive, even satanic. All religions are not created equal. It is time to tell people that if they take certain trips to "bliss," they'll be taken for a ride. In the words of the psalmist, God gave them their hearts desire, but sent leanness unto their souls.[37]

The question for bishop and biblical scholar Krister Stendahl is "How do I sing my song to Jesus with abandon, without telling dirty stories about others?"[38] Christians need to find themselves more comfortable in situations that make them more uncomfortable than in situations that make them feel right at home. Can we find home away from home? The differences in the human family are as profound and important and lasting as the similarities.

The global world that is emerging must be built on differences as well as similarities. Our differences can unite us as much as our similarities. Indeed, similarities can be more divisive than our differences.

It is the easiest thing in the world for USAmerican Christians to "put yourself in their shoes" when "their shoes" are those of the white suburban, middle-aged, middle class. The Simi Valley jury in the first trial of the police officers who beat Rodney King proved this explicitly. The challenge is to put oneself in the shoes of people who are different from you. The mark of postmodern maturity is the ability to inhabit someone else's space who is entirely different from you, to live and think in their world.

Clovis Chappell loved to say that everyone had a right to enter the kingdom of heaven, but no one has the right to shut anyone out. Or in the thesis of Hans Küng's recent book, there will be no peace among the nations of the world without peace among the religions of the world.[39] We have much to learn about God from outside our own ranks of the faith.

7. Any Adjectives in Heaven?

Will the postmodern era be the Postdenominational Age? Will the denominations continue their slow slide into world irrelevancy? There is no doubt that denominations have become unadaptive mascots of modernity and some of the great mastodons of the postmodern world. There is little argument that denominational differences are relevant or significant anymore. Yet the religious establishment spends much of its time defending them as if they were.

Interest in denominational matters may be hardening among clergy, but decreasing among people in the pews. To see this one only has to look as far as denominational publications. *The American Baptist Magazine*, for example, is the oldest religious magazine with continuous publication in the western hemisphere. It began in 1803 as a Baptist missions magazine in Massachusetts. Its circulation dropped from a modern high of 75,000 to less than 24,000. It ceased publication with the July-August 1992 issue.

So why do we do so little to work together? Joan Campbell has engraved this postmodern sensibility with these memorable words: "The question for our day is not, 'Can we identify to which flock we belong?' The question for our day is, 'Can we hear the shepherd's voice, and are we prepared to respond to the call?' "[40] In heaven, as in heaven on earth, God will be "all in all."

There is a widespread delegitimation of traditional institutions and a disdain for large organizations like unions, political parties, charities, denominations. People don't trust "institutions," even the church. According to George H. Gallup Jr., the military has replaced organized religion as the nation's most trusted "institution."[41]

This "anti-affiliation movement" is coterminous with people wanting to

183

seek unencumbered alliances and form grassroots networks like never before. New public spheres, styles, and movements, or what some are calling the "proliferation of multiple micropublic spheres," testifies to the emergence of a distinctly postmodern politics. One of the keys to the success of the 1992 Clinton campaign, for example, was his early "depoliticization" by his handlers, and their portrayal of the candidate as not just another conventional politician.

Similarly, people are turning away from traditional or institutional religion at warp speed. Unlike William James, who at the conclusion of his classic *The Varieties of Religious Experience* (1902), confessed that while he could find no reason for believing in "God," yet he believed in religion because it was a prime human exercise and provided comfort and solace for people like himself; today people find not faith in God difficult but organized religion difficult or impossible. When they do show up at the doors of organized religion, they come to participate, but not to join. The New Age movement has been extremely popular partly because it has found ways of delivering a spirituality without the trappings, apparatus, and constraints of organized religion. "Organized religion" represents to postmoderns "dead and often intolerable structures affixed for social control in service of the state."[42]

In much the same way eighteenth century evangelicals like Wesley, Whitefield, and Edwards became deeply skeptical, even distrustful of the ability of governments to lead in any reformation of religion,[43] so today people are skeptical of denominations and other centralized bureaucracies to lead in any revitalization of religion. It is not simply the mavericks who are hurling gauntlets before the organized religion establishment. From every angle there is a turning instead to local initiatives, spiritual sources, and an outpouring of the Holy Spirit for an awakening of God's presence in the world. Evelyn Woodward, the Director of the Cara Centre for Clergy and Religions in New South Wales, has already written a handbook on how the religious and their communities can emerge from "garrison Catholicism" and deinstitutionalize: "We can no longer be satisfied to operate solely in institutional ministries. The call to be pilgrims is louder than ever before."[44]

Yet the social form known as the denominations, however inadequate, will never go away. Associations are a vital supplement but not a substitute for denominations. Those who are predicting the disappearance of the denomination ("If you're riding a dead horse," they say, "dismount") in the new reconfiguration of American religion are speaking too soon. It will be a while yet before the bell tolls for denominations, if ever. Denominations may even get stronger. But denominations will find health only as heritages not as hierarchies. They will get stronger only if they get smaller, as netweaves not as judicatories. They will get stronger more on a micro level than on the macro level of national systems and bureaucracies. They will get stronger only if they reconstitute through a higher form of integration.

Most of what denominational agencies have offered churches are already being delivered in better quality and cheaper quantity through parachurch organizations or entrepreneurs.[45] Denominations may yet decide, however, to go the way of the Amish or Hasidim if they keep on doing things as they're used to doing them. Those in holes are ill-advised to keep digging. And digging deeper at the same hole is what denominations are doing when they keep acting more like organizations and less like connections. The institutional church must become a missional and connectional church.

But the growing gap between the religious and the spiritual is best bridged by denominational bodies. Only by becoming a member of some religious tribe can a Christian pledge abiding allegiance to religious faith over some diffuse "spirituality," which polymath Martin E. Marty rightly calls a "contemporary code word for gaseous, noncommittal religion, that evasive term that may refer to little more than a warm tingle in the toes."[46]

Discipleship is not noncommittal. Discipleship is not an easy, everything-for-nothing affair. Every individual must pay a price to be embodied in the life of Jesus Christ. There are personal levies, holy compromises involved in membership in the Body of Christ. There are personal sacrifices that must be made to living in community. Sometimes one can only get "half a loaf" progress.

Two people have helped me to say with feeling "I am a loyal member of an organized religious tribe." The first is George Bernard Shaw, an activist in the British Labour Party who, when he heard that a Labour Party Candidate for Parliament (Joseph Burgess) refused to compromise on an issue, retorted:

> When I think of my own unfortunate character, smirched with compromise, rotted with opportunism, mildewed by expediency, dragged through the mud of borough council and Battersea elections, stretched out of shape with wire-pulling, putrefied by permeation, worn out by twenty-five years pushing to gain an inch here, or straining to stem a backrush, I do think Joe might have put up with just a speck or two on those white robes of his for the sake of the millions of poor devils who cannot afford any character at all because they have no friend in Parliament. Oh these moral dandies, these spiritual toffs, these superior persons. Who is Joe, anyhow, that he should not risk his soul occasionally like the rest of us?[47]

The second ever-present help in time of trouble is this affirmation from Rabbi Lionel Blue, which I keep with me as spiritual medicine to counteract the denominational declension disease:

> Organized religion is not religion itself, but it is a powerful stimulant to it. If you decide to go into it, it is better to dive right in than to wander round the edges of the pool, putting in a toe and complaining that the water is too cold. . . .

I like Organized Religion. It does not solve any religious problem by itself, but you are forced to get to the point of the problem quicker without wasting so much time.[48]

To those who say "I don't like organized religion" I now reply: "You don't like organized language? You don't like organized meetings? You don't like organized stores? You don't like organized air-traffic?"

8. Be a World Christian

We are now living in a borderless world, where natural boundaries are irrelevant. Borders are just dotted lines on a map. They have no more reality for the egrets (our natural environment) than for the entrepreneurs (our economic environment).

Nakasone, when prime minister of Japan, launched a drive to persuade the Japanese to buy more imports. So sales went up of Del Monte Ketchup, Wilson tennis rackets, Kleenex and Scotties tissues. Unfortunately, all of these items were made in Taiwan, Portugal, Hong Kong, and Japan. One can no longer talk about an "American product" or a "Japanese product" or a "German product" and still mean anything. We no longer have economics divided into discrete national units.

What nation-states were to the modern world, transnational enterprises are to the postmodern world. They move across national boundaries through telecommunications technology. In the postmodern world, nation-states are being replaced by nations within states.

One of the most unprecedented phenomena in the history of the globe is that all peoples on this planet are sharing the same experiences. Another way of analyzing this phenomenon is through the democratizing effect of media. Even though a government may not be a political democracy, there is a worldwide "consumer democracy" that is being created by the media.

President Truman liked to say that if you could put a Sears and Roebuck catalog in every home behind the Iron Curtain on Friday, by Monday communism would be finished. "In a sense," writes one economist, "that is just what the fax machine has done."

> Information empowers people. Governments can't fool the people any longer. In the technological age, a new set of weapons has emerged. Computers, printers, photocopiers, fax machines, and telephones are the new guns of liberty. Technology has replaced tanks. The seventy-year iron reign of the communists proved that they could control tanks, but that they could not control fax machines.[49]

Theology hatched in the WASP nest is culturally bound. Western theology does no more than give biblical answers to Western questions. What about

African questions? Asian questions? Latin American questions? Eastern questions? William A. Dryness shows how theology can be both faithfully Christian and yet flexibly and authentically cultural.[50] It can be as Paul of Tarsus once boasted about the gospel "all things to all people." The gospel can speak with a multitude of voices to a multitude of peoples.

New paradigm churches in the Americas should enter into close relationships with other religious communities around the world, both within the Christian faith (e.g., 10 percent of Iraqis are Christians) and without (Islam, Hindu, etc.). One theologian has even made this the Bible's golden rule of mutual recognition: "Interpret [the existence of] others as you would have them interpret [your existence]."[51]

I love truth wherever I find it.

JOHN WESLEY TO SAMUEL FURLY

---

9. Live and Let Live

If ever we needed the motto "Live and let live," it is during these dog days of dogma. The grand or meta-narratives—Marxism, structuralism, psychoanalysis—are either dead or dying.[52] The very notion of an all-embracing system is suspect. Life lived in submission to a single, fixed, dominant principle is over. Part of the new paradigm is the existence of multiple paradigms through the realization that each paradigm is to a significant degree socially conceived and constructed.

There is no reigning meta-paradigm in the postmodern world. Who hasn't felt like the person who confessed, "I want to put my foot down, but I can't find a place to put it"? We don't answer to the "doctrines" of the faith anymore, which theologian George Lindbeck says should not be understood as truth claims anyway but as rules for speech. The days are long gone when people can laugh lovingly, as nineteenth century students did, when chanting this doggerel about the great Victorian classicist Benjamin Jowett:

> Here I stand, my name is Jowett
> If there's knowledge, then I know it.
> I am the master of this college:
> What I know not, is not knowledge.

Indeed, the reigning postmodern concept is as much uncertainty as the reigning modern scientific notion was certainty. Heisenberg's "Uncertainty Principle" has the same metaphysical standing for postmoderns that Descartes' "Cogito, Ergo Sum" had for moderns beginning in the seventeenth century.[53]

187

All of life is seen less as something under the central control of command headquarters than a synergy of chaotic, complex, even contradictory, but always surprisingly interdependent processes. Life is less obeying certain rules than it is living in a certain spirit.

> The Methodists alone do not insist on your holding this or that opinion; but they think and let think. Neither do they impose any particular mode of worship; but you may continue to worship in your former manner, be it what it may.
>
> JOHN WESLEY

Instead of churches aspiring to be communities of shared assumptions ("Here I stand"), churches should consider aspiring to be communities of shared ambitions with a diversity of assumptions about how to get there ("There we go"). Just observe the odd mix of people Jesus chose to be his disciples— the political radical Simon the Zealot, the fiscal conservative Judas Iscariot, the wealthy but despised Matthew the Tax Collector, the social pariah Peter the Fisherman. The multiples are unified by a common commitment to Christ and the mission of God in the world.

J. Christiaan Beker has taught us how the apostle Paul himself proved to be "exceedingly flexible for the sake of multiformity within the unity of the church" as long as the truth of the gospel was not at stake.[54] There is no one gospel truth, no single expression of the truth of Jesus Christ. The gospel is for everyone, just as food is for everyone. What one digestive system thrives on, however, causes another to throw up—or even sometimes go into anaphylactic shock. In 1529 after months of frustrating discussion with other Reformers about the presence of Christ in the Eucharist, Martin Bucer concluded: "I have never yet seen two men who agree exactly on any one thing. This also applies to theology."[55]

Truth is tolerance. When we claim to have arrived at the Truth that ends all truth, we cheat ourselves and condemn others. It is the sense of the frailty rather than finality of interpretation that strikes postmoderns and that opens them to further insights, illuminations, inspirations, and so on. Gerald Kennedy tells the story about a missionary outpost where the closest hospital was a hundred miles away, the closest garage a half-day's drive, and the "car" an absolute life-line to both the missionaries and the community they served.

I was visiting a mission station in the Belgian Congo, staffed by two young missionaries and their families. The two men were far apart in their theology and I wondered how they got along. They were cut off from other preachers and thrown closely together. One of them said to me, "We get along fine. We do not talk theology. We talk cars."[56]

The postmodern church, if it is to be a missional church rather than an institutional church, needs to learn "car-talk."

Postmodern culture keeps a humbler and broader church than ever before. However broad the church, however humble the pluralism, many postmoderns will be only happy as heretics. But once one accepts the humbling fact that the best we can do is approximate final solutions, one is released to accept more than one answer to the problems and paradoxes of life. There must be learned a peaceful coexistence of contradictions and anomalies that are produced by differing methodological approaches.

But truth is also intolerance. Postmodern culture may be more probabilistic, less absolutistic than ever before. But this shyness of interpretation can allow all answers to any question, as the postmodern temptation is to be committed to not being committed ("I'm just keeping my options open"). As we saw in faithquake 1, adhesion (adding another commitment onto previous commitments, even to the point of a shuffling-of-the-cards spirituality) becomes the norm rather than conversion (turning from one set of commitments to another). Swarthmore psychology professor Kenneth Gergen shows in his new book *The Saturated Self* (1992) how the postmodern personality becomes populated with growing numbers of selves as it becomes bombarded by an ever-increasing number of potential relationships (TV, travel, telephones, faxes, computers, etc.).

All too quickly the self can spiral toward what Gergen calls "multiphrenia," in which a drowning, overpopulated self swims frantically about trying to take advantage of the sea of quirky, murky choices. As The Slaughterman remarks severely in Peter Barnes's BBC monologue: "I came to the conclusion that all the big ideas about God, faith and grace were for playing with and not for committing myself to."[57]

Populist relativism ("there are no absolutes") is false. It is not true "everything is relative." Not everything. There is one absolute—God. God is absolute. Everything else is relative. God is the fundamental, the final absolute. And that absolute of God relativizes everything else—all our thoughts (which are flawed), all our beliefs (which are partial), all our customs (which are contingent), all our realities (which are "trendy")—all are relativized by the one absolute: God. God is the one truth that ascends the moral summits and transcends all dictions and diversities, whatever they may be.

Because God is absolute, it is not true that there are no better or worse answers. Because God is absolute, it is not true that all answers are of the same weight, that it's all "a matter of opinion." Because God is absolute, there are standards; there are canons; there are wrong answers. It is time the church stuck its neck out and announced that some ways of living are better than others. It is time that Christians started showing people how to make value judgments again. Postmodern Christians must not give up on the idea of Truth.

What there is not any more is a last word about anything—unless that word be Christ. Only God has the last word, and that word, the Word whose ring would silence the universe, has not been said. There is Truth. But Truth allows more to be said.

CHAPTER EIGHT

MissionQuakes

SocioQuake 8: *S.O.S.*

The problems of New York City are so severe, one wit has commented, that they are considering changing their area code from
212 to 911.

One does not have to have been born within sight of Times
Square to realize that the culture is sending out what Popcorn calls S.O.S. signals: "Save Our Society."[1] In USAmerican society alone, each year there are
4.7 million assaults, a million plus robberies, and 22,000 homicides. Indeed,
humans can be such an unlovable and irresponsible species that it is a wonder
God hasn't treated us like the pterodactyl and tyrannosaurs and phased us out
of the evolutionary process.

Popcorn predicts the 1990s will be "The Decency Decade" and will in some
ways bring back the social conscience and moral rightness of the 1960s, especially in the three "E's" areas where the horsemen of the apocalypse are riding
most furiously: "Environment, Education, Ethics." Or as another observer has
written, "nothing which is not socially or ecologically responsible [will] make
it out of this decade alive."[2]

Many businesses are already finding their identity not in profit but in service—a tradition as American as Fuller Brush to Herbalife which transforms
"sales" into "service" through businesses finding missions larger than themselves—with profit the reward for making the world a better place. Most amazing, Popcorn challenges American corporations to go even further and
develop a soul, or what others are calling a "service ethic." Popcorn hopes that
"the status that an M.B.A. held for marketers in the '80s will be replaced by
the status of a new M.B.S. (Masters of Business Soul)."[3]

One hears similar utterances from other advisors and consultants to the
business community, such as Harvard's Rosabeth Moss Kanter:

Money should never be separated from mission. It is an instrument, not an end. Detached from values, it may indeed be the root of all evil. Linked effectively to social purpose it can be the root of opportunity.[4]

Peter Block's leadership manual portrays the key to effective management as *Stewardship: Choosing Service Over Self-Interest* (1993). He calls for a redistribution of power that replaces traditional management tools of control, efficiency, and predictability with responsibility, accountability, and compassion. So too argues Peter M. Senge in his management textbook on systems thinking entitled *Fifth Discipline: Mastering the Five Practices of the Learning Organization* (1992), which argues for a more spiritual and missional basis for organizational development and leadership.

Such instruction is already having an effect. Five percent of all 1992 MBA graduates now select Mother Teresa as the person they most admire (she wasn't even on the last list; missing now is Michael Milken and even Lee Iacocca). An amazing 79 percent of the graduates signaled their resolve never to work for tobacco producers.[5] Wendy's founder R. David Thomas ("Dave" to his TV commercial fans) requires an MBA of all of his employees—a "Mop Bucket Attitude" that puts service, honesty, and goodness above everything else.[6] The busters and after-busters are letting go the easy pitch. They are going after the tough challenge.

That many in the business community have adopted a service orientation is also evident in the growing prominence of the "stakeholder" rather than "shareholder" philosophy of business. "The mission of NCR," it was announced at the award-ceremony for the 1992 Prize for Non-Fiction, "is to create value for all our Stakeholders—customers, shareholders, employees, suppliers, and the community in which we operate."[7] The economic "moves" of many multinationals are increasingly vibrating to more notes than those struck by market positionings and extendings.

One also sees concern to help humankind in the actions of corporations like Stride Rite Corporation, which views public service as a business investment and which earmarks 5 percent of its pretax earnings for philanthropy in the form of the Stride Rite Foundation. Covenant Investment Management of Chicago has even found that socially responsible companies or what Popcorn would like to call "S.O.S" companies produce higher returns to stockholders than others.[8] Journalists Mary Scott and Howard Rothman were so struck by the bandwagon of "caring capitalism," as the founders of Ben & Jerry's Ice Cream call it, that they explored such firms as Shorebank Corporation, Patagonia, Smith & Hawken, Celestial Seasoning, Esprit de Corps, and others and published their findings under the title *Companies with a Conscience*.[9]

FaithQuake 8: *MissionQuakes*

It is hard not to be a moral alarmist about the three "E's." Indeed, the church is located to travel (notice I did not say "speak out on") the grim social terrain of all three fronts. Society needs the church to help move it from its fixated self-centeredness to public-spiritedness.

> The Church is the
> Church only when it
> exists for others.
>
> DIETRICH BONHOEFFER

Or at least this is the argument of sociologist Virginia A. Hodgkinson, who concludes her analysis of benevolence activity in the United States with the stunning prediction that "if a new progressive movement ushers in the twenty-first century, its birthplace will not be in political parties or in government but in the local congregations and adjutant religious organizations of America." Why here? Because it is religious organizations, she says, that "provide the opportunity for communal gatherings that permit the kind of discourse necessary to create the possibility of a new national consensus on values that can recognize and reconcile the diversity and pluralism of our current society."[10]

The most recent research on service, altruism, and volunteerism is that there is a self-referential and self-reinforcing component to helping others. Called the "helper's high" or the "Mother Teresa effect," there accrues to people who help others measurable physical and mental benefits. When we do something about the problems of the world, instead of finding ourselves dragged down, we feel pumped up; people who help others are more exuberant, stress-free, and happier than those who don't.[11]

"What specifically can I do to make a difference," you ask? Take out of the library *The Encyclopedia of World Problems and Human Potential* (1991). It lists over 1,000 problems affecting planet Earth. Pick one. There are over 450,000 nonprofit organizations in this country dedicated to moral betterment (out of 1.2 million tax-exempt organizations). Pick one.

There are three picks, however, that are essential or foundational to many of the other causes. The church needs to call itself to three "helper's highs" in its mission to this postmodern world.

1. Look Through a Glass Greenly

The first helper's high comes from making Christianity green again.[12] Christianity is vapid unless it deconstructs its unhealthy relationships with nature and relates to the world around us as a living being. Christians are called to become friends of the planet once again. Will the church be a force for getting humans back on speaking terms with the universe, or will it distance humans further from the rest of creation?

> *You can't save the soul while the biosphere crumbles.*
>
> THEODORE ROSZAK

David Brower is one of the leading lights of the twentieth-century environmental movement. Speaking to a class of law students on the Mission Point Peninsula beach at Michigan's Grand Traverse Bay, Brower held his thumb and forefinger out in front of him, two inches apart, and said:

Imagine if you will our entire planet reduced to this, the size of an egg. . . . If the planet Earth were reduced to the size of an egg, what do you think the proportionate volume of all its air, its atmosphere, would be? And what would be the total volume of the water that, along with air and sunlight, sustains life on this Earth? . . . According to the computations I've seen, the sum total of atmosphere veiled around this egg planet Earth would be equivalent of no more than the volume of a little pea wrapped around the globe. And the water? That would be no more than a matchhead, a tiny volume spread thin enough to fill the oceans, rivers and lakes of the world.

Looking at the students, Brower asked:

Thinking of those limits, can you any longer not believe that our planet is a tremendously vulnerable little system, totally dependent on this fragile tissue of air and water, a thin fabric of life support made up of all the air and water the Earth will ever have?[13]

Since Ernst Haeckel first used the word *ecology* in 1866, nature has gone from being a threat to be conquered to a resource to be consumed. Images of planet Earth such as those of the astronaut's "ball," Brower's "egg," and Steven's "spaceship" are helping us come around to Haeckel's sense of nature as an organism with which humans need to be in communion.

Perhaps the greatest achievement of the environmental movement of the 1970s and 1980s has been to widen the world's horizons into realizing that acid rain, ozone depletion and the destruction of the rain forests are the first truly global crises planet Earth has faced.[14] Something is seriously awry when nature's most life-giving fluids—mother's milk and semen—have become death fluids filled with dioxins, furans, and viruses.

The environment deserves to be what it portends to be—if the Environmental Summit in Rio de Janeiro is any indication—the centering, unifying political issue of the 1990s, or in Albert Gore's formulation, the "central organizing principle" for a new civilization.[15] In a post-Cold War, Hot-Peace world, national security thrusts are less military than they are environmental, as environmental security and international equity assume center stage in political and economic relations. Environmental concerns must become central to all policies.

The consumer class of the world is ruining the planet while fighting over the costs of saving it. In Kurt Vonnegut's novel *Hocus Pocus*, character Ed Bergeron proposes that a gigantic epitaph be carved in the Grand Canyon "for the flying saucer people to find" after humans had all gone "belly up like guppies in a neglected fishbowl":

> WE COULD HAVE SAVED IT,
> BUT WE WERE TOO DARN CHEAP AND LAZY.[16]

And too unloving. God's love has never left the world, but our love has. James Hillman observes:

> Great Mother Nature no longer provides our support; we are now obliged to care for her. Nature today is on dialysis, slowly expiring, kept alive only by advanced technology. What can stir our depths equal to the depths of ecological need? Duty, wonder, respect, guilt, or the fear of extinction are not enough. Only love can keep the patient alive—a desire for the world which affords the vitality, the passionate interest on which all other efforts rest.[17]

It is important for the church to understand that the environment is not just another social justice issue. Planet Earth is the playing field on which all other social justice issues stand or fall.

But the environment is not only the unifying political issue of our time, flouting ideological boundaries and diverse political bases like no other issue. The environment is most particularly a *status confessionis* (confessional moment) in the history of the church. Will we keep and renew God's first covenant, the covenant with Noah? Or will we be found in breach of that covenant, and add another breach rather than a bridge over the troubled fluids, both hydrosphere and atmosphere, of planet Earth?

Noah saved the world in its infinite variety. The world will be saved only if its infinite variety is protected by us who have been chosen by God to be "trustees" of planet earth, or in James Lovelock's preferred phrase, "shop stewards" for our fellow species: "We are just shop stewards, workers chosen because of our intelligence as representatives for the others, the rest of life on our planet."[18]

The problem is that the shop stewards themselves are consuming rather than stewarding the shop. As Jean Chesneaux points out in his *Brave Modern World* (1992), if every single resident of planet Earth consumed and polluted as much as the 5 percent who live in USAmerica, the Earth would be stripped bare and die in no time. Of all the prescription drugs sold in USAmerica over the past 25 years, 25 percent were extracted from tropical plants. Of 250,000 higher plant species, only 2 percent (5,000) have been screened for healing properties.[19] The world's best and biggest drug store is literally going up in flames, and nature's richest treasurehouse of cures—the rainforest—is being cut down and burned away. According to Pulitzer prize-winning scientist Edward O. Wilson, humans are bringing on the sixth "great extinction" of planet Earth, with a 20 percent species extinction a strong possibility in the global diversity of "close to 10 million or as high as 100 million species."[20] How much force does it take to break the crucible of emergence? We are now finding out.

The environment is an area where the church needs to sit at the feet of its children. The number one issue in juvenile USAmerica today? The environment. As any reading of the bimonthly children's magazine *Stone Soup* makes clear, our children are the ones educating us in how to look "through a glass greenly." They are the leaders in a new worldwide phenomenon, environmental activism; these kids who have largely turned green may even be the first wave of environmental martyrs.

Eco-kids from across USAmerica are already forming "Natural Guards" to protect the trees, ponds, and animals of their neighborhoods. National groups already in place include CAPE (Children's Alliance for Protection of the Environment), Kids FACE (Kids For A Clean Environment), Kids STOP (Kids Save Our Planet), KSE (Kids for Saving the Earth). A grass-roots children's environmental group in Wisconsin recently bought five acres of rainforest in Costa Rica with proceeds from a walk-a-thon.[21]

The fight between the tree cutters and the tree huggers that is tearing so much of booster culture to shreds has already been decided by the busters and their children, for whom issues of the environment (along with children's rights) rank highest in the S.O.S. scale. Booster George Bush's "clean" campaign attacks on boomer Al Gore for being a "prairie fairy" and a "fern-feeler" demonstrate just how out of touch one generation can become with what follows it. Indeed, the booster generation, who has destroyed more wildlife in the past forty years than in the previous four million years combined, would be horrified if they knew how their hazy equivocations caused the upcoming buster and Benetton generations not just to "see green," but to give in to "ecotage" fantasies—even to give a green light to environmental terrorism, a phenomenon with which the boomers, awash in an environmental mess of theirs and the boosters' making, will need to contend.

If the only eagle many of the booster generation want to protect is on the back of a dollar bill, the buster generation is willing to sacrifice lots of the latter for a few of the former. The boomers and the busters are united in their demand for products that are "eco-packaged" and good for the environment. The younger members of the buster generation are literally demanding environmental studies programs at colleges and universities until about one in ten are offering environmental science as a major.[22] The Christian futurist Tom Sine shows how "we are already witnessing the emergence of a whole new generation of environmental activists that range from aerial crusaders to environmental martyrs."[23]

The slowness of "traditional religion" to come to terms with an Earth ethic has meant that, for some like novelist, rancher, and fly-fisherman Thomas McGuane, the conservation movement has replaced denominational religion as a religious force in life (witness *Nothing But Blue Skies* [1992]). It is not merely for the more revolutionary "greens" like Jesse Hardkin, also known as "Live Wolf," for whom deep ecology is the liberation theology for "a unified planet-body." Similar impulses range through the more moderate "greens" represented by realist ecologists like Bill McKibben and Wes Jackson.

It is time the church led the world into "geo-justice" and a "planetary Pentecost," in James Conlon's unforgettable phrasings.[24] The problem is a pervasive sense that nothing can be done. Or in the words of Donella Meadows, one of the co-authors of the original *Limits to Growth* (1972) in her introductory remarks to its sequel *Beyond the Limits* (1992): "I don't know which is going to be harder to do twenty years after *Limits to Growth*. To convince people that economic and ecological collapse is possible, even probable within twenty or thirty years. Or that a sustainable future is possible, even probable within twenty or thirty years if we don't stop trying to solve our problems by that which has caused our problems—growth. The former was harder twenty years ago. The latter, I suspect, will be harder today."[25]

According to sociologists Virginia Hodgkinson, M. S. Weitzman and A. D. Kirsch, churches and synagogues are least likely to be involved in environmental issues.[26] The ethic of trusteeship that moral traditions in USAmerica have pioneered must extend to and embrace the environment. Every time we open our wallets we vote for or against the environment. Every time we drink a cup of coffee during "Fellowship Hour" we cast a ballot for or against the future. How many of our churches continue to "throw away" rather than recycle, drink out of styrofoam rather than ceramic and glass mugs? McDonald's should really not be ahead of the church in its environmental sensitivity.

In fact, churches should be leading the way in showing people how to keep the First Commandment—tend the garden; attend the Gardener (i.e., conserve and co-create)—by starting with its own garden and tending that. What wonderful things would happen if the church became a green thumb in the world, or what Redwood National Park Ranger Linda Mealue calls a "day-glo, neon-green thumb." In a world that specializes in violence, there is a desperate need for communities who will raise violets.

What an impact the church might have if pastors saw themselves as priests, not only of humans, but as priests of all creation with a prime pastoral responsibility to all earthlings. Mark 16:5 instructs us to preach the gospel to the whole creation. The church must lift up a multiple-species vision of nature and wilderness that does not exclude humans. What can churches do? Partner with the International Network for Religion and Animals in celebration of the interfaith "World Week of Prayer for Animals" the first full week in October. During this week Christian, Hindu, Buddhist, Jewish, Muslim, Native American, and other religious traditions pray not only for those animals that share hearth and heart with us, but also those "endangered" species and "abused" animals that are threatened daily by our disregard. This would be a good week to study emerging statements on animals such as "A Pronouncement on Christian Responsibility Toward Animal Creation: A Declaration of Independence" (UCC), or gather signatures for "The Glauberg Confession," a postmodern Barmen Declaration issued by Protestant and Catholic Christians in Europe.

> We confess before God, the Creator of the Animals,
>   and before each other:
> We have failed as Christians,
>   because we forgot the animals in our faith.
> As theologians we were not prepared to stand up
>   against scientific and philosophical trends
>   inimical to life with the Theology of Creation.
> We have betrayed the diaconal mission of Jesus,
>   and not served our least brethren,
>   the animals.
> As pastors we were scared to give
>   room to animals
>   in our churches and parishes.
> As the Church, we were deaf to the "groaning in travail" of our mistreated and
>   exploited fellow-creatures.[27]

What can churches do? Why not celebrate January 17 with a "The Blessing of the Animals" service. This is the feast day of St. Antony the Abbot, patron saint of animals. An ancient ceremony still practiced in Mexico and parts of Texas has families on this day bringing their pets and family creatures to the priest to be blessed. The animals' collars and cages are usually decorated with pieces of folk art, which are now highly sought-after museum prizes.[28]

What can churches do? Why not celebrate "The World's Oldest Profession

Day" on September 1, the feast day of St. Fiacre de Breuil—the seventh century patron saint of gardeners. Lift up those in the church who are members of that most ancient of human occupations, and arrange for special visits to their gardens. Offer "Adam and Eve" awards (bonsai trees? handcarved wooden apples? metal sculptured fig leaves?) to those who have done the most to make the church into a garden. Get people to see themselves as "gardeners" regardless of what they are doing or working with—right now I'm gardening words with my word processor, thereby fulfilling the "First Commandment." Gardeners work with notes, stones, wood, paper, paint, dreams, and visions as well as plants. Do everything imaginable to give professional "gardeners" the same professional standing as doctors, lawyers, teachers, and preachers. Why not a "Minister of Planet Earth" (i.e., gardener) on the church masthead who helps the community learn how to plant a tree, how to grow one's own food, how to compost, and so on? Why not put in the budget support for S.A.F.E. (Sustainable Agriculture, Food, and Environment) and other such groups that pay attention to the top six inches of soil upon which all life depends? Why not donate to local businesses chrysanthemums, spider plants, and philodendrons for offices, since according to NASA these plants clean office air better than machines, their pores virtual vacuum cleaners for fumes from cigarettes, paints, and other toxic sources.

> MUCH OF THE ENVIRONMENTAL DEGRADATION WITNESSED TODAY IS DUE . . . TO TWO GROUPS—THE TOP BILLION RICHEST AND THE BOTTOM BILLION POOREST."
>
> EARTH ISLAND JOURNAL

What can churches do? The church itself could "live more lightly" on the earth. It could conserve energy resources by cutting back on conferences and travel costs—try teleconferencing instead. High-cost, low-return denominational assemblies and task forces no longer make effective change-agents anyway. It could model in its architecture, as First United Church of Christ in Jupiter, Florida, has done, a style that gives a feel of being indoors and outdoors at the same time.

What can churches do? Besides being comprised of the "consumer class" of the world's population (this one-fifth of the world's population is destroying the planet),[29] the church is a big property owner. Instead of planting flowers that look pretty and require gallons upon gallons of "cides" and water and manicuring, why not have churches become urban and suburban wildlife corridors and habitats for birds and wildlife, allowing animals free movement through urban and suburban areas and providing citizens with nature trails.

Why can't churches become urban wildlife sanctuaries, even wildlife corridors, planting native perennials, shrubs and trees, grasses that provide food, cover, water and living space for fauna.

What can churches do? The church could be known for its flower, food, and bird gardens. Instead of those boring taxus bushes, why not plant some "butterfly bushes," or species that provide food for caterpillars and provide nectar for adult butterflies? Instead of more flagpoles, why not erect nesting structures and bird feeders? Instead of fountains for pennies and coins, why not construct small ponds that might attract and sustain wildlife? Why not have tree nurseries or forests on church grounds rather than mowed lawns? Willard Sherman is a seventy-nine-year-old retired machinist who decided in 1987 to get the kids of his church in Marietta, Georgia, to put in a garden. In the beginning Sherman could interest only thirty boys and girls. In 1992, over one hundred kids received with Sherman a 1992 National Gardening Grant.

What can churches do? Become ecological evangelists. Ansel Adams, whom some say is the greatest photographer who ever lived, made as a part of his life a resolution. He resolved to do one good deed a day for the environment. He would write a letter, he would read an article, he would pick up litter, he would make a phone call, he would talk to somebody about recycling, and so on. But everyday he would do at least one good deed for the planet Earth.

What can churches do? Green the Christian consciousness by bringing back handkerchiefs to replace paper tissues ("What right do we have to wipe our noses on the lungs of the Earth?" asks scientist Helen Caldicott[30]). Sponsor "Hanky Panky" flea markets where vintage handkerchiefs can be rescued and restored, or "Hanky Panky" worship where people can wave old or new cloth (clean) handkerchiefs like a flag.[31] Instead of yelling to our children "Go to your room!" where their lives are constricted and cramped, perhaps it is time the church helped create communities where parents could feel safe in yelling "Go outside!"

What can churches do? Create pantheistic rituals that celebrate the gift of living together on this "morally deep world."[32] In his workshops Matthew Fox suggests a Lenten meditation that demonstrates the tragedy of rain forest destruction, a "cosmic mass" that helps worshipers appreciate the wonder of God's creation of the human body (Fox himself does this by projecting color slides in a darkened room that resemble extraterrestrial landscapes but that actually are microscopic photographs of tissue from twenty-six human organs), and a ceremony where Christians will commit themselves to asceticism (if not total abstinence) in the consumption of red meat.

The disturbing schism between minorities and environmentalism is beginning to be bridged by the churches, as the First National People of Color Environmental Leadership Summit (1991) made clear. The poor and disenfranchised rightly fear that there is a shortage of love out there, and that love for the environment means less love for them. It is up to the church to demonstrate the magic, mystery, and miracle of love: the more love is given away, the more love there is to go around.

Norris McDonald is one of a growing number of African American leaders who are active in the environmental movement. The current president of the Center for the Environment, Commerce and Energy (CECE), McDonald argues that the degradation of the environment affects minority communities more than any other community. Where are the toxic waste dumps located? What part of communities get the industrial polluters as neighbors? Which people inhale the bulk of our lethal breathings?[33] Benjamin F. Chavis, Jr., the new head of the NAACP, spearheaded a pioneering document "Toxic Waste and Race in the United States" (1987), which exposes the disproportionate share of air, land, and water pollution borne by people of color.[34]

When you live in a shopping mall culture, where everything bears a human imprint, whom do you worship?

ESSAYIST BILL MCKIBBEN

But the church also must monitor the causes that stand behind the inverse relationship between social scale and environmental concerns. Of course the rich are "interested in keeping the planet nice," British columnist and novelist Julie Burchill writes in her warning of "Greenism"; "they hold the property rights."[35] As we think and act less humanocentric or anthropocentric and more earthcentric, the church must not leave the trinity of race, class, and gender issues behind. Only then can be healed the long-ruptured links between humans and one another, flora, fauna, the Earth, and the divine. And we must prepare for an antienvironmental backlash, already present in earnest form through the "Wise-Use" and "Sahara Club" movements. The church must help to educate those who are creating the backlash.

2. Education That Grows Down, Not Simply Grows Up

Several months before the *Challenger* launch on January 28, 1986, President Reagan commented on the significance of the selection of high school teacher Christa McAuliffe as the "first civilian astronaut."

> When that shuttle lifts off—all America will be reminded of the crucial role teachers and education play in the life of our nation. I can't think of a better lesson for our children, and our country.[36]

Unfortunately, the lesson USAmerica learned about "public education" (or perhaps better called state-run education) from that tragically self-destructing shuttle was not exactly the one President Reagan had in mind. The charred remains from the blown-up *Challenger* reflected the reality of this nation's loss of public faith in its educational institutions more than a peaceful projectile launched into the "wild, blue yonder." Education is the most "vexing problem of social policy in the United States."[37]

So-called public education provides us with the kind of statistics and stories that could convince a suicide that they were in their right mind. It is almost too easy to tick off the mess we've made of things in our educational systems. Statistics provide a truly infernal picture of the state of affairs in our public schools. According to the federal government's Center for Disease Control (CDC), one out of five high school students in America admits to carrying a gun, knife, or other weapon with the intention of using it if necessary. Among boys alone, the horrifying figure is one out of three. Not just in cities, but in towns of all sizes. And to cap off the nightmare, the CDC admits that these figures are an "underestimate."

Seventeen percent of America's teachers live with fear of physical attack. Twelve percent of America's high school teachers are threatened with violence every month. One government report concluded: "conflict, confrontation and carnage have replaced the 3 Rs in many of the nation's schools." A 1991 University of Alabama at Birmingham study showed that 43 percent of inner-city children age 7 to 19 say they have actually witnessed a homicide. Another sociologist at Hays State University studied a class of 26 high school students in a town within 150 miles of Hays, Kansas. In four years of high school, 14 of those 26 students had attempted suicide, one successfully, two ending up in a persistent vegetative state, and the other 11 survived. In 1991, there were 150,000 live births in USAmerica to kids aged 9 to 14 (this does not include abortions, miscarriages, etc.). Our sex-obsessed, drug-clogged, violence-riddled, suicide-driven, school-blazered children are the casualties of a consumerist "Toys R Us" culture. Toys R Us, literally.[38]

Conditions had deteriorated in a large, urban high school until the mayor called the principal into his office. "What is your biggest problem?" the mayor asked. "Dropouts," the principal said. "In the past month alone, we've had fourteen dropouts." "That's intolerable," replied the mayor. "We've got to find out what we're doing wrong, make the necessary changes, and get those kids back into the classrooms." "I'm afraid you don't understand," replied the principal. "The fourteen dropouts were teachers."

USAmerican education is in spiritual crisis. The solution is not to make the factory model of education more efficient (more homework, more school weeks, more pay for teachers, more standardized national curriculum), which has become a profitable growth industry in educational circles today (alas, "there is good money to be made out of bad schools"[39]). The solution is in breaking out of the bureaucratic, mass-production, factory mode and coming up with a human-scale, minischool, noncompetitive, choice-based, electronic model of education where the student is the subject and not the object of education.

This means education must get more freewheeling, freethinking, and freelance. It means educators must become more like sideline coaches and standby tutors than up-front "teachers." It means that interactive, in-context learning is the way forward. It means that education must face and outface what is being called "the biggest school system" of them all—television and the full panoply of electronic culture. It means that other sectors of society must work out partnership arrangements with schools.

It means most decidedly that the era of mass education and regimented learning is over. The era of transformation education has just begun, a holistic methodology of creative learning that attends to the moral, intellectual, and spiritual fronts of a diverse array of students without snipping those "trailing clouds of glory" (Wordsworth) which every student tugs to the educational task. Transformation education hence facilitates children in "growing down" into the depths of life's meaning, morals, and mystery, as well as "growing up" into the mastery of some career.

Why can't churches help prove that public schools themselves can change into more holistic directions[40] by adopting a class in the public school system like some businesses are doing? What is preventing denominations from partnering with Educational Alternatives, Inc. or Whittle Communications, both of whom are working on the front lines to reinvent an educational system (the former public, the latter private) fit for the postmodern era? Or when more and more families are opting for "home schooling," why not "church schooling"—micro-schools run by churches, even possibly using fiber optic technology and distance education?

Why couldn't a church group serve as para-parents, or work with the real parents, or actually take over some of the classroom work of teaching? Churches could supervise public school students in required community service teams (clean up neighborhood, build homes, care for the poor) as part of students' "field education." More radically, Alvin and Heidi Toffler wonder whether education doesn't need to become "holographically distributed through all the institutions of society, rather than allocated to schools alone."[41]

Why can't the churches adopt themselves, as well as help school systems put in place, service-learning models of education where there is a diversity of entry points, a diversity of commitment levels, and one gets to choose direct, nondirect, or indirect engagements?[42] Some examples of this action/reflection model of education, where faith is nurtured in motion, include (1) direct service within community agencies or programs (e.g., prison ministries, homeless shelters, Habitat for Humanity, and school community projects); (2) advocacy or social justice organizations (e.g., Amnesty International, Bread for the World, Pax Christi, Greenpeace); (3) immersion experiences both at home and transculturally (e.g., direct experiences of the poor and hurting).

Finally, why don't churches and synagogues collaborate with school systems to help in the "character formation" components so conspicuously and nihilistically absent in our schools? William K. Kilpatrick's *Why Johnny Can't Tell Right from Wrong* offers in depressing detail evidence of the wrong-headedness of values clarification and virtues impartiality. The graduates of our public schools enter the adult world as "moral illiterates," without the intellectual girders or spiritual moorings requisite for any "good society" regardless of religious persuasion.[43]

3. What's Right, What's Wrong

My economics instructor, explaining the ruling power of "value-free economic laws," used to say, "Don't mix economics with ethics." An ethics-free economics has brought us to the place where John Sharp, Comptroller of the State of Texas, can say about their state's proposed lottery: "Never mind the morality, just think about all of that money."[44] Or Donald J. Trump who, in his *second* autobiography, can subtitle the chapter on his divorce from Ivana "Undoing the Deal."[45] The title alone reveals how economic exchanges came to define every aspect of life; even personal relationships and social bonds are reduced to the "cash nexus." In a society of hyperconsumption, human values and relationships may themselves be shaped into a field of commodified images.

Postmoderns are feeling the need to spend more time in their conscience closet. A "new economics" is quickly taking the world (but not fast enough) away from the 1980s, the economic era when Ivan Boesky could claim that "greed is good." Coca-Cola is now running social-market advertising; Levi Strauss has adopted global sourcing policies that prevent their doing business in countries with oppressive regimes and human-rights violations.

> We learned anew some curious facts.
> First, everybody is an expert on ethics.
> Second, nobody knows what ethics really is.
> And finally, times change.
>
> JEFFERSON GRIGSBY

Service-learning models are being adopted almost faster by business communities than by religious or educational communities. This is partly because business managers already recognize that the big money to be made in future franchising revolves around a four letter-word: Care. The post-S&L-BCCI motto—"Who Cares, Wins"—finds expression in burgeoning new franchises in lawn care, pet care, elder care, home care, as well as in manuals for "squeaky clean" dealings like James J. Lynch's *Ethical Banking*.[46] AT&T now celebrates the almost mystical connections that tie us together in the global village. Diet Coke offers some spiritual principles of life as its fundamental "Facts of Life." The business world is returning to what financier J. P. Morgan once termed "glass pocket" dealings—everything done openly, above board, and with the highest of ethics.

In calling for a new moral authority to accompany the world's maturing global consciousness before selfish materialism rips it apart, former National Security Adviser Zbigniew Brzezinski admits that "The dogmatic certainties of the modern age must yield to the recognition of the inherent uncertainty of the human condition." But he also contends that "in a world of contingency, moral imperatives then become the central, and even the only, source of reassurance."[47]

This moralizing strain in postmodern culture is partly due to a loss of faith in its epistemological claims. "If we can't tell you what's true and what's false—the thought goes—we'll at least tell you what's right and what's wrong. What's wrong? Racism, colonialism, oppression, cultural imperialism, patriarchy, epistemic violence."[48] The moral earnestness of postmodernism is based on this awareness that without ethics, both environmental ethics and economic ethics, the free enterprise and free government movements sweeping

205

the globe will turn into nightmares. Moral passion and genuine tolerance are not mutually exclusive. Indeed, postmoderns are proclaiming their own moral convictions like never before at the same time they are acknowledging other points of view like never before.

Many people are calling for a new Bill of Rights, a commercial bill of rights that emphasizes not the rights of corporations, but the rights of the people who work within them and are served by them. Here are the first, third, and seventh rights as defined by one of the best of these bills of rights: "The right to create products and participate in processes that do not harm others. . . . The right to a job that is meaningful, worthy, and constructive. . . . The right not to exploit other people or other forms of life."[49]

But an ultimate ethic must be a religious ethic, not merely a humanist ethic. Six USAmerican adults in ten (61 percent) believe that religion can answer all or most of today's problems. Disagreeing are 17 percent who hold the opinion that religion is largely old-fashioned and out of date, and an additional 22 percent are uncertain about the ability of religion to address today's issues. Those who believe religion has the answers to life's problems increased from 56 percent in 1984 to 61 percent in 1989.[50] If the *humanum* is not grounded in the *divinum*, the *humanum* can be controlled more by market forces than by moral vision.

In the business world, business "soul" can be too quickly a matter of simply having the right style, or what Popcorn calls "hot-branding." In the 1990s hot-branding is "not about being marked by designer initials, but by a deeper 'branding': character, style, eccentricity." Or as she puts this earlier in her book, "Companies will have to realize that you don't sell only what you make. You sell who you are."[51] But what kind of person you should be is too easily molded by market-based powers and establishment principalities without a religious ethic.

The Mormons have perhaps realized this better than any other faith tradition. For Christian communities, however, it has not always been an identity issue. Who are we? Christ offers a new identity to people—both a new individual identity and a new communal identity as partners with God in the continuing of Creation. Is the church marked, or as Popcorn would put it "hot-branded," by the character and spirit of Christ?

There We Go

There is an old Chinese saying that there are five points to the compass. There is north, south, east, west, and where you are pointing. Where are you pointing? Where are we headed? Where is everyone going?

FaithQuakes is based on the premise that we are poised today at a terra nova juncture in the journey through time, that this is a new moment in American culture. In the words of the Dorie Ellzey hymn "We are Gathered":

> We're traveling on a road we've never seen before
> And oh, it's hard to know which way to go.

Admittedly, this Great Transition theme can get to be a little too much. The poet Wallace Stevens noticed how "it is one of the peculiarities of the imagination that it is always at the end of an era."[52] More to the point about "crossroads," Yogi Berra said more than once, "When you've arrived at a fork in the road, take it." Woody Allen in his already classic commencement address, "My Speech to the Graduates," declares:

> More than any other time in history, mankind faces a crossroads. One path leads to despair and utter hopelessness. The other, to total extinction. Let us pray we have the wisdom to choose correctly.[53]

The choice the church faces in its pilgrimage is not the hopelessness or extinction of Woody Allen-land (what planet is he living on, anyway?).

But the choice we face may not be what most others think it is either: whether to turn to the Right or to the Left.[54] A Tennessee bumper sticker asks "Which Way to Heaven?" It answers its own question in the form of a traffic sign, signaling a sharp turn to the right.

Partisans of the right are proud of the way the right symbolically prevails from the vantage of comparative ethnography in ceremonial customs and social etiquette; left-sidedness is associated with clumsiness, superstition, and unluckiness. In the Second Testament Jesus "will set the sheep on his right hand, but the goats on the left" (Matt. 25:33) and most renderings of the devil portray him as left-handed. Forces of evil are on the left in medieval Judaism, and even in Buddhism the "right" path leads to enlightenment while the "left" way to peril.

Partisans of the left are quick to counter by pointing out that the left is the side of the heart, while the right is the side of the liver and bile. God split the Adam on the left side. *The Left-Hander Syndrome*[55] is but the most recent in many studies designed to rehabilitate "lefties" from their reputations and associations.

The imaginative geography of "Left" and "Right," which has oriented almost all Western political and intellectual life since it started in Versailles in August 1789, no longer works. Indeed, the dividing up of political space into "Left" and "Right" as we know it today derives from the seating arrangements of the constituent assembly, when one voting bloc sat on the right of the President's desk, the other on his left.[56]

We don't sit down that way anymore.

The familiar idioms *liberal* and *conservative* derive from social distinctions that surfaced in the nineteenth century. We don't make sense of our world that way anymore. "Left" and "Right" are the seating distinctions of a sedentary, status quo political establishment. More than that, the polarization of left and right, as people are expected to "choose up sides" and "come down" on this side or that lest they remain "up in the air," embodies the larger breakdown of America's faith communities, perhaps even portending massive "culture wars."

The issues of the times do not track well with traditional right/left, conservative/liberal distinctions.[57] Postmoderns don't think that way anymore, either. If there is a bivalent confrontation in cultural matters, it may more properly be between what Robert Hughes calls the "two PCs—the politically correct and the patriotically correct," the former headquartered in our universities and academic centers, the latter in America's coffee shops, bars, boardrooms, and brokerage houses.[58]

Postmodern choices transcend the dividing factions and cliched faultlines between the liberal or conservative, left or right political belief-camps. In the words of historian Christopher Lasch, the ideologies of left and right "have exhausted their capacity either to explain events or to inspire men and women to constructive action."[59] People can't find a place for themselves in the traditional spectra of politics or ecclesiastics anymore, not so much because they are against such distinctions as they feel somehow above and beyond them. Left and right labels others pin to us (or us to the labels) are now caricatures that abuse the very things and people they pretend to represent. If ever the old adage "All labels are libels" were true, it is now.

FaithQuakes was born out of the belief that authentic theology emerges from the praxis of the front lines: a *theologia viatorum*, a theology-on-the-way. It is time to tell the church to move forward and become God's missionary people again. The motto of those ecological freedom fighters known as Greenpeace, the largest environmental organization in the world (over two million contributors in 1990), is this: "Neither left nor right, but in front." The choice today is whether faith communities are going to be on the front lines, out front in the "contact zones"[60] where the in-breaking Spirit is working with and missionizing this age, or whether they are safely in the rear, part of the rear guard, bringing up the rear in witness and ministry.

The two roads faith communities face at this crossroads of time may be the same as the Israelites faced when Moses was leading them into the Land of Canaan. The people were groaning and grumbling, stewing and brewing over the challenges they were being asked to confront, hankering after the good old days of Egyptian flesh pots.

"Did you have to bring us out here in the desert to die? . . . Didn't we tell you before we left that this would happen? We told you to leave us alone and let us go on being slaves in Egypt" (Exod. 14:11-12 GNB). They even formed a "Back-to-Egypt Committee" that every priest or pastor knows about. Moses himself became an ex-officio member of this committee, as he began wishing for the good old days, wondering whether they could really do what God was calling them to do. All the odds were against them.

But Yahweh said to Moses: "Tell the people to move forward. Lift up your walking stick and hold it out over the sea. The water will divide and the Israelites will be able to walk through the sea on dry ground" (Exod. 14:15b-16 GNB). In the Exodus imagery, the Israelites had the choice of whether to *refuse* the experience of moving forward and turn around or to *embrace* the experience of the unknown future and move forward. The choice was not a "bounded set" of belief, but a "directional set" of mission.

It would be difficult to find a more adventurous analysis than the relationship between the "mission of the church" and media change. Missiologists David Bosch, Lesslie Newbigin, and Charles Van Engen have spoken eloquently about the theological imprecision of talking about the church having a "mission." The church does not have a mission, they argue. It is God who has a mission, and the missionary of God is the Holy Spirit. The question is whether the mission of God has a church, and whether the missionary activity of the Holy Spirit has an ecclesiastical partner and place with which to bring God's work to fulfillment.[61]

Out front, a missionary people can follow the *Heilige Geist* (Holy Spirit) and shape the spirit of the age by putting the gospel and their bodies on the line. As part of the rear guard, an establishment people can only or mainly be shaped by the *Zeitgeist* (spirit of the times), or be the product of an unhealthy *Zeitgeist*. The Civil War General Nathan Bedford Forrest put it most memorably: "If the enemy is in our rear, then we're in his." The church has been at the wrong end of things for too much of its history. Indeed, movement people and missionary churches need not worry about the rear, or their butt being kicked soundly, for "the glory of the LORD shall be your rear guard" (Isa. 58:8).

Actually, the choice the Hebrews faced was more pointed than what theologian Ray S. Anderson insightfully calls a "mission theology" versus a "church theology."[62] Their real choice was either life or death. They couldn't go back. They had to pass through the Red Sea, which Carl Jung sees as "the healing and transforming baptismal water." They either had to find ways forward together, or die. "The Red Sea is a water of death for those that are 'unconscious' but for those that are 'conscious' it is a baptismal water of rebirth and transcendence."[63] There is no way around the waves and the waters. There is no escape from the future. Which faith communities will be submerged and drown? Which will cross the waters on dry ground and enter the new land?

We now can reach Mt. Everest by phone. The road less traveled by the church is the road people are on, the mediated-road into the future where the world is traveling. Is it the church's role to take the road less taken, to stray down the many interesting side streets and back alleys of postmodernity? Or is the church to travel the road (the electronic highway or soon-to-be 500-channel "vidway") people are on?

The reasons for this historic decision not to take the road out front which the people are actually on may be as complex as some of the arguments in this book or as simple as this: It is safer to choose death than life. Bob Dylan has a line in one of his songs, "He not busy being born is busy dying." Living means constantly to be enduring labor pangs, dark channels, sudden propulsions. Living is a very dangerous trajectory.

Dying, on the other hand, is a very safe thing to do. The Greek word for "experience" means "pass through." Experience, anthropologist Victor Turner argues, conveys simultaneously and cumulatively the notions of a journey, a test, a ritual passage, an exposure to peril or risk, and a source of fear.[64] No wonder the masses of people born have simply memorized their lines, huddled together with others of like mind, and gone quietly to their deaths. No wonder the prevalence of the middle-of-the-road mindlessness that does in ministry only what was done yesterday. No wonder the way of the dodos, the ditherers, and the defunct. When we approach the reality depicted by the Mexican novelist Juan Rulfo, whose *Pedro Páramo* (1953) portrays a world where the living cannot tell who among them is alive and who is already dead, then we are living a nightmare.

At this crossroads Christians can choose to bear witness to the truth in another time, the era of modernity, at best giving breathless accounts of ideas no longer fresh. Or Christians can bear witness to the truth in this time, the "postmodern era." Theologian and ethicist Don Shriver has suggested that a key to the difference between the mentalities of the modern versus "the postmodern era" is in the difference between, "Here I stand; I can do no other" and "This way we walk." We cannot go back.[65] The difference between the two is the difference between the reformational model of modern, propositional theology and a missional model of postmodern, informational theology.

In the modern era, three talismanic words of Martin Luther helped inaugurate and in some ways shape modernity: Here I stand. Similar words may also be seen to have ended modernity five hundred years later, with Rosa Parks' refusal to go to the back of the bus: Here I stay. Each one of these words captured an essence of the modern spirit. The shibboleth of the modern consciousness was based on representation: Take a Stand. The shibboleth of the postmodern consciousness is based on participation: There We Go, or better yet, Take a Hike!

Each one of these three words—*There, We, Go*—does not so much return us to a period before the Reformation/Enlightenment as to build upon their contributions to our understanding of truth and move us beyond them. There can be no sneaking back to a pre-Enlightenment innocence, no shelving of the Enlightenment heritage. There can be, however, an evading of the Enlightenment's slip-ups while taking up its challenges.

It is time for faith and ministry to get mobile. In a postmodern sense, truth is not the stand you take. Truth is the path you tread. Truth is not a standpoint. Truth is a walkway. The postmodern church doesn't need leaders today who will simply take a stand. It needs leaders today who will take a hike.

Taking a stand in the postmodern era is not a static, stationary thing. It is not position-taking but post-taking—taking a post alongside those in need; taking a walk with someone is a form of taking a stand for them. Faith as a walking is how some old slave preachers and some new theologians put it.

If the modern era was into the present, the postmodern era is into the future. The question becomes how we face the future as a community? One occupies the there of tomorrow by not leaving behind the then of yesterday, an AncientFuture sensibility.

The truly new is not antagonistic to the old; it simply reconceptualizes and recontextualizes it. For example, Einstein didn't eliminate classical Newtonian physics—he just gave the world a new perspective to look at it. Quantum physics recontextualized Einstein, and superstring theory, complexity theory, and twister physics are doing the same for quantum. The postmodern mythic revival, spurred by Joseph Campbell's celebration of the power of myths to carry the human spirit forward, is a graphic example of postmodernism's old-new way of being in the world. In the words of Wallace Stevens, postmoderns seek a new account of everything old.[66]

Does the church want to move into the postmodern world? Much of the church doesn't want to budge. In fact, there are those who contend the church has become primarily a party of resistance. Isn't *resistance* after all part of its mission statement? While "in" the world, the church is to resist being "of" the world. But what is the church resisting? Is its resistance primarily to the powers and principalities of the world? Or is its resistance to the future?

It can be argued that in large measure the church today has not decided to live its own story, to connect the gospel story to the people's own postmodern story. Or put historically, has the church inhabited the postmodern era by incarnating the faith into the language of postmodern public life without enculturating the gospel? Or put theologically, has the postmodern church decided to receive as a gift the moment in which God has chosen it to live?

The modern era put its cards on the table (Here I Stand). The postmodern era lays its body on the line (There We Go).

It's time to go.

N O T E S

INTRODUCTION: MINDQUAKES

1. *What Do We Mean When We Say God?* ed. Deidre Sullivan (New York: Doubleday, 1991), 12.
2. O. B. Hardison, *Disappearing Through the Skylight: Culture and Technology in the Twentieth Century* (New York: Viking, 1989).
3. See Robert A. Markus, *The End of Ancient Christianity* (Cambridge: Cambridge University Press, 1991).
4. Roger Scruton, "In Inverted Commas," *TLS: Times Literary Supplement* 18 (December 1992), 4.
5. Quoted in Russell Chandler, *Racing Toward 2001: The Forces Shaping America's Religious Future* (San Francisco: HarperSanFrancisco, 1992), 216.
6. Gordon C. Goodgame, "Applied Theology: Radical Righteousness and Quality Discipleship," Bishop Nolan B. Harmon Lecture in Practical Theology, unpublished paper given at Candler School of Theology, 18 March 1992, 1.
7. As quoted in "While We're At It," *First Things*, January 1992, 62.
8. William R. O'Brien, "Southern Baptists' Changing Age," unpublished paper given at the Baptist Public Relations Association, San Francisco, April, 1991.
9. Quoted in Hannah Josephson, *Jeannette Rankin: First Lady in Congress* (Indianapolis: Bobbs-Merrill, 1974), 135.
10. Martin E. Marty explores this theme of "altered landscapes" in his "Introduction: Religion in America 1935-1985," *Altered Landscapes,* ed. John F. Wilson and David Lotz (Grand Rapids, Mich.: Eerdmans, 1989), 1-16.
11. Peter F. Drucker, *Management: Tasks, Responsibilities, Practices* (New York: Harper and Row, 1974), 128.
12. As told by Herb Miller in his foreword to R. Robert Cueni, *The Vital Church Leader* (Nashville: Abingdon Press, 1990), 13.
13. As examples from the world of literary criticism, see Frank Kermode's *The Sense of an Ending* (New York: Oxford University Press, 1967) followed by Edward Said's *Beginnings: Intention and Method* (New York: Basic Books, 1975).
14. Marshall Blonsky, ed. *On Signs* (Baltimore: Johns Hopkins University Press, 1985).
15. The phrase is that of Frederic and Mary Ann Brussat. See their editorial introduction to "The Spiritual Elders" issue of *Values & Visions* 23, no. 5-6 (1992): 3.
16. See Elizabeth Achtemeier, *Preaching from the Old Testament* (Louisville: Westminster/John Knox Press, 1989), 109-35; Achtemeier, *Jeremiah* (Atlanta: John Knox Press, 1987); Achtemeier, *Nahum-Malachi* (Atlanta: John Knox Press, 1986; Achtemeier, *The Community and Message of Isaiah 56–66: A Theological Commentary* (Minneapolis: Augsburg Publishing House, 1982), esp. 9-11.
17. I first ran across this phrase "with-it-ry" in the writings of Joseph Epstein, editor of *The American Scholar*. The analogy of the weathervane on the back porch emerged from a table-talk conversation on "reading the signs of the times" sponsored by the Lilly Endowment, Inc.

18. Faith Popcorn, *The Popcorn Report: Faith Popcorn on the Future of Your Company, Your World, Your Life* (New York: Doubleday, 1991).
19. *Popcorn Report*, 21.
20. Neil Howe and William Strauss, "The New Generation Gap," *Atlantic*, December 1992, 68.
21. This has been effectively broached by George Barna, *Marketing the Church* (Colorado Springs: NavPress, 1988), 64-65.
22. Popcorn's seventh and eighth "socioquakes," "Staying Alive" and "The Vigilante Consumer" respectively (*Popcorn Report*, 62-77) I am exploring separately in subsequent studies.
23. This is a phrase coined by financier/philanthropist/Princeton Seminary trustee Sir John M. Templeton and chemist Robert L. Herrmann in their *The God Who Would Be Known: Revelations of the Divine in Contemporary Science* (San Francisco: Harper & Row, 1989).
24. Father Mackonochie is quoted in *Speeches, Sermons, Pictures, and Official Documents from The Episcopal Synod of America Founded at Fort Worth, Texas, June 3, 1989*, ed. A. Donald Davies (Harrisburg, Penn.: Morehouse Publishing, 1990), 92.

1. HomeQuakes

1. Faith Popcorn, *The Popcorn Report: Faith Popcorn on the Future of Your Company, Your World, Your Life* (New York: Doubleday, 1991), 27.
2. Ibid., 4.
3. Ibid.
4. Ibid., 29.
5. The best story of how one can spend a lifetime amassing a fortune, only to end one's life consuming a fortune to "protect" that fortune is Tom Sine's account of the Massachusetts couple Mr. and Mrs Rose, as found in *Why Settle for More and Miss the Best?* (Waco, Tex.: Word Books, 1987), 3.
6. Thanks to John M. Buchanan of Fourth Presbyterian Church, Chicago, for alerting me to journalist Bob Greene's editorial pointing this out.
7. *Crime in the U.S.* (1992): 187.
8. See Vicki Robin and Joe Dominguez, *Your Money Or Your Life* (New York: Viking, 1992).
9. John Urry, *The Tourist Gaze: Leisure and Travel in Contemporary Societies* (London: SAGE Publications, 1990).
10. Anne-Marie Willis, "Will Your Fingers Do the Shopping?" *World Monitor* 6 (May 1993): 60-62. "The best-case scenario goes beyond stimulating a desire for individual gratification to encouraging a desire for ecological well-being. Thus the shopping of the future will be delivered by shopping for the future" (62).
11. "Nike Town" attracts 5,000 to 6,000 daily visitors on weekends, compared with an average 3,600 people who visit their neighbor on Michigan Avenue, the Art Institute of Chicago. See the *Wall Street Journal*, 11 March 1993, B1.
12. As quoted in John Huey, "New Frontiers in Commuting," *Fortune*, 13 January 1992, 58.

13. Kurt Vonnegut, *Fates Worse Than Death: An Autobiographical Collage of the 1980s* (New York: G. P. Putnam's Sons, 1991), 33.
14. *The Popcorn Report*, 32.
15. "The Living Room Kitchen," *Metropolitan Home* 24 (May 1992): 84-90.
16. *The Popcorn Report*, 32.
17. Merrill Markoe, "The Dating Game," *Time*, Special Issue, Fall 1992, 53.
18. Eudora Welty, *One Writer's Beginnings* (Cambridge, Mass.: Harvard University Press, 1984), 31.
19. See George G. Hunter III, *How to Reach Secular People* (Nashville: Abingdon Press, 1992), 23.
20. Neil Howe and William Strauss, "The New Generation Gap," *Atlantic Monthly*, December 1992, 74.
21. I owe this word to William O'Brien, Director of The Global Center at Samford University.
22. In the 1940s when her first collection of fiction and poetry appeared, the book jackets carried blurbs by Nelson Algren, Sinclair Lewis, Carl Sandburg, and others.
23. Lesslie Newbigin, *Mission in Christ's Way* (Geneva: WCC Publications, 1987), 21.
24. Richard C. Carlson, *2020 Visions: Long View of a Changing World* (Stanford, Calif.: Stanford Alumni Association, 1990), 193.
25. When Massachusetts Mutual Insurance Company asked respondents to choose their definition of a family from a list, 75 percent chose "a group who love and care for each other." See Arthur Kornhaber, "A Nation of Families," *Vital Connections: The Grandparenting Newsletter* 7 (Summer 1991): 4.
26. In inner cities, the figure runs at 80 percent and above. See Andrew Hacker's *Two Nations: Black and White, Separate, Hostile, Unequal* (New York: Macmillan, 1991), 67.
27. Gerald, Schlabach, *And Who Is My Neighbor: Poverty, Privilege, and the Gospel of Christ* (Scottdale, Pa.: Herald Press, 1990), 123-25.
28. Colin Morris, *Wrestling With an Angel: Reflections on Christian Communication* (London: Collins, 1990), 181.
29. Benton Johnson, Dean R. Hoge and Donald A. Luidens, "Mainline Churches: The Real Reason for Decline," *First Things*, March 1993, 13-18, esp. 17.
30. See also Susan Sherwin's insistence that organized religions are "repressive to women" in *No Longer Patient: Feminist Ethics and Health Care* (Philadelphia: Temple University Press, 1992), 17.
31. As quoted in *New Republic*, 5 July 1993, 5.
32. See Gore Vidal, *Live From Golgotha* (New York: Random House, 1992). For Lubow quotes, see Arthur Lubow, "Gore's Lore," *Vanity Fair*, September 1992, 126, 132.
33. Camille Paglia, *Sex, Art, and American Culture* (New York: Vintage Books, 1992), 31.
34. Thomas Moore, *Care of the Soul: A Guide for Cultivating Depth and Sacredness in Everyday Life* (New York: HarperCollins, 1992), 66-67.
35. Christopher Hitchens, "Minority Report," *Nation*, 13 April 1992, 474, and Hitchens, *For the Sake of Argument: Essays and Minority Reports* (New York: Verso, 1993).
36. John E. Mack, "Blowing the Western Mind—An Essay," *ReVision* 14 (Fall 1991): 108-10.

37. The best narrative of the process of "deconversion" from Christianity is found in Philip Yancey's story of "Richard" in *Disappointment with God: Three Questions No One Asks Aloud* (Grand Rapids, Mich.: Zondervan, 1988), 27-33.
38. See Victor Shklovsky's famous 1917 article "Art as Technique," as reprinted in *Russian Formalist Criticism*, trans. and with an intro. by Lee T. Lemon and Marion J. Rice (Lincoln: University of Nebraska Press, 1965), 3-57.
39. See Father Leo Booth's *When God Becomes a Drug: Breaking the Chains of Religious Addiction and Abuse* (Los Angeles: J. P. Tarcher, 1991).
40. Paul Ricoeur, *Freud and Philosophy: An Essay on Interpretation* (New Haven: Yale University Press, 1970), 26-32.
41. *Mythemes* is a term used by Bernard Brandon Scott, *Hear Then the Parable: A Commentary on the Parables of Jesus* (Minneapolis: Fortress Press, 1989), 37-38.

2. ExperienceQuakes

1. Faith Popcorn, *The Popcorn Report: Faith Popcorn on the Future of Your Company, Your World, Your Life* (New York: Doubleday, 1991), 34.
2. See Ken Jowitt, *New World Disorder: The Leninist Extinction* (Berkeley: University of California Press, 1992), esp. 248-331.
3. See John Urry, *The Tourist Gaze: Leisure and Travel in Contemporary Societies* (London: Sage Publications, 1990), 5.
4. Figures are from World Travel and Tourism Council, as reported in "Tourism Fuels Jobs," *USA Today*, 14 April 1992, 1B.
5. David Lodge, *Paradise News: A Novel* (New York: Viking, 1992).
6. See Sally Banes, "Will the Real . . . Please Stand Up: An Introduction to the Issue," Drama Review 34 (1990): 21, and Jean Baudrillard, *Simulations* (New York: Semiotext, 1983).
7. Gilbert Adair, *The Postmodernist Always Rings Twice: Reflections on Culture in the 90s* (London: Fourth Estate, 1992), 190, 192.
8. Christian Smith, *Going to the Root: Nine Proposals for Radical Church Renewal* (Scottdale, Penn.: Herald Press, 1992), 125.
9. Judith A. Adams, *The American Amusement Park Industry: A History of Technology and Thrills* (Boston: Twayne, 1991), 98-99.
10. See Eugene Sloan, "Today's Museums Make Stuffy Exhibits History," *USA Today*, 10 December 1992, 7D.
11. Mary Midgley, *Wisdom, Information, and Wonder: What Is Knowledge For* (New York: Routledge, 1989), 20.
12. Quoted in Brennan Manning, *The Ragamuffin Gospel: Good News for the Bedraggled, Beat-Up and Burnt Out* (Portland, Ore.: Multnomah Press, 1990), 149.
13. Umberto Eco, *Travels in Hyper-Reality* (San Diego: Harcourt Brace Jovanovich, 1986).
14. See, for example, *The United Methodist Book of Worship* (Nashville: United Methodist Publishing House, 1992), 425.
15. *Reminisce's* address is 5927 Memory Lane, P.O. Box 3088, Milwaukee, Wisconsin, 53201.

16. Quoted by Bart Schneider, "Facing Fear: An Interview with Cecil Williams," *Hungry Mind Review*, Fall 1992, 23.

17. Cecil Williams with Rebecca Laird, *No Hiding Place: Empowerment and Recovery for Our Troubled Communities* (San Francisco: HarperSanFrancisco, 1992).

18. Andrew Sung Park, "Theo-Orthopraxis," *Journal of Theology* 97 (1993): 59-72; see also Park, *The Wounded Heart of God: The Asian Concept of Han and the Christian Doctrine of Sin* (Nashville: Abingdon Press, 1993).

19. See Daniel C. Dennett's marvelous *Consciousness Explained* (Boston: Little, Brown, 1991).

20. See Leonard I. Sweet, *Quantum Spirituality: A Postmodern Apologetic* (Dayton: Whaleprints, 1991), 84-91.

21. Quoted by Nena Bryans, *Full Circle: A Proposal to the Church for an Arts Ministry* (San Carlos, Calif.: Schuyler Institute for Worship and the Arts, 1988), 15.

22. Charles L. Rice, *The Embodied Word: Preaching as Art and Liturgy* (Minneapolis: Fortress Press, 1990), 86-87.

23. You can find this sermon published as "The World's Saving Gesture: The Line and the Circle," in *Homiletics* 5 (April-June 1993): 27-30.

24. James Gaughan, "How Ecumenical Are We," *Christian Century*, 23 January 1985, 78, expanding on James F. White, *Sacraments as God's Self-Giving* (Nashville: Abingdon Press, 1983): "No mournful dirge this; the eucharist was a joyful feast for the early church, unlike the penitential rite it all too frequently has been since the late Middle Ages" (54).

25. See Margaret Miles, *Augustine on the Body* (Missoula, Mont.: Scholars Press, 1979); Miles, *Practicing Christianity: Critical Perspectives for an Embodied Spirituality* (New York: Crossroad, 1988); Miles, *Carnal Knowing: Female Nakedness and Religious Meaning in the Christian West* (Boston: Beacon Press, 1989).

26. As told in Diane Bailey, "The Illustrated Sendak," *US Air Magazine*, February 1992, 39.

27. See for example Marilyn Sewell, ed., *Cries of the Spirit: A Celebration of Women's Spirituality* (Boston: Beacon Press, 1991).

28. Michael Heim, "The Metaphysics of Virtual Reality," in *Virtual Reality: Theory, Practice, and Promise*, ed. Sandra K. Helsel and Judith Paris Roth (Westport, Conn.: Meckler, 1992), 27.

29. "The Ultimate Interface," *Informationweek*, 25 June 1990, 46-48.

30. Meredith Bricken's quote is from Brenda Laurel, "Virtual Reality Design: A Personal View," in *Virtual Reality*, ed. Helsel and Roth, 95. Michael B. Spring defines *virtual reality* as "a fact or real event that is such in essence, but not in fact" in "Informating with Virtual Reality," in Ibid. 6. Ever since the *New York Times* plastered on its front page "What is Artificial Reality?" (10 April 1989), what is now called virtual reality has been a hot media topic. An up-to-date, state-of-the-art guide to the VR phenomenon is British writer Benjamin Woolley's *Virtual Worlds: A Journey in Hype and Hyperreality* (New York: Cambridge University Press, 1992).

31. Scott S. Fisher, "Virtual Environments: Personal Simulations & Telepresence," in *Virtual Reality*, ed. Helsel and Roth, 102.

217

32. This definition emerged from the First Conference on Cyberspace, 11 November 1989, at the University of Texas at Austin, as quoted in Joseph Henderson's "Designing Realities: Interactive, Media, Virtual Realities and Cyberspace," in *Virtual Reality*, ed. Helsel and Roth, 67.

33. Randal Walser, "Elements of a Cyberspace Playhouse," *Virtual Reality*, ed. Helsel and Roth, 51.

34. Timothy Ferris is already speculating about "the morality of sexual encounters between individuals thousands of miles apart, who may never meet, and who may, furthermore, elect to present themselves in the VR environment dressed in faces and bodies that do not resemble their own" in *The Mind's Sky: Human Intelligence in a Cosmic Context* (New York: Bantam Books, 1992), 51n.

35. For the forces behind this phenomenon, see Vary T. Coates, "The Future of Information Technology," *Annals of the American Academy of Political and Social Science* 522 (July 1992): 48.

36. See Woolley, *Virtual Worlds*.

37. See R. Gustav Niebuhr, "If U Cn Rd Ths U Cn Rd the Bible; If Not, C the Moo-v," *Wall Street Journal*, 2 March 1992, front page.

38. Roger Housden, *Soul and Sensuality: Returning the Erotic to Everyday Life* (London: Rider Books, 1993).

39. See Ann-Janine Morey, *Religion and Sexuality in American Literature* (New York: Cambridge University Press, 1992).

40. Louis Menand, "What Are Universities For?" *Harper's*, December 1991, 49.

41. Mervyn Laurence Peake, *Gormenghast* (London: Eyre and Spottiswoode, 1950).

42. Virginia Ramey Mollenkott, *Sensuous Spirituality: Out from Fundamentalism* (New York: Crossroad, 1992).

43. James Purdy, *Out With the Stars* (London: P. Owen, 1992). See also Gore Vidal, *Live from Golgotha* (New York: Random House, 1992).

44. Joanna Macy, *World as Lover, World as Self* (Berkeley, Calif.: Parallax Press, 1992), 8-9.

45. Jerome W. Berryman, *Godly Play: A Way of Religious Education* (San Francisco: HarperSan Francisco, 1991), 8.

46. Anthony de Mello, *Sadhana: A Way to God* (St. Louis: The Institute of Jesuit Sources, 1979), 59-62, quote on 59-60.

47. See the provocative study of the role of fairy tales in indoctrinating children into "official culture" and disciplining their sensibilities by Maria Tatar entitled *Off With Their Heads! Fairy Tales and the Culture of Childhood* (Princeton: Princeton University Press, 1992).

48. Madonna, *Truth or Dare* (Van Nuys, Calif.: LIVE Home Video, 1991).

49. Avery Brooke, *Hidden in Plain Sight: The Practice of Christian Meditation* (Nashville: Upper Room, 1986), 13.

50. Gregory Bateson and Mary Catherine Bateson, *Angels Fear: Towards an Epistemology of the Sacred* (New York: Macmillan, 1987), 197.

51. Nancey C. Murphy, "Does Prayer Make a Difference?" in *Cosmos as Creation: Theology and Science in Consonance*, ed. Ted Peters (Nashville: Abingdon Press, 1989), 244.

52. Kenneth A. Briggs, "America's Return to Prayer," *New York Times Magazine*, 18 November 1984, 108.
53. Thomas Ryan, *Fasting Rediscovered: A Guide to Health and Wholeness for Your Body-Spirit* (Ramsey, N.J.: Paulist Press, 1981).
54. Mark Rider, "Mental Shifts and Resonance: Necessities for Healing," *Revision* 14 (Winter 1992), 149-57.
55. "Prayer for Peace," *Peace Prayers: Meditations, Affirmations, Invocations, Poems, and Prayers for Peace* ed., Carrie Leadingham, Joanne E. Moschella, and Hilary M. Vartanian (San Francisco: HarperSanFrancisco, 1992), 127.
56. *The Sermons and Devotional Writings of Gerard Manley Hopkins*, ed. Christopher Devlin (New York: Oxford University Press, 1959), 200-1.
57. Doug Murren, *The Baby Boomerang: Catching the Baby Boomers as They Return to Church* (Ventura, Calif.: Regal Books, 1990), 188-212.
58. Jill Purce, "Re-enchanting our Lives," in *The Way Ahead: A Visionary Perspective for the New Millennium*, ed. Eddie and Debbie Shapiro (Rockport, Mass.: Element, 1992), 127.
59. Dietrich Bonhoeffer, *Life Together* (New York: Harper & Row, 1954), 61.
60. Purce, "Re-enchanting our Lives," 128.
61. See R. Gustav Niebuhr's "So It Isn't Rock of Ages, It Is Rock, and Many Love It," *New York Times*, 9 December 1991.
62. John Koenig, *Rediscovering New Testament Prayer: Boldness and Blessing in the Name of Jesus* (San Francisco: HarperSanFrancisco, 1992), 66-80.
63. See "To Archibald T. Davison, 22 September 1949," *Selected Letters of Virgil Thomson*, ed. Tim Page and Vanessa Weeks Page (New York: Summit, 1988), 238.
64. Leander E. Keck, "Caught in the Act: Praise and Renewal in the Church," *Christian Century*, 6 December 1992, 171.
65. Abraham Heschel, *Who is Man?* (Stanford, Calif.: Stanford University Press, 1965), 116.
66. Thomas W. Mann, *To Taste and See: Exploring Incarnation and the Ambiguities of Faith* (Cleveland, Ohio: Pilgrim Press, 1992), 113.
67. For further elaboration of themes struck in this section, see Sweet, *Quantum Spirituality*, 150-63.

3. MicroQuakes

1. For another good discussion of "IDI-ology," see Tom Sine, *Wild Hope* (Dallas, Tex.: Word Publishing, 1991), 160.
2. See Martin E. Marty's quote from *Chronicle of Higher Education* in *Context*, 5 January 1992, 2.
3. Faith Popcorn, *The Popcorn Report: Faith Popcorn on the Future of Your Company, Your World, Your Life* (New York: Doubleday, 1991), 40.
4. Brennan Manning, *The Ragamuffin Gospel: Good News for the Bedraggled, Beat-Up, and Burnt Out* (Portland, Ore.: Multnomah Press, 1990), 118.
5. Nathan O. Hatch, "The Perils of Being a Professional," *Christianity Today*, 11 November 91, 27.

6. See W. Kip Viscusi's *Fatal Tradeoffs: Public and Private Responsibilities for Risk* (New York: Oxford University Press, 1992).

7. Loren B. Mead, *The Once and Future Church: Reinventing the Congregation for a New Mission Frontier* (New York: Alban Institute Publication, 1991), 2.

8. Quoted in David L. McKenna, *The Coming Great Awakening: New Hope for the Nineties* (Downers Grove, Ill.: InterVarsity Press, 1990), 74.

9. Nicholas Dawidoff, "One for the Wolves," *Audubon* 92 (July-August 1992): 38-45.

10. Juan Carlos Ortiz, *Call to Discipleship* (Plainfield, N.J.: Logos International, 1975), 3.

11. As quoted in William Pannell, *Evangelism From the Bottom Up* (Grand Rapids, Mich.: Zondervan, 1991), 20.

12. See Elmer L. Towns's *An Inside Look at 10 of Today's Most Innovative Churches* (Ventura, Calif.: Regal Books, 1990).

13. John G. Stackhouse, Jr., "Getting the Small Picture," *Christianity Today*, 27 April 1992, 34.

14. See also Christopher Mogil and Anne Slepian, *We Gave Away a Fortune: Stories of People Who Have Devoted Themselves and Their Wealth to Peace, Justice and the Environment* (Philadelphia: New Society Publishers, 1992). The best novelistic account of what can happen when a decision is made to invest one's wealth in the poor and needy rather than bequeath it to the family is the story of the dying woman Elisabeth Gompertz in Heinrich Böll, *Der Engel Schwieg* (Cologne: Kiepenheuer und Witsch, 1992).

15. Alan Thein Durning, *How Much Is Enough? The Consumer Society and the Future of the Earth* (New York: W. W. Norton, 1992), 26-27.

16. As quoted in Jacques-Yves Cousteau and the Staff of the Cousteau Society, *The Cousteau Almanac: An Inventory of Life on Our Water Planet* (Garden City, N.Y.: Doubleday, 1981), 752.

17. Bill McKibben, "Christmas Already in the Air Challenges Christians," *The United Methodist Record: News and Notes Edition* 2 (October 1992), 5.

18. For gift ideas under $10, as well as "green" tips on how to celebrate a more simple and environmental friendly Christmas (e.g., wrap presents in reusable items like bandannas, scarves, pillowcases, etc.) see Noel Pax and Mary Thompson, *Simply Christmas: Great Ideas for a Noncommercial Holiday* (New York: Walker and Company, 1992).

19. "Music's Discipline of the Means: An Interview with Ernest McClain," *Parabola* 16 (Winter 1991): 90-91.

20. See Geoffrey L. Simons, *Silicon Shock: The Menace of the Computer Invasion* (New York: Basil Blackwell, 1985).

21. David Ruelle, *Chance and Chaos* (Princeton, N.J.: Princeton University Press, 1991), 67, 75-76.

22. Ibid., 77.

23. Edward O. Wilson, *The Diversity of Life* (Cambridge, Mass.: Harvard University Press, 1992), esp. 14, 180-81.

24. James Gleick, *Genius: The Life and Science of Richard Feynman* (New York: Pantheon Books, 1992), 5.

25. "Are We Becoming a Country of Haters?" Interview in *USA Today*, 2 September 1992, 9A.

26. See the column by George Kovanis, *Detroit Free Press*, 20 December 1991, Metro ed., 3F.
27. Lyle E. Schaller, *The Seven-Day-A-Week Church* (Nashville: Abingdon Press, 1992), 15.
28. Ibid., 50.
29. See also Schaller's *Seven-Day-A-Week Church*.
30. Steven Waldman, "The Tyranny of Choice," *New Republic*, 27 January 1992, 23.
31. "Open All Weekend: Saturday Services," *Christianity Today*, 9 November 1992, 68.
32. Steven Waldman, "The Tyranny of Choice," *Newsweek* 22-25.
33. For a fuller elaboration of this theme, see Leonard I. Sweet and K. Elizabeth Rennie, "AYOR (At Your Own Risk)," *Homiletics* 4 (July-September 1992): 27-30.
34. I wish to thank David Lowes Watson for his help in formulating this position.
35. Mary Hunt, as quoted in Paul V. Mankowski, "What I Saw At the American Academy of Religion," *First Things*, March 1992, 41.
36. Eugene D. Genovese, "Pilgrim's Progress," *New Republic*, 11 May 1992, 38.
37. Garrett Keizer, *A Dresser of Sycamore Trees* (New York: Viking, 1992), 66.
38. Thanks to business guru Kenneth Blanchard for this wonderfully insightful acronym.
39. Colin M. Morris, *Out of Africa's Crucible* (London: Lutterworth Press, 1960), 99.
40. Sergei Hackel, "Paths to Reconciliation," *Epiphany Journal* 6 (Summer 1986): 34.
41. Wendy Kaminer, *I'm Dysfunctional, You're Dysfunctional: The Recovery Movement and Other Self-Help Fashions* (Redding, Mass.: Addison-Wesley, 1992), 27.
42. Robert Wuthnow, *Acts of Compassion: Caring for Others and Helping Ourselves* (Princeton, N.J.: Princeton University Press, 1991), 87.
43. Howard Jacobson, *The Very Model of a Man* (London: Viking, 1992), 1.
44. See George Barna, *User Friendly Churches: What Christians Need to Know About the Churches People Love to Go to* (Ventura, Calif.: Regal Books, 1991), 98. See also Norman Shawchuck, Philip Kotler, Bruce Wrenn, and Gustave Rath, *Marketing For Congregations: Choosing to Serve People More Effectively* (Nashville: Abingdon Press, 1992).
45. As quoted by Jeremiah A. Wright, Jr., "A Black Congregation in a White Church," *Good News in Growing Churches*, ed. Robert L. Burt (New York: Pilgrim Press, 1990), 47.
46. Barna, *User Friendly Churches*, 43.
47. John Naisbitt and Patricia Aburdene, *Megatrends 2000: Ten New Directions for the 1990's* (New York: William Morrow, 1990), 62.
48. See John Macquarrie, *Jesus Christ in Modern Thought* (Philadelphia: Trinity Press International, 1990), 15.
49. See Parker Palmer, "The Woodcarver: A Model for Right Action," in his *The Active Life: Wisdom for Work, Creativity, and Caring* (San Francisco: HarperSanFrancisco, 1991), 55-77.
50. For such calls from within the business community, see Peter M. Senge, *The Fifth Discipline: The Art and Practice of the Learning Organization* (New York: Doubleday/Currency, 1990), 141.

4. DesignerQuakes

1. Faith Popcorn, *The Popcorn Report: Faith Popcorn on the Future of Your Company, Your World, Your Life* (New York: Doubleday, 1991), 43-44.
2. I wish to thank liturgist Kendall Kane McCabe for his insightful probings and stimulating conversations in this area.
3. As quoted in *Research Recommendations*, 25 March 1991, 3.
4. Stuart Ewen, *All Consuming Images: The Politics of Style in Contemporary Culture* (New York: Basic Books, 1988).
5. See John Roberts's *The Triumph of the West* (Boston: Little, Brown, 1985). For the domination of Western pop-music and pop-cinema throughout Asia, see Pico Iyer, *Video Night in Kathmandu and Other Reports from the Not-So-Far East* (New York: Alfred A. Knopf, 1988).
6. T. C. Frank, "The American Nonconformist in the Age of the Commercialization of Dissent," *The Baffler* 3 (Winter/Spring 1992): 6, 70. See also Paul Rudnick, "Everybody's a Rebel," *Spy*, March 1992, 52-58.
7. John Urry, *The Tourist Gaze: Leisure and Travel in Contemporary Societies* (London: Sage Publications, 1990), 4.
8. See John David Webb, *How to Change the Image of Your Church* (Nashville: Abingdon Press, 1993).
9. Pierre Babin, *The New Era in Religious Communication* (Minneapolis: Fortress Press, 1991), 65.
10. For additional examples see the chapter "Feeding the Baby Boomers," in William Easum, *How to Reach Baby Boomers* (Nashville: Abingdon Press, 1991), 73-92.
11. Martin Lloyd-Jones, *Growing in the Spirit: The Assurance of Our Salvation* (Westchester, Ill.: Crossway Books, 1989), 42.
12. I am heavily indebted here to the insights of Alison Lurie, *The Language of Clothes*, rev. ed. (London: Bloomsbury, 1992).
13. George Barna, *User Friendly Churches: What Christians Need to Know About the Churches People Love To Go To* (Ventura, Calif.: Regal Books, 1991), 69.
14. Frank Burch Brown, "Sin and Bad Taste: Aesthetic Criteria in the Realm of Religion," *Soundings* 70 (Spring/Summer 1987): 65-80.
15. Richard Lachmann, "Graffiti as Career and Ideology," *American Journal of Sociology* 94 (1988): 237.
16. As quoted in Joseph Bryan, *Gallimaufry to God: Puns, Put-downs and Other Curiosities* (New York: Dell Publishing, 1991), 206.
17. Diana T. Meyers, *Self, Society, and Personal Choice* (New York: Columbia University Press, 1989), 53.
18. George G. Hunter, *How to Reach Secular People* (Nashville: Abingdon Press, 1992).
19. "The Greening of the Self," Joanna Macy, *World as Lover, World as Self* (Berkeley: Parallax Press, 1991), 183-92.
20. Colin Campbell, *The Romantic Ethic and the Spirit of Modern Consumerism* (New York: Basil Blackwell, 1987).
21. Calvin, *Institutes*, 3.7.5.
22. Ibid., 4.1.3.

23. Nobel physicist Erwin Schrödinger puts this in extreme form: "The mind by its nature is a *singulare tantum*, I should say: the overall number of minds is just one." See his *What is Life? The Physical Aspect of the Living Cell and Mind and Matter* (London: Cambridge University Press, 1969), 145.

24. See Karl H. Pibram, *Brain and Perception: Holomomy and Structure in Figural Processing* (Hillsdale, N.J.: Lawrence Erlbaum Associates, 1990). See also his earlier works, especially, *What Makes Man Human* (New York: American Museum of Natural History, 1971) and *Mood, States and Mind: Selected Readings* (Baltimore: Penguin Books, 1969).

25. See David Bohm, *Wholeness and the Implicate Order* (Boston: Routledge and Kegan Paul, 1981).

26. His Holiness The Dalai Lama, "The Global Community and Universal Responsibility," *The Way Ahead: A Visionary Perspective for the New Millennium*, ed. Eddie and Debbie Shapiro (Rockport, Mass.: Element, 1992), 51.

27. Myron L. Smith, Johann N. Bruh, and James B. Anderson, "The Fungus *Armillaria Bulbosa* Is Among the Largest and Oldest Living Organisms," *Nature*, 2 April 1992, 428-31: "By comparison, *Sequoiadendron giganteum*, the largest plant on earth, attains a mass of over 1,000 tonnes, most of which is non-living wood that has accumulated during thousands of years of growth. In contrast to these more highly integrated organisms, fungi may undergo dramatic fluctuations in mass, for example, up to threefold within a few years, depending on recent forest history" (431).

28. Shortly after this "discovery" scientists supposedly discovered an even larger fungus, an *Armillaria ostoyze* covering two-and-a-half square miles in the state of Washington. See *New York Times*, 8 May 1992, 12A.

29. Emilia Askari, "Trees, Not Fungus, Called Biggest," *Detroit Free Press*, 25 November 1992.

30. Smith, Bruh, and Anderson, "The Fungus *Armillaria Bulbosa*." See also William Ecenbarger, "The Humongous Fungus Debate," *Audubon* 94 (September-October 1992): 20-21.

31. Stephen Jay Gould, "A Humongous Fungus Among Us," *Natural History*, July 1992, 10-18.

32. Gould says there are five properties to an "individual" organism: (1) they are born; (2) they die; (3) they are stable enough during their lifetime to have some character; (4) they reproduce; (5) the offspring both resemble parents and embody their own differences. See Gould, "A Humongous Fungus Among Us," 16.

33. As quoted in Macy, *World as Lover*, 184.

34. As quoted in Michael Thompson, *Rubbish Theory* (New York: Oxford University Press, 1989), 1.

35. Alan Watts, *The Book: On the Taboo Against Knowing Who You Are* (New York: Collier Books, 1967), 51.

36. As quoted by James Roose-Evans, *The Inner Stage: Finding a Center in Prayer and Ritual* (Cambridge, Mass.: Cowley, 1990), 29.

37. "In the Mouths of Babes: No More Cavities?" *Science News*, February 1992, 70.

38. See Shirley MacLaine, *Don't Fall Off the Mountain* (New York: W. W. Norton, 1970), 141.

39. Andres Serrano's 1989 photograph, "Piss Christ," received a grant from the National Endowment for the Arts.

40. As suggested by a Portland minister in *Hungry Mind Review*, Spring 1993, 9.

41. Christopher R. Browning, *Ordinary Men: Reserve Police Battalion 101 and the Final Solution in Poland* (New York: HarperCollins, 1992). Quote is from 184.

42. James Hillman and Michael Ventura, *We've Had a Hundred Years of Psychotherapy—And the World's Getting Worse* (San Francisco: HarperSanFrancisco, 1992), 43.

43. *The New Individualists: The Generation After the Organization Man* (New York: HarperCollins, 1991), 381-83.

44. Lyle Schaller, *The Seven-Day-A-Week Church* (Nashville: Abingdon Press, 1992), 75.

45. Stanley Hauerwas with David Burrell, "From System to Story" (15-39) and "Story and Theology" (71-81) in Hauerwas, *Truthfulness and Tragedy: Further Investigations in Christian Ethics* (Notre Dame, Ind.: University of Notre Dame Press, 1977).

46. Helen M. Luke, *Dark Wood to White Rose: Journey and Transformation in Dante's Divine Comedy* (New York: Parabola Books, 1989), 5.

47. See Charles L. Rice, *The Embodied Word: Preaching as Art and Liturgy* (Minneapolis: Fortress Press, 1990), 99.

48. Babin, *The New Era in Religious Communication*, 146.

49. Former General Secretary of the World Council of Churches Philip Potter uses this analogy to define the kind of leadership required in the church today. The analogy is quoted in "One Flock, One Shepherd," by Joan B. Campbell, *Bread Afresh, Wine Anew: Sermons by Disciples Women*, ed. Joan Campbell and David Polk (St. Louis: Chalice Press, 1991), 147.

50. Madeleine L'Engle, *A Circle of Quiet* (New York: Farrar, Straus and Giraux, 1972), 99.

51. As quoted by Joel Schwartz in "The Moral Environment of the Poor," *Public Interest* 103 (Spring 1991): 29.

52. Thanks to Walter W. Burghardt for this story. See his *Dare to Be Christ: Homilies for the Nineties* (New York: Paulist Press, 1990), 26.

53. John Gruidl and Steven Kline, "What Happens When a Large Discount Store Comes to Town?" *Small Town*, March-April 1992, 20-25. Quote is on 25.

54. Jane Bosveld, "Life According to Gaia," *Omni* 14 (October 1991): 67.

55. See David Beaty, *The Naked Pilot: The Human Factor in Aircraft Accidents* (London: Methuen, 1992).

56. William Irwin Thompson, *Passages About Earth: An Exploration of the New Planetary Culture* (New York: Harper & Row, 1981), 82.

57. The surveys were conducted and paid for by Cotton, Inc. and Levi Strauss.

58. As found in *Executive Speechwriter Newsletter* 7, no. 2 (1992): 5.

59. Ardie Kendig-Higgins, "Where in Heaven Is Angels Camp?" *Good News in Growing Churches*, ed. Robert L. Burt (New York: Pilgrim Press, 1990), 195.

60. James D. G. Dunn, "Another Test Case: Church Ministry (2)" in *New Testament Theology in Dialogue*, ed. Dunn and James P. Mackey (London: SPCK, 1987), 133.

61. *The Popcorn Report*, 45.

62. David Friend and the Editors of Life, *More Reflections on the Meaning of Life* (Boston: Little, Brown, 1992), 27.

63. Harold Bloom, *The American Religion: The Emergence of the Post-Christian Nation* (New York: Simon & Schuster, 1992), 30, 37.

64. Peter Russell, *The White Hole in Time: Our Future Evolution and the Meaning of Now* (San Francisco: HarperSanFrancisco, 1992).

65. As reported in "Lifeline," *USA Today*, 4 January 1993, 1D.

66. As quoted in Mark Bernstein, "The Roller-Coaster King Is Dead," *Ohio Magazine* 15 (July 1992): 15.

67. P. J. O'Rourke, *Give War a Chance: Eyewitness Accounts of Mankind's Struggle Against Tyranny, Injustice and Alcohol-Free Beer* (New York: Atlantic Monthly Press, 1992), 90.

68. Bruce W. Nelan, "How the World Will Look in 50 Years," *Time*, Special Issue, Fall 1992, 36.

69. Louis de Bernières, *The Troublesome Offspring of Cardinal Guzman* (London: Secker and Warburg, 1992), 1-2.

70. See Chris McGinn and Michael McCauley, "Bush Administration Opens Backdoor to Gut Health, Safety Standards Via Trade Pacts," *Public Citizen* 12 (September/October, 1992): 14-17.

71. Robert S. Bachelder, "Churches Building Bridges," *Christian Century*, 21 October 1992, 924.

72. As found in Joe Dominquez and Vicki Robin, *Your Money Or Your Life: Transforming Your Relationship With Money and Achieving Financial Independence* (New York: Penguin Books, 1992), 160.

73. My thanks to William Robert McClelland for help in seeing this. See McClelland, *Worldly Spirituality: Biblical Reflections on Money, Politics and Sex* (St. Louis, Mo.: CBP Press, 1990), 12-13.

74. Manfred Max-Neef, "Ecological Economics," *Resurgence*, November/December 1992, 7.

75. See Angelo B. Henderson and Janice Hayes, "Communities Built on Faith," *USA Today*, 10 August 1992, 3A.

76. Louis Menand, "Don't Think Twice: A Retrospective on the Decade that Wouldn't Die," *New Republic*, 9 October 1989, 22.

77. Neil Postman, *Technopoly: The Surrender of Culture and Technology* (New York: Alfred A. Knopf, 1992).

78. Stuart Ewen, *All Consuming Images: The Politics of Style in Contemporary Culture* (New York: Basic Books, 1988).

5. WorkQuakes

1. See also Richard and Linda Eyre, *Lifebalance: Priority Balance, Attitude Balance, Goal Balance in All Areas of Your Life* (New York: Ballantine Books, 1988): "It's not the sparse simplicity of too little but the crowded complexity of too much that plagues our lives" (16). For the postmodern preference for field images over linear ones, see Leonard I. Sweet, *Quantum Spirituality: A Postmodern Apologetic* (Dayton, Ohio: Whaleprints, 1991), 230-40.

2. Faith Popcorn, *The Popcorn Report: Faith Popcorn on the Future of Your Company, Your World, Your Life* (New York: Doubleday, 1991), 50

3. Research Recommendations, 10 August 1992, 3.

4. *The Popcorn Report*, 54.

5. See George Barna, *The Barna Report: What Americans Believe* (Ventura, Calif.: Regal Books, 1992), 165-66, where it is reported that 72 percent of adults deemed having a close relationship with God very desirable.

6. *Washington Spectator*, 15 November 1992, 1-2.

7. Richard Wolkomir, "Trying to Decipher Those Inscrutable Signs of Our Times," *Smithsonian* 24 (September 1993): 66.

8. "Have a Nice Life," *Sunday Sermons*, 8 September 1991, 9-10.

9. Jonathan Raban, "Ideal Cities," Pat Rogers' response, *TLS: Times Literary Supplement*, 8 September 1992, 12.

10. Andres Duany and Elizabeth Plater-Zyberk, "The Second Coming of the American Small Town," *Wilson Quarterly* 16 (Winter 1992): 28.

11. Quentin Crisp in *Hungry Mind Review*, Fall 1992, 12.

12. See Kirkpatrick Sale, *Dwellers in the Land: The Bioregional Vision* (San Francisco: Sierra Club Books, 1985); see also Scott Russell Sanders, *Staying Put: Making a Home in a Restless World* (Boston: Beacon Press, 1993).

13. This is the only statistic one needs to understand why Cuomo isn't driven to seek the U.S. presidency. I found this statistic buried in Sidney Blumenthal, "The Coward: The Last Gasp of Mario Cuomo," *New Republic*, 6 March 1992, 12.

14. Wallace Stegner, *Where the Bluebird Sings to the Lemonade Springs* (New York: Random House, 1992), 206.

15. Alfred Meyer, "The Rise of New America," Interview with Jack Lessinger, *Mother Earth News* 110 (March/April 1988), 68-72.

16. Tom Morganthau, "Are Cities Obsolete," *Newsweek*, 9 September 1991, 42-44.

17. See Joel Garreau, *Edge City: Life on the New Frontier* (New York: Doubleday, 1991).

18. HRH Prince Charles, "Age Without Spirit," *Resurgence*, July/August, 1992, 5.

19. See Gary Moll and Stanley Young, *Growing Greener Cities: A Tree-Planting Handbook* (Los Angeles: Living Planet Press, 1992).

20. See urban design theorist Rob Krier, *Urban Space* (New York: Rizzoli International, 1979); see also Léon Krier's introduction to *Urban Transformations* (London: Architectural Design, 978).

21. The highway construction of the future will be financed by the ISTEA (Internodal Surface Transportation Efficiency Act) of 1991—"iced tea" to the initiates.

22. Vernon Mays, "Neighborhoods by Design," *Progressive Architecture*, June 1992, 92.

23. For example see Wally Bowen, "Lost Public Space Risks Democratic Dialogue," *Media & Values* (Winter 1992): 20 and Elizabeth Plater-Zybeck, Richard Sennett, James Wines and Elyn Zimmerman, "Whatever Became of the Public Square," *Harper's*, July 1990, 49-60.

24. Floyd McClung, *Seeing the City with the Eyes of God* (Tarrytown, N.Y.: Fleming H. Revell, 1991), 58, 94.

25. David Rusk, *Cities Without Suburbs* (Washington, D.C.: Woodrow Wilson Center Press, 1993).

26. Tom Sine, *Wild Hope* (Dallas: Word Publishing, 1991), 145.

27. Milenko Matanovic, *Meandering Rivers and Square Tomatoes: The Art of Crafting Visions* (Issaquah, Wash.: Morningtown Press, 1988), 23.
28. James Patterson and Peter Kim, *The Day America Told the Truth: What People Really Believe About Everything That Really Matters* (New York: Prentice-Hall Press, 1991), 4, 172.
29. Duany and Plater-Zyberk, "The Second Coming of the American Small Town," 25.
30. For the car as a cultural symbol, see Wolfgang Sachs, *For Love of the Automobile: Looking Back into the History of Our Desires* (Berkeley: University of California Press, 1992).
31. Duany and Plater-Zyberk, "The Second Coming of the American Small Town," 28.
32. European Green Party Secretary Sara Parkin, as quoted by Lester R. Brown, "Worldwatcher's Warning," *World Monitor* 5 (May 1992): 19.
33. Paul Karr, "The High Cost of Cars," *Sanctuary: The Journal of the Massachusetts Audubon Society* 31 (May/June 1992): 13-14.
34. See Margaret Marsh, *Suburban Lives* (New Brunswick, N.J.: Rutgers University Press, 1990).
35. David Mohney and Keller Easterling, *Seaside: Making a Town in America* (New York: Princeton Architectural Press, 1991).
36. Mark Westmoreland, private conversation with author. A novel on the obsessions of small town living is G. B. Hummer, *Red Branch* (London: Sinclair-Stevenson, 1993).
37. Lewis Mumford, *The Myth of the Machine: Technics and Human Development* (New York: Harcourt, Brace and World, 1967) contains the best description ever written of the virtue of small town life; see esp. "Archaic village culture," 156-62.
38. Kathleen Norris talks about "the holy use of gossip" in her account of small-town living entitled *Dakota: A Spiritual Geography* (New York: Ticknor and Fields, 1993), 69-77.
39. A summary of such voices can be found in Mark B. Lapping, "On the Necessity of Porches and the Recovery of the Public Voice," *Small Town* 23 (July-August 1992): 20-23. I am indebted to Fred Smith of Leadership Network for this reference.
40. Thomas Rawls, *Small Places* (Boston: Little, Brown and Company, 1990). Rawls terms the newcomers "weeds."
41. Pierre Clavel, *Opposition Planning in Wales and Appalachia* (Philadelphia: Temple University Press, 1983).
42. As cited in Russell Chandler, *Racing Toward 2001: The Forces Shaping America's Religious Future* (San Francisco: HarperCollins, 1992), 21.
43. This is mentioned in Witold Rybcaynski, *Waiting for the Weekend* (New York: Viking, 1992), 18.
44. Hans-Georg Gadamer, *Truth and Method*, 2d rev. ed. (New York: Crossroad, 1989), 102.
45. For the American obsession with work, see Juliet Schor, *The Overworked American* (New York: Basic Books, 1991).
46. Robert S. DeRopp, *The Master Game: Pathways to Higher Consciousness Beyond the Drug Experience* (New York: Delcourt Press, 1968), 11.
47. Miroslav Volf, *Work in the Spirit: Toward a Theology of Work* (New York: Oxford University Press, 1991).

48. James Robertson, "A New Future for Work," *Resurgence*, July/August 1992, 12. See also Robertson's *Future Work: Jobs, Self-Employment and Leisure After the Industrial Age* (New York: Universe Books, 1985).

49. Charles Handy, "Work Is More Than a Job," *Resurgence*, May/June 1993, 7-9.

50. As quoted by Joe Treen, "Search for Tomorrow," *People*, 2 December 1991, 114.

51. The phrase is that of Bernard Cooke in his *The Distancing of God: The Ambiguity of Symbol in History and Theology* (Minneapolis: Fortress Press, 1990). Cooke traces the way God is made to appear far away ("afar off") from the laity or "common Christian" through systematic theology, ritual and church order.

52. Newsman Arthur (Bugs) Baer as quoted by Jimmy Breslin in *Damon Runyon: A Life* (New York: Tickner and Fields, 1992), 140.

53. As reported in *National and International Religion Report*, 3 July 1992, 8.

54. A move in this direction is Anne Rowthorn, *The Liberation of the Laity* (Wilton, Conn.: Morehouse-Barlow, 1986).

55. Christian Smith, *Going to the Root: Nine Proposals for Radical Church Renewal* (Scottdale, Penn.: Herald Press, 1992), 37. For a provocative analysis of the causes of lay-clergy friction, see Richard K. Fenn's thesis about "The Daedalus Complex" in *The Secularization of Sin* (Louisville, Ky.: Westminster/John Knox Press, 1991), 173ff.

56. Gordon D. Fee, "Laos and Leadership Under the New Covenant" *Crux* 25 (1989), 6.

57. J. Christiaan Beker, *Paul the Apostle* (Philadelphia: Fortress Press, 1980), 320.

58. James D. G. Dunn, "Another Test Case: Church Ministry," *New Testament Theology in Dialogue*, ed. Dunn and James P. Mackey (London: SPCK, 1987), 123. See also 124-26.

59. F. R. Barry, *Asking the Right Questions* (London: Hodder and Stoughton, 1960), 84, as referenced by John A. T. Robinson, "Taking the Lid Off the Church's Ministry," *New Ways with the Ministry*, ed. John Morris (London: Faith Press, 1960), 13.

60. See Edward Schillebeeckx, *The Church with a Human Face: A New and Expanded Theology of Ministry* (New York: Crossroad, 1985).

61. E. L. Mascall, *The Recovery of Unity* (London: Longmans Green, 1958), 5-6 as referenced by Robinson, "Taking the Lid Off," 14.

62. This was a comment in a speech by John "Pete" Hammond, director of the Inter-Varsity Marketplace in the U.S., at the Second International Congress on World Evangelization, entitled "The Laity," in *Proclaim Christ Until He Comes: Lausanne II in Manilla* (Minneapolis: World Wide Publications, 1990), 81.

6. AgeQuakes

1. See Albert Rosenfeld, "Stretching the Span," *Wilson Quarterly* 9, no. 1 (1985): 96.

2. This is the argument of Howard P. Chudacoff, *How Old Are You? Age Consciousness in American Culture* (Princeton, N.J.: Princeton University Press, 1989).

3. Census statistics compiled from "The Elderly in America," *Wilson Quarterly*, 9, no. 1 (1985): 96 and Rosenfeld, "Stretching the Span," 99.

4. Faith Popcorn, *The Popcorn Report: Faith Popcorn on the Future of Your Company, Your World, Your Life* (New York: Doubleday, 1991), 57.

5. Ibid., 59.

6. Ibid., 57.

7. As quoted in Judy Foreman, "Aging: Scientists Rethink Limits on Life Span," *Denver Post*, 8 October 1992, 37A.

8. See e.g., Roy L. Walford, *The 120-Year Diet: How to Double Your Vital Years* (New York: Simon and Schuster, 1988).

9. Martin Elkort, *The Secret Life of Food: A Feast of Food and Drink History, Folklore and Fact* (Los Angeles: Jeremy P. Tarcher, 1990), 86-87.

10. See Melinda Beck et al., "Attention Willard Scott," *Newsweek*, 4 May 1992, 75.

11. Sally Lehrman, "The Fountain of Youth?" *Harvard Health Letter*, 7 (June 1992): 1-3.

12. Janet Raloff, "Paring Protein," *Science News*, 21 November 1992, 346.

13. *Johns Hopkins Medical Letter*, September 1993.

14. See the pioneering work by Duke psychologists James A. Blumenthal, David J. Madden, Thomas W. Pierce; Boston Deaconess Hospital physician William C. Siegel; and Vanderbilt University psychologist Mark Applebaum, "Hypertension Affects Neurobehavioral Functioning," *Psychosomatic Medicine* 55 (January-February 1993): 44-50, 1.

15. Marilyn Elias, "When to Worry about Forgetting," *Harvard Health Letter*, 7 (July 1992): 1-3. Statistics are on 2.

16. Lehrman, "The Fountain of Youth?" 1.

17. As quoted in Foreman, "Aging," 29A.

18. Rosenfeld, "Stretching the Span," 97.

19. See Peter Laslett's celebration of the "third age" in his *A Fresh Map of Life: The Emergence of the Third Age* (Cambridge, Mass.: Harvard University Press, 1991).

20. The work of Donald Joy is absolutely critical for every parent and every church. See his *Bonding: Relationships in the Image of God* (Waco, Tex.: Word Books, 1985).

21. K. A. Fackelmann, "Brave New Biology: Granny Gives Birth," *Science News*, 3 February 1993, 100.

22. A similar percentage of those over 85 also rated their health as excellent, very good, or good in this nationwide survey. See *University of California at Berkeley Wellness Letter*, August 1993).

23. Priest/novelist/sociologist Andrew Greeley, criticized for his *Wages of Sin* (New York: Putnam, 1992) depiction of two older characters lusting after one another, released a study which reveals that 37 percent of married people over 60 have sex at least once a week, and one in six more often than that. Greeley also discovered from his survey that married men who are sexually active after 60 are happier with their sex lives than 20-year-old sexually active single males with multiple partners. See Kenneth L. Woodward and Karen Springen, "Better Than a Gold Watch," *Newsweek*, 24 August 1992, 71.

24. Samuel S. Janus and Cynthia L. Janus, *The Janus Report on Sexual Behavior* (New York: John Wiley and Sons, 1993), 25.

25. Laurence A. Levine, as quoted in "The New Middle Age," by Melinda Beck, *Newsweek*, 2 December 1992, 54.

26. Marilyn Elias, "Late-Life Love," *Harvard Health Letter* 18 (November 1992): 2. This article reports the growing number of third agers seeking help from sex therapists. As for the fear of a heart attack? "Fewer than 1 percent of sudden coronary deaths occur during intercourse, and seven out of ten of these happen to explorers in extramarital territory—*flagrante delicto*" (2).

27. Beverly Merz, "Why We Get Old," *Harvard Health Letter*, Special Supplement, October 1992, 9-12, quote is on 10.

28. See William Graebner in *A History of Retirement* (New Haven: Yale University Press, 1980) for his analysis of how the meaning of retirement shifted to a leisure concept.

29. Virginia A. Hodgkinson, "The Future of Individual Giving and Volunteering: The Inseparable Link Between Religious Community and Individual Generosity," Robert Wuthnow and Hodgkinson, *Faith and Philanthropy in America: Exploring the Role of Religion in America's Voluntary Sector* (San Francisco: Jossey-Bass, 1990), 287.

30. As the succession of footnotes will readily reveal, I am heavily dependent here on Richard Cornuelle's research in "New Work for Invisible Hands," *TLS: Times Literary Supplement*, 5 April 1991, 5-6.

31. Ibid., 6.

32. Hodgkinson, "The Future of Individual Giving," 286.

33. Cornuelle, "New Work for Invisible Hands," 6.

34. Ann Swidler, "Inequality and American Culture: The Persistence of Voluntarism," *American Behavioral Scientist* 35 (March/June 1992): 606-29.

35. Hodgkinson, "The Future of Individual Giving," 299.

36. See Ralph Nader's foreword to Edgar Cahn and Jonathan Rowe, *Time Dollars* (Emmaus, Penn.: Rodale Press, 1992), ix-xiii.

37. *Research Recommendations*, 26 April 1993, 3.

38. Nader, foreword, x.

39. Douglas M. Lawson, *Give to Live: How Giving Can Change Your Life* (La Jolla, Calif.: ALTI Pub., 1991). See esp. ch. 2, "The Extraordinary Benefits of Giving," 19-34.

40. See Arthur Kornhaber and Kenneth L. Woodward, *Grandparents/Grandchildren: The Vital Connection* (Garden City, N.Y.: Anchor Press, 1981).

41. See Paul Thompson, Catherine Itzin and Michele Abendstern, *I Don't Feel Old* (New York: Oxford University Press, 1990).

42. These are itemized and outlined in Kornhaber and Woodward's *Grandparents/Grandchildren*, 167-79.

43. Bernie and Bobbie Siegel, "A Torch to Light our Way" in *The Way Ahead: A Visionary Perspective for the New Millennium*, ed. Eddie and Bobbie Shapiro (Rockport, Mass.: Element, 1992), 113.

44. See "The Risk of Evolution: An Interview with Joseph Chilton Pearce," *Parabola* 17 (May 1992): 58.

45. Chris Waddington, "Passionate Interest: An Interview with Maurice Sendak," *Hungry Mind Review*, Winter 1992–93, 12.

46. *The Popcorn Report*, 60.

47. Jaan Kaplinski, *The Wandering Border* (Port Townsend: Copper Canyon Press, 1987), 44.

48. John Javna, *Cool Tricks! A Grown-Ups Guide to All the Neat Things You Never Learned to Do as a Kid* (Chicago: Contemporary Books, 1989). Illustrations are from 85, 48-49, 68, 75, 90-94, respectively.

49. See James Hillman and Michael Ventura, *We've Had A Hundred Years of Psychotherapy—And the World's Getting Worse* (San Francisco: HarperSanFranciso, 1992), 25. Hillman is paraphrasing Ivan Illich here.

50. Ibid., 6.

51. Tom Wakefield, *Lot's Wife* (London: Serpent's Tail, 1989), 71.

52. See Paula Payne Hardin, *What Are You Doing With the Rest of Your Life? Choices in Midlife* (San Rafael, Calif.: New World Library, 1992).

53. As quoted in Dan Wakefield, "Coming Back to Religion: What It Can Add to Your Life," *New Choices—For Retirement Living*, May 1992, 29.

54. Stephanie Coontz, *The Way We Never Were* (New York: Basic Books, 1992), 29.

55. See Sally Sontheimer, ed., *Women and the Environment: A Reader: Crisis and Development in the Third World* (New York: Monthly Review Press, 1991).

56. As quoted in Frederic A. Brussat, "Spiritual Elders," *Values & Visions* 23, nos. 5-6 (1992): 5.

57. See Lois W. Banner, *In Full Flower: Aging, Women, Power and Sexuality: A History* (New York: Alfred A. Knopf, 1992); also Germaine Greer, *The Change: Women, Aging and the Menopause* (New York: Alfred A. Knopf, 1992).

7. ColorQuakes

1. John Cage, *Silence* (Middletown, Conn.: Wesleyan University Press, 1961), 93, and quoted in John Dominic Crossan, "A Metamodel for Polyvalent Narration," *Semeia* 9 (1977), 105-6.

2. Faith Popcorn, *The Popcorn Report: Faith Popcorn on the Future of Your Company, Your World, Your Life* (New York: Doubleday, 1991), 78.

3. Katherine Mansfield went on: "What with complexes and repressions and reactions and vibrations and reflections, there are moments when I feel I am nothing but the small clerk of some hotel without a proprietor, who has all his work cut out to enter the names and hand the keys to the wilful guests." *The Letters and Journals of Katherine Mansfield: A Selection*, ed. C. K. Stead (London: Allen Lane, 1977), 173.

4. See for example Daniel Dennett's *Consciousness Explained* (Boston: Little, Brown, 1992).

5. As quoted from Jacqueline Rose, "Faking It Up with the Truth," a review of Diane W. Middlebrook, *Anne Sexton: A Biography* (Boston: Houghton Mifflin, 1991), *TLS: Times Literary Supplement*, 1 November 1991, 8-9.

6. Hazel Markus and Paula Nurius, "Possible Selves," *American Psychologist* 41 (1986): 954.

7. See Daniel C. Dennett and Marcel Kinsbourne, *Consciousness Explained* (Boston: Little, Brown, 1991).

8. Edward R. Wolpow, "After the Fall," *Harvard Health Letter* 16 (April 1991): 2-3.

9. As quoted by Deborah Houy, "Islands, the Universe, Home," *Buzzworm* 4 (March/April 1992): 14.

10. Jerome Bruner quotes Freud and makes this point in *Acts of Meaning* (Cambridge, Mass.: Harvard University Press, 1990), 42.

11. Ted Peters, "The Dimensions of God's Life," *Christian Century*, 6-13 January 1993, 24-27.

12. See Leonard I. Sweet, *Quantum Spirituality: A Postmodern Apologetic* (Dayton, Ohio: Whaleprints, 1991), 268-71.

13. *The Popcorn Report*, 81.

14. Ibid., 83.

15. Stephanie Culp, *Streamlining Your Life: A 5-Point Plan for Uncomplicated Living* (Cincinnati: Writers Digest Books, 1991).

16. Ken Blanchard and Spencer Johnson, *One Minute Manager* (New York: William Morrow, 1982).

17. Frank C. Laubach, *Prayer: The Mightiest Force in the World* (New York: Fleming H. Revell, 1946), 56.

18. This chart can be found in Kirkpatrick Sale, *Human Scale* (New York: Coward, McCann and Geoghegan, 1980), 57-58.

19. R. S. Thomas, "Pilgrimages," *Frequencies* (London: Macmillan, 1978), 51.

20. See Robert H. Waterman, *Adhocracy: The Power to Change* (Knoxville, Tenn.: Whittle Direct Books, 1989).

21. See Peter Emerson, *Consensus Voting Systems* (Belfast: P. J. Emerson, 1991).

22. Rustum Roy, *An Appropriate God for a Technological Culture*, Gross Memorial Lecture: 1991 (Valparaiso, Ind.: Valparaiso University, 1992), 21.

23. Jonathan Z. Smith, "Differential Equations: On Constructing the 'Other,'" Thirteenth Annual University Lecture in Religion, Arizona State University, 5 March 1992.

24. Christopher Ricks and William L. Vance, eds., *The Faber Book of America* (Boston: Faber and Faber, 1992), xvi.

25. Joan Huber and William H. Form, *Income and Ideology: An Analysis of the American Political Formula* (New York: Free Press, 1973); Mary R. Jackman and Robert W. Jackman, *Class Awareness in the United States* (Berkeley: University of California Press, 1983); James R. Kluegel and Elliot R. Smith, *Beliefs About Inequality: Americans' Views of What Is and What Ought to Be* (New York: de Gruyter, 1986).

26. Charles Murray, "Class and Underclass," a review of *American Apartheid* by Douglas S. Massey and Nancy A. Denton, *TLS: Times Literary Supplement*, 21 May 1993, 9.

27. Carl Degler, "In Search of the Un-hyphenated American," *Kettering Review*, Summer 1992, 43.

28. Louis Menand, "Being an American," *TLS: Times Literary Supplement*, 30 October 1992, 4.

29. See James Davison Hunter, *Culture Wars: The Struggle to Define America* (New York: Basic Books, 1991). Sociologist Hunter calls the two diverse moral systems the orthodox party versus the progressivist party.

30. This is the thesis of Ross Chambers' study of oppositional narratives entitled Room for Maneuver: Reading [the] Oppositional [in] Narrative (Chicago: University of Chicago Press, 1991).

31. David Bosch, *Transforming Mission* (Maryknoll, N.Y.: Orbis Books, 1991), 454.

32. Benjamin R. Barber, "Jihad vs. McWorld," *Atlantic Monthly*, March 1992, 53.

33. Michael Walzer, "The New Tribalism: Notes on a Difficult Problem," *Dissent* 39 (Spring 1992): 164-71; quote is from 171.

34. Thomas W. Ogletree, *Hospitality to the Stranger: Dimensions of Moral Understanding* (Philadelphia: Fortress Press, 1985), 119.

35. Hans Küng, *Global Responsibility: In Search of a New World Ethic* (New York: Crossroad, 1991).

36. For Judaism as a missionary religion, see Heinrich Graetz' classic essay, "The Significance of Judaism for the Present and the Future," *Jewish Quarterly Review* 1 (1889): 4-13; 2 (1890): 257-69.

37. Clark Pinnock's third chapter on "Religions Now" is helpful in exploring why not all religions are pathways to God. See his *A Wideness in God's Mercy: The Finality of Jesus Christ in a World of Religions* (Grand Rapids, Mich.: Zondervan, 1992), 81-113.

38. Interview with Krister Stendahl, *Books & Religion* 19 (Spring 1992): 14.

39. Küng, *Global Responsibility*.

40. Joan B. Campbell, "One Flock, One Shepherd," *Bread Afresh, Wine Anew: Sermons by Disciples Women*, ed. Joan Campbell and David Polk (St. Louis, Mo.: Chalice Press, 1991), 148-49.

41. *Religion in America: 1990* (Princeton, N.J.: Princeton Religion Research Center, 1990), 54.

42. John Pereault, "The Transformative Vision," *DesignSpirit*, Winter/Spring 1990, 16.

43. See Michael J. Crawford, *Seasons of Grace: Colonial New England's Revival Tradition in Its British Context* (New York: Oxford University Press, 1991).

44. Evelyn Woodward, *Poets, Prophets & Pragmatists: A New Challenge to Religious Life* (Notre Dame, Ind.: Ave Maria Press, 1987), 16, 25.

45. Lyle Schaller, "The Changing Face of American Christianity," *Seven-Day-A-Week Church* (Nashville: Abingdon Press, 1992), 17-36.

46. Martin E. Marty, "How My Mind Has Changed," *Christian Century*, 10-17 July 1991, 703.

47. James M. Penning, "Politics, Compromise, and Justice," *Reformed Journal* 29 (December 1979): 3.

48. Lionel Blue, *Day Trips to Eternity* (London: Darton, Longman and Todd, 1987), 41.

49. Senior economist, National Center for Policy Analysis, Barry Asmus, "Building an Unlimited Future," *Imprimis* 21 (January 1992): 4.

50. William A. Dyrness, *Learning About Theology from the Third World* (Grand Rapids, Mich.: Zondervan, 1990).

51. Brayton Polka, *The Dialectic of Biblical Critique: Interpretation and Existence* (London: St. Martin's Press, 1986), 17.

52. For the postmodern "incredulity toward metanarratives" (Jean-François Lyotard), see Charles Jencks, *What Is Post-Modernism?* (London: Academy Editions, 1986), 36.

53. It should be noted that Descartes' principle of certainty was foreshadowed by pre-Renaissance figures (such as St. Augustine) just as Heisenberg's uncertainty principle has been similarly foreshadowed by figures like Hildegaard of Bingen, St. John of the Cross, etc.

54. J. Christiaan Beker, *Paul the Apostle* (Philadelphia: Fortress Press, 1990), 312.
55. As quoted in Alastair Hamilton, "Variations in a New Religion," *TLS: Times Literary Supplement*, 2 July 1991, 22.
56. Gerald Kennedy, *The Parables: Sermons on the Stories Jesus Told* (New York: Harper, 1960), 128.
57. Peter Barnes, *The Spirit of Man and More Barnes' People: Seven Monologues* (London: Methuen Drama, 1990), 64.

8. MissionQuakes

1. Faith Popcorn, *The Popcorn Report: Faith Popcorn on the Future of Your Company, Your World, Your Life* (New York: Doubleday, 1991), 85.
2. Caroline Casey, as quoted in Suzi Gablik's *The Reenchantment of Art* (New York: Thames and Hudson, 1991), 144.
3. *The Popcorn Report*, 163.
4. Rosabeth Moss Kanter, "Money is the Root," *Harvard Business Review*, May-June, 1991, 10.
5. A 1992 Knight-Ridder News Service press release.
6. Interview by Jere Van Dyk in *Profit*, July/August 1992, 18.
7. As quoted in *TLS: Times Literary Supplement*, 29 May 1992, 14.
8. As cited in "Seeing Public Service As an Investment," *Newsweek*, 4 May 1992, 60.
9. Mary Scott and Howard Rothman, *Companies with a Conscience: Intimate Portraits of Twelve Firms That Make a Difference* (Secaucus, N.Y.: Carol Publishing, 1992).
10. Virginia Hodgkinson, "The Future of Individual Giving and Volunteering: The Inseparable Link Between Religious Community and Individual Generosity," Hodgkinson and Robert Wuthnow, *Faith and Philanthropy in America: Exploring the Role of Religion in America's Voluntary Sector* (San Francisco: Jossey-Bass, 1990), 286.
11. See Leonard I. Sweet and K. Elizabeth Rennie, "The Mother Teresa Effect," *Homiletics* 5 (January-March 1993), 51-54 and Allan Luks, *The Healing Power of Doing Good* (New York: Fawcett Columbine, 1991).
12. See Ian Bradley, *God is Green: Christianity and the Environment* (New York: Doubleday, 1990). "The Christian faith is intrinsically Green . . . the good news of the Gospel promises liberation and fulfillment for the whole of creation and . . . Christians have a positive and distinctive contribution to the salvation of our threatened planet" (1).
13. Zigmunt J. B. Plater, Robert H. Abrams, William Goldfarb, *Environmental Law and Policy: Nature, Law, and Society* (New York: West Publishing Company, 1992), xxvii.
14. Bill McKibben, Heck Lectures, United Theological Seminary, 21-22 April, 1992.
15. Albert Gore, Jr., *Earth in the Balance: Forging a New Common Purpose* (Boston: Houghton, Mifflin, 1992).
16. Kurt Vonnegut, *Hocus Pocus* (New York: G. P. Putnam, 1990), 140.
17. James Hillman, "The Practice of Beauty," *Resurgence* 157 (March/April 1993): 35.
18. James Lovelock, "Planetary Medicine: Stewards or Partners on Earth," *TLS: Times Literary Supplement*, 13 September 1991, 8.
19. Timothy Ferris, *The Mind's Sky: Human Intelligence in a Cosmic Context* (New York: Bantam Books, 1992), 196.

20. Edward O. Wilson, *The Diversity of Life* (Cambridge, Mass.: Belknap Press of Harvard University, 1992). Wilson admits that we may be able to limit the environmental damage to 10 percent. "At first glance the difference may seem bearable. It is not; it amounts to millions of species."

21. For more examples of what eco-kids are doing to protect the Earth, see *Kid Heroes of the Environment*, ed. Catherine Dee (Berkeley, Calif.: Earth Works Press, 1991).

22. Holly Brough, "Environmental Studies: Is It Academic?" *WorldWatch*, January/February 1992, 26-34.

23. Tom Sine, *Wild Hope* (Waco, Tex.: Word, 1991), 21.

24. James Conlon, *Geo-Justice: A Preferential Option for the Earth* (Winfield, British Columbia: Wood Lake Books, 1990).

25. These words were spoken at a private briefing at the American Red Cross headquarters in Washington for the USA division of the Club of Rome, 13 April 1992.

26. V. A. Hodgkinson, M. S. Weitzman, A. D. Kirsch, *From Belief to Commitment: The Activities and Finances of Religious Congregations in the United States* (Washington, D.C.: Independent Sector, 1988), 18-19.

27. If interested in adding your own personal declaration or signatures to the document, write to C. & M. Blanke, D6475, Glauberg, Germany. See also Marc A. Wessels, "Voices Within the Church: Part Two," *InRoads*, Summer/Fall 1992, 4-6.

28. See "The Blessing of the Animals" exhibit at the Institute of Texan Cultures, San Antonio, Texas. See also "A Service of Blessing of Animals," *The United Methodist Book of Worship* (Nashville: United Methodist Publishing House, 1992), 608-10.

29. See Alan Durning's *How Much Is Enough? The Consumer Society and the Future of the Earth* (New York: W. W. Norton, 1992), where he argues that the world's consumer class bears the largest blame for releasing virtually all ozone-depleting chemicals, two-thirds of greenhouse gases, and pollutants that cause acid rain.

30. Helen Caldicott, "Creating a Sane and Caring Society" in *The Way Ahead: A Visionary Perspective for the New Millennium*, ed. Eddie and Bobbie Shapiro (Rockport, Mass.: Element, 1992): "The Japanese use the equivalent of one forest a day in disposable chopsticks. We use trees to blow our noses on. It is medically contra-indicated to use trees to blow our noses because if we do this then we are killing the earth" (160).

31. Studio Dry Goods handkerchiefs are works of art. They can be contacted at 4820 Carpenter Avenue, North Hollywood, CA 91607.

32. See Lawrence E. Johnson's *A Morally Deep World: An Essay on Moral Significance and Environmental Ethics* (New York: Cambridge University Press, 1991).

33. See also David Holstrom, "Pollution in U.S. Cities Hits Minorities Hardest," *Christian Science Monitor*, 7 January 1993, 8.

34. See Benjamin Chavis, "Race, Justice and the Environment," *Nature Conservancy* 7 (September/October 1992): 38. For specific documentation on how the poor of Los Angeles suffer the most from that city's notoriously dirty air, see Eric Mann's *L.A.'s Lethal Air: New Strategies for Policy, Organizing and Action* (Los Angeles: Labor/Community Strategy Center, 1991). For the argument that "injustice is not a socially or ecologically sustainable proposition," see Victor Lewis, the founder of Environmentalists Against Racism, in "A Message to White Environmentalists," *Earth Island Journal* 7 (Fall 1992): 41.

35. Julie Burchill, *Sex and Sensibility* (London: Grafton, 1992), 153.
36. *New York Times*, 28 August 1984, 3C, as quoted in David H. Hopper, *Technology, Theology, and the Idea of Progress* (Louisville: Westminster/John Knox Press, 1991), 26.
37. So argues Senator Daniel Patrick Moynihan in his article "Defining Deviancy Down," *American Scholar*, Winter 1993, 22.
38. See Leonard I. Sweet and K. Elizabeth Rennie, "Toys 'R' Us. NOT!" *Homiletics* 4 (October-December 1992): 19-21.
39. Moynihan, "Defining Deviancy Down," 23.
40. George H. Wood, *Schools That Work: America's Most Innovative Public Education Programs* (New York: Dutton, 1992).
41. See Alvin and Heidi Toffler's "L.A.'s Lessons for the World," *World Monitor*, June 1992, 18.
42. See the excellent work by campus minister Erin D. Swezey, "Grounded in Justice: Service Learning from a Faith Perspective," *New Directions for Student Services*, 50 (Summer 1990), 77-90, on which this discussion heavily draws.
43. William K. Kilpatrick, *Why Johnny Can't Tell Right from Wrong: Moral Illiteracy and the Case of Character Education* (New York: Simon and Schuster, 1992).
44. Quoted by Rev. William H. Hinson, "The Lottery: Selling the Poor for Less Than a Pair of Shoes," *United Methodist Reporter*, First United Methodist Church of Houston, Texas edition, 25 October 1991, 1.
45. Donald Trump, "Trump vs. Trump: Undoing the Deal," chapter 3 of *Trump: Surviving at the Top* (New York: Random House, 1990), 61-82.
46. James J. Lynch, *Ethical Banking: Surviving in an Age of Default* (New York: St. Martin's Press, 1991).
47. Zbigniew Brzezinski, "Power and Morality," *World Monitor* 6 (March 1993): 28.
48. Henry Louis Gates, Jr., "Good-bye Columbus? Notes on the Culture of Criticism," *American Literary History* 3 (1991):718.
49. Paul Hawken, "The Ecology of Commerce," *Resurgence* 157 (March/April 1993): 15.
50. *Religion in America 1990* (Princeton, N.J.: Princeton Religion Research Center, 1990), 58.
51. *The Popcorn Report*, 6-7.
52. Wallace Stevens, *The Necessary Angel: Essays on Reality and the Imagination* (New York: Vintage Books, 1951), 22.
53. Woody Allen (aka Allen Konigsberg), *Side Effects* (New York: Random House, 1980), 57.
54. For example, see Princeton sociologist Robert Wuthnow's belief expressed as *The Struggle for America's Soul* (Grand Rapids, Mich.: Eerdmans, 1989) that will be resolved by a paradigm shift either to the right or the left.
55. Stanley Coren, *The Left-Hander Syndrome* (New York: Free Press, 1992).
56. See Steven Lukes, "What Is Left?," *TLS: Times Literary Supplement*, 27 March 1992, 10, where he says that it was "not until the early nineteenth century that the distinction became current as a means of representing divisions within the National Assembly, and thence in the nation at large; and in the process the dichotomy became a continuum. Then it spread to Piedmont and Italy and thence throughout Europe and the entire world."

57. French sociologist Eugen Weber is surely on target in his observation that "while Right and Left have been buried, resurrected and reburied more often than vampires, no one has yet managed to drive a stake through their palpitating hearts. Opinion surveys since 1989 show how two-thirds of the French find their dichotomy beside the point of our times, yet—also by two-thirds—continue to classify themselves as either of the Left or of the Right." See Weber's "Fascism, Religion and the French Right," *TLS: Times Literary Supplement*, 9 July 1993, 10.
58. Robert Hughes, "The Fraying of America," *Time*, 3 February 1992, 46.
59. Christopher Lasch, *The True and Only Heaven: Progress and Its Critics* (New York: W. W. Norton, 1991), 21.
60. I have been persuaded by Mary Louise Pratt that "contact zone" is a better language than "frontier" because of what she calls the latter's "reductive diffusionist perspective." See Pratt, *Imperial Eyes: Travel Writing and Transculturation* (New York: Routledge, 1992).
61. See David Bosch, *Transforming Mission: Paradigm Shifts in Theology of Mission* (Maryknoll, N.Y.: Orbis Books, 1991); also Lesslie Newbigin, *Mission in Christ's Way* (Geneva: WCC Publications, 1987), 20; and Charles Van Engen, *God's Missionary People: Rethinking the Purpose of the Local Church* (Grand Rapids, Mich.: Baker Book House, 1991).
62. Ray S. Anderson, *The Praxis of Pentecost: Revisioning the Church's Life and Mission* (Downers Grove, Ill.: InterVarsity Press, 1993). Anderson argues that this distinction emerged as early as the New Testament period, with the mission theology position conveyed most powerfully by Paul.
63. *The Collected Works of C. G. Jung*, ed. Herbert Read, Michael Fordham, and Gerhard Adler (New York: Pantheon Books, 1963), 199.
64. See Victor Turner, *From Ritual to Theatre: Human Seriousness of Play* (New York: Performing Arts Journal Publications, 1982).
65. Donald W. Shriver, Jr., "Response to the Future of Mission in a Pluralistic World," *Theological Education* 27 (Autumn 1990): 51.
66. "St. Armorer's Church from the Outside," in *The Collected Poems of Wallace Stevens* (New York: Alfred A. Knopf, 1985), 529. See also Leonard I. Sweet *Quantum Spirituality: A Postmodern Apologetic* (Dayton: Whaleprints, 1991), 255.